CUMULATIVE INDEX TO
KIERKEGAARD RESEARCH:
SOURCES, RECEPTION AND RESOURCES

Tome III: Index of Subjects
Overview of the Articles in the Series

Kierkegaard Research: Sources, Reception and Resources
Volume 21, Tome III

Kierkegaard Research: Sources, Reception and Resources
is a publication of the Søren Kierkegaard Research Centre

Cumulative Index to
Kierkegaard Research:
Sources, Reception and Resources

Tome III: Index of Subjects
Overview of the Articles in the Series

KATALIN NUN STEWART

Routledge
Taylor & Francis Group

LONDON AND NEW YORK

First published 2018
by Routledge
2 Park Square, Milton Park, Abingdon, Oxon OX14 4RN

and by Routledge
711 Third Avenue, New York, NY 10017

Routledge is an imprint of the Taylor & Francis Group, an informa business

British Library Cataloguing-in-Publication Data
A catalogue record for this book is available from the British Library

Library of Congress Cataloging-in-Publication Data
A catalog record for this book has been requested

ISBN: 978-1-138-08098-0 (hbk)
ISBN: 978-1-315-11311-1 (ebk)

Typeset in Times New Roman
by Apex CoVantage, LLC

Contents

Overview of *Kierkegaard Research: Sources, Reception and Resources*

Section I: Kierkegaard Sources

Volume 1:
Kierkegaard and the Bible
1.I: *Kierkegaard and the Bible*, Tome I, *The Old Testament*, ed. by Lee C. Barrett and Jon Stewart, Farnham and Burlington: Ashgate 2010.
1.II: *Kierkegaard and the Bible*, Tome II, *The New Testament*, ed. by Lee C. Barrett and Jon Stewart, Farnham and Burlington: Ashgate 2010.

Volume 2:
Kierkegaard and the Greek World
2.I: *Kierkegaard and the Greek World*, Tome I, *Socrates and Plato*, ed. by Katalin Nun and Jon Stewart, Farnham and Burlington: Ashgate 2010.
2.II: *Kierkegaard and the Greek World*, Tome II, *Aristotle and Other Greek Authors*, ed. by Katalin Nun and Jon Stewart, Farnham and Burlington: Ashgate 2010.

Volume 3:
Kierkegaard and the Roman World
3: *Kierkegaard and the Roman World*, ed. by Jon Stewart, Farnham and Burlington: Ashgate 2009.

Volume 4:
Kierkegaard and the Patristic and Medieval Traditions
4: *Kierkegaard and the Patristic and Medieval Traditions*, ed. by Jon Stewart, Aldershot and Burlington: Ashgate 2008.

Volume 5:
Kierkegaard and the Renaissance and Modern Traditions
5.I: *Kierkegaard and the Renaissance and Modern Traditions*, Tome I, *Philosophy*, ed. by Jon Stewart, Farnham and Burlington: Ashgate 2009.
5.II: *Kierkegaard and the Renaissance and Modern Traditions*, Tome II, *Theology*, ed. by Jon Stewart, Farnham and Burlington: Ashgate, 2009.
5.III: *Kierkegaard and the Renaissance and Modern Traditions*, Tome III, *Literature, Drama and Music*, ed. by Jon Stewart, Farnham and Burlington: Ashgate 2009.

Volume 6:

Kierkegaard and His German Contemporaries

6.I: *Kierkegaard and His German Contemporaries*, Tome I, *Philosophy*, ed. by Jon Stewart, Aldershot and Burlington: Ashgate 2007.

6.II: *Kierkegaard and His German Contemporaries*, Tome II, *Theology*, ed. by Jon Stewart, Aldershot and Burlington: Ashgate 2007.

6.III: *Kierkegaard and His German Contemporaries*, Tome III, *Literature and Aesthetics*, ed. by Jon Stewart, Aldershot and Burlington: Ashgate 2008.

Volume 7:

Kierkegaard and His Danish Contemporaries

7.I: *Kierkegaard and His Danish Contemporaries*, Tome I, *Philosophy, Politics and Social Theory*, ed. by Jon Stewart, Farnham and Burlington: Ashgate 2009.

7.II: *Kierkegaard and His Danish Contemporaries*, Tome II, *Theology*, ed. by Jon Stewart, Farnham and Burlington: Ashgate 2009.

7.III: *Kierkegaard and His Danish Contemporaries*, Tome III, *Literature, Drama and Aesthetics*, ed. by Jon Stewart, Farnham and Burlington: Ashgate 2009.

Section II: Kierkegaard Reception

Volume 8:

Kierkegaard's International Reception

8.I: *Kierkegaard's International Reception*, Tome I, *Northern and Western Europe*, ed. by Jon Stewart, Farnham and Burlington: Ashgate 2009.

8.II: *Kierkegaard's International Reception*, Tome II, *Southern, Central and Eastern Europe*, ed. by Jon Stewart, Farnham and Burlington: Ashgate 2009.

8.III: *Kierkegaard's International Reception*, Tome III, *The Near East, Asia, Australia and the Americas*, ed. by Jon Stewart, Aldershot and Burlington: Ashgate 2008.

Volume 9:

Kierkegaard and Existentialism

9:   *Kierkegaard and Existentialism*, ed. by Jon Stewart, Farnham and Burlington: Ashgate 2011.

Volume 10:

Kierkegaard's Influence on Theology

10.I: *Kierkegaard's Influence on Theology*, Tome I, *German Protestant Theology*, ed. by Jon Stewart, Farnham and Burlington: Ashgate 2012.

10.II: *Kierkegaard's Influence on Theology*, Tome II, *Anglophone and Scandinavian Protestant Theology*, ed. by Jon Stewart, Farnham and Burlington: Ashgate 2012.

10.III: *Kierkegaard's Influence on Theology*, Tome III, *Catholic and Jewish Theology*, ed. by Jon Stewart, Farnham and Burlington: Ashgate 2012.

15.II: *Kierkegaard's Concepts*, Tome II, *Classicism to Enthusiasm*, ed. by Steven M. Emmanuel, Jon Stewart, and William McDonald, Farnham and Burlington: Ashgate 2014.

15.III: *Kierkegaard's Concepts*, Tome III, *Envy to Incognito*, ed. by Steven M. Emmanuel, Jon Stewart, and William McDonald, Farnham and Burlington: Ashgate 2014.

15.IV: *Kierkegaard's Concepts*, Tome IV, *Individual to Novel*, ed. by Steven M. Emmanuel, Jon Stewart, and William McDonald, Farnham and Burlington: Ashgate 2014.

15.V: *Kierkegaard's Concepts*, Tome V, *Objectivity to Sacrifice*, ed. by Steven M. Emmanuel, Jon Stewart, and William McDonald, Farnham and Burlington: Ashgate 2015.

15.VI: *Kierkegaard's Concepts*, Tome VI, *Salvation to Writing*, ed. by Steven M. Emmanuel, Jon Stewart, and William McDonald, Farnham and Burlington: Ashgate 2015.

Volume 16:
Kierkegaard's Literary Figures and Motifs

16.I: *Kierkegaard's Literary Figures and Motifs*, Tome I, *Agamemnon to Guadalquivir*, ed. by Katalin Nun and Jon Stewart, Farnham and Burlington: Ashgate 2014.

16.II: *Kierkegaard's Literary Figures and Motifs*, Tome II, *Gulliver to Zerlina*, ed. by Katalin Nun and Jon Stewart, Farnham and Burlington: Ashgate 2015.

Volume 17:
Kierkegaard's Pseudonyms

17: *Kierkegaard's Pseudonyms*, ed. by Katalin Nun and Jon Stewart, Farnham and Burlington: Ashgate 2015.

Volume 18:
Kierkegaard Secondary Literature

18.I: *Kierkegaard Secondary Literature*, Tome I, *Catalan, Chinese, Czech, Danish and Dutch*, ed. by Jon Stewart, Farnham and Burlington: Ashgate 2016.

18.II: *Kierkegaard Secondary Literature*, Tome II, *English, A–K*, ed. by Jon Stewart, Farnham and Burlington: Ashgate 2016.

18.III: *Kierkegaard Secondary Literature*, Tome III, *English, L–Z*, ed. by Jon Stewart, London and New York: Routledge 2016.

18.IV: *Kierkegaard Secondary Literature*, Tome IV, *Finnish, French, Galician and German*, ed. by Jon Stewart, London and New York: Routledge 2016.

18.V: *Kierkegaard Secondary Literature*, Tome V, *Greek, Hebrew, Hungarian, Italian, Japanese, Norwegian, and Polish*, ed. by Jon Stewart, London and New York: Routledge 2016.

18.VI: *Kierkegaard Secondary Literature*, Tome VI, *Portuguese, Romanian, Russian, Slovak, Spanish, and Swedish*, ed. by Jon Stewart, London and New York: Routledge 2016.

Volume 19:
Kierkegaard Bibliography

19.I: *Kierkegaard Bibliography*, Tome I, *Afrikaans to Dutch*, ed. by Peter Šajda and Jon Stewart, London and New York: Routledge 2017.

19.II: *Kierkegaard Bibliography*, Tome II, *English*, ed. by Peter Šajda and Jon Stewart, London and New York: Routledge 2017.

19.III: *Kierkegaard Bibliography*, Tome III, *Estonian to Hebrew*, ed. by Peter Šajda and Jon Stewart, London and New York: Routledge 2017.

19.IV: *Kierkegaard Bibliography*, Tome IV, *Hungarian to Korean*, ed. by Peter Šajda and Jon Stewart, London and New York: Routledge 2017.

19.V: *Kierkegaard Bibliography*, Tome V, *Latvian to Ukrainian*, ed. by Peter Šajda and Jon Stewart, London and New York: Routledge 2017.

19.VI: *Kierkegaard Bibliography*, Tome VI, *Figures A–H*, *Figures*, by Peter Šajda and Jon Stewart, London and New York: Routledge 2017.

19.VII: *Kierkegaard Bibliography*, Tome VII, *Figures I–Z*, by Peter Šajda and Jon Stewart, London and New York: Routledge 2017.

Volume 20:
The Auction Catalogue of Kierkegaard's Library

20:   *The Auction Catalogue of Kierkegaard's Library*, ed. by Katalin Nun, Gerhard Schreiber, and Jon Stewart, Farnham and Burlington: Ashgate 2015.

Volume 21:
Cumulative Index to Kierkegaard Research:
Sources, Reception and Resources

21.I: *Cumulative Index to Kierkegaard Research: Sources, Reception and Resources*, Tome I, *Index of Names, A–K*, by Katalin Nun Stewart, London and New York: Routledge 2018.

21.II: *Cumulative Index to Kierkegaard Research: Sources, Reception and Resources*, Tome II, *Index of Names, L–Z*, by Katalin Nun Stewart, London and New York: Routledge 2018.

21.III: *Cumulative Index to Kierkegaard Research: Sources, Reception and Resources*, Tome III, *Index of Subjects. Overview of the Articles in the Series*, by Katalin Nun Stewart, London and New York: Routledge 2018.

Index of Subjects

A

Aaben Skrivelse til den danske Rigsdag fra Kjøbenhavnske Præster,
20, U 8
abasement,
1.II, 75, 159, 160, 164, 179
abjection,
13, 187, 188
absolute, the,
7.II, 3, 257, 279, 341; **10.I**, xii, 77, 78, 86, 197, 200, 213, 216, 323, 337, 350, 356, 357, 360, 362, 366, 386, 387; **11.I**, 40; **12.I**, 25–7, 32, 38, 102; **15.I**, *1–4*
absolute and relative,
9, 36, 41, 50, 52; **11.II**, 4, 14–16, 18, 19, 119, 123; **12.I**, 26, 176; **14**, 46, 63, 111–13, 126, 165, 199, 268
absolute decision,
8.I, 38
absolute dependence,
10.I, 18
absolute idea,
7.II, 341
absolute idealism,
5.I, 36, 41, 44
absolute infinite negativity. *See* negativity, absolute infinite
absolute knowing,
6.III, 57, 140; **11.II**, 52, 122, 244, 248, 252
absolute other, the,
2.I, 146
absolute paradox,
4, 5
abstraction,
2.I, 46–8, 51, 54, 62, 63, 69, 70, 99, 107, 191; **2.II**, 37, 61, 82, 83, 140–2;

5.I, 28, 35, 42–4; **10.I**, 323; **11.I**, 34, 128, 158
absurd, absurdity,
1.I, 52, 67–9, 75, 124; **1.II**, 18, 23, 24, 26, 29, 30, 109, 268; **2.II**, 93, 241; **4**, 47, 58, 89, 131–8; **5.I**, 39; **7.II**, 58, 59, 65, 69, 76–85 passim, 90–2; **8.I**, 249, 441, 442, 445, 449, 453; **8.II**, 92, 225, 226, 260, 294; **8.III**, 75, 85, 231; **9**, 49, 63–72 passim, 76–81, 84–8, 90, 142, 150, 174, 177, 179, 180, 187, 265, 273, 274, 277–9, 279, 280, 282, 367; **10.II**, 11–13, 16, 18, 19, 32, 36, 39, 42, 151, 152; **10.III**, 33, 64, 182, 191, 199, 200, 202, 209; **11.I**, 14, 152, 171, 297; **11.II**, 26–8, 101, 104, 212, 236, 237, 240–2, 245, 249, 250, 252; **11.III**, 37, 76, 77, 80, 123, 124; **12.I**, 22, 79, 104, 129, 154, 185, 207; **12.II**, 146; **12.III**, 29, 40, 43; **12.IV**, 3, 17, 66 n, 154, 207; **12.V**, 9, 10, 29, 70, 71, 78, 81, 84, 144; **13**, 61, 62, 66, 69, 72, 143, 187, 317, 318; **14**, 37, 47, 65, 233, 234, 238–40; **15.I**, *5–10*; **16.I**, 118, 269; **17**, 153, 154, 190
accommodation,
4, 48, 53, 58
acedia,
13, 89; **14**, 116
acosmism,
4, 245–7, 251; **6.III**, 253; **9**, 43, 44, 45, 48, 57, 131, 166, 170, 171, 183; **10.III**, 71; **11.I**, 272, 279; **13**, 71, 266–8
acoustic illusion,
14, 201

acting,
　17, 107–15
actuality,
　1.I, 20, 25, 30, 35, 69–71, 76, 90, 91,
　122, 133, 134, 158, 163, 164, 167,
　175, 222; **2.II**, 18, 26, 30, 37, 38, 50,
　63, 73, 75, 96, 113, 139–41, 187; **4**,
　56, 174, 175, 212, 214, 215, 225; **5.I**,
　42–4, 66, 69, 71, 93, 99, 174, 184–6;
　6.I, 4, 7, 83, 84, 101, 102, 104, 115,
　120, 121, 123, 127, 256, 315, 324,
　325, 329; **6.III**, 34, 70, 71, 143, 198,
　218, 224, 201, 202, 206–8, 211, 215,
　216, 219–21, 223, 227, 242, 254–8,
　261–5, 306; **7.I**, 48, 62, 63, 120, 127,
　199, 207, 245, 253, 296, 308, 313;
　7.II, 4, 8, 9; **8.III**, 8, 54, 240; **10.I**,
　204, 345; **10.II**, 35, 37; **11.I**, 152,
　227, 259, 262; **11.II**, 5, 6, 9, 87, 99,
　213, 216, 228, 242, 249; **12.V**, 69,
　109–11, 113, 116, 167; **13**, 70, 163,
　222, 223, 300, 312; **16.II**, 27, 59, 79,
　82, 143, 144, 150, 158, 159, 184
actuality and possibility,
　10.I, 363
admiration,
　15.I, *17–22*
Advisory Estates Assembly,
　7.III, 108, 127, 133
Aeneid,
　16.I, 98
Ærens Torne-Vej,
　20, M 1465
aestheticism,
　16.I, 192, 197, 198; **17**, *1–25*, 147,
　305
aestheticism, reflective,
　17, 3, 5, 12
aesthetics,
　1.II, 61, 62; **2.I**, 251, 259; **2.II**,
　51, 61, 71, 72, 77–9, 83; **5.III**, 44,
　47; **7.I**, 35, 38, 50, 55, 56, 68, 215;
　7.III, 97, 110, 135, 145, 157, 172,
　178, 179, 182, 209, 210, 214, 227,
　259, 265, 279, 281; **8.I**, 67–9, 79,
　81, 89; **10.I**, xii, 17, 19, 59, 81, 82,

86, 97, 202, 213, 301, 322, 339,
355, 365, 380, 381, 387; **10.II**, 16,
27; **10.III**, 11, 13–16, 19–22, **11.I**,
21, 56, 59, 60, 70; **11.II**, 9, 30, 32,
58, 59, 66, 79, 86, 97, 103, 105,
116, 143, 149, 152, 162, 182, 185,
189; **11.III**, 30, 55–61, 66, 110,
123, 125, 127–9; **12.I**, 2, 9, 11, 12,
25, 34, 35, 38, 48, 71, 72, 76, 80–7,
95, 96, 101, 103, 105, 147, 152,
160, 166, 173, 177, 188, 238, 241;
12.II, 55; **12.III**, 3, 4, 46, 61, 155;
12.V, 28, 113; **13**, 2, 8–11, 45, 60,
67, 116, 125–8, 143, 153, 167, 186,
206, 262, 263, 266, 268, 302–5,
317, 318; **15.I**, *23–30*; **16.I**, 10, 43,
55, 128, 147–9, 190; **16.II**, 20, 24,
27, 59; **17**, 58, 59, 61, 74, 148, 159,
172, 179, 185
affectation,
　7.I, 107, 112, 123, 144–9, 218
agape. See love, *agape*
agnosticism,
　10.III, 83
ahistoricism,
　8.I, 334
akedah,
　1.I, 45–63 passim, 67, 69, 74, 76, 78,
　79; **9**, 55; **11.II**, 119; **13**, 132
alchemy,
　5.II, 43, 46, 47, 51, 222
alienation,
　6.II, 13, 15, 244; **6.III**, 192, 199,
　200, 206, 207, 250; **8.I**, 432; **8.II**,
　171; **8.III**, 57, 117, 119, 233; **9**, 47,
　56, 68, 70, 108, 113, 210; **10.I**, 357,
　366, 369; **10.II**, 122, 123; **10.III**,
　115–18, 128; **11.I**, 13, 164, 167, 171;
　11.II, 71, 74, 163, 249; **12.I**, 19, 119,
　201, 225, 238; **12.III**, 46; **12.IV**, 28,
　37, 55, 102, 130, 177, 178, 199, 214,
　224; **12.V**, 10, 18; **13**, 8, 10, 96, 98,
　184, 207, 220, 262, 263; **14**, 128,
　130, 163, 244, 269
allegory,
　11.III, 40–2; **15.I**, *31–6*

Allgemeine deutsche Real-
Encyklopädie für die gebildeten
Stände,
20, M 1299–1310
Allgemeine Encyklopädie der
Wissenschaften und Künste,
20, M 1311–1363
Allgemeines Repertorium für die
theologische Literatur und kirchliche
Statistik,
20, M 36–66
Alter-Bog for Danmark,
20, M 381
alterity. *See also* other, the/otherness
11.II, 112; **15.V**, *23–8*
ambiguity,
9, 1, 8, 9, 14, 247, 248, 254, 255,
304, 334, 385, 407; **10.I**, 127, 132,
135, 217, 342, 345, 353, 358, 367;
11.I, 28, 35; **11.II**, 27, 66, 113, 117;
12.I, 26, 204; **12.V**, 83; **13**, 206; **14**,
102, 203, 223, 244, 268; **15.I**, *37–44*
American Psychological Association,
13, 218, 239
Anabaptism,
1.II, 36, 38; **5.II**, 182; **7.II**, 241
analogia entis,
10.III, 135–40, 144
anamnesis,
16.I, 265
anarchism,
14, 117, 152
Anfægtelse. See spiritual trial
Anfechtung,
5.II, 24; **10.III**, 7
angst. *See* anxiety
anguish. *See* anxiety
anonymity,
15.I, *45–52*
anthropocentrism,
10.I, 16, 18
anthropology,
7.II, 268; **9**, 33, 35, 48, 52, 53, 57,
67, 88–90, 128, 238, 245, 407; **10.I**,
20, 22, 23, 32, 65, 69, 85, 112, 113,
119, 133, 173, 192, 197, 241–74,

251, 302, 321, 323; **10.II**, 20, 45,
59, 96, 130, 143, 148, 150; **10.III**,
15, 35, 36, 53, 68, 70, 71, 136, 149;
11.I, xi, 14, 15, 31, 35, 39, 188, 194;
11.II, 44, 46, 215, 234; **12.I**, 17, 109
n, 144; **13**, 1, 21, 29, 34, 36, 37, 41,
43, 84, 124, 125, 135, 140, 143, 144,
222, 288, 293; **14**, xv, 47, 79, 100,
215, 217, 219, 220, 227; **15.I**, *53–8*
antinomianism,
5.II, 83, 85, 86, 90, 100, 176, 182,
183, 194, 195, 205
Antiochene creed,
4, 51
anti-Semitism,
7.III, 106, 126–8; **10.III**, 99; **11.I**,
35, 36; **11.III**, 100; **12.I**, 161, 206,
207; **12.II**, 25; **12.IV**, 205, 206, 226;
13, 83; **14**, xii; **16.II**, 238, 245
anxiety,
1.I, 4, 25, 31–3, 36–9, 64–6, 70, 95,
127, 167, 214; **1.II**, 66, 141, 144,
146, 182; **2.I**, 64, 146; **2.II**, 305,
318–21; **3**, 140; **4**, 127; **5.II**, 29, 43,
54, 56, 105, 106, 198, 201; **5.III**, 72,
215–20, 223; **6.I**, 6, 8, 9, 12, 80, 86,
259, 303–5; **6.II**, 8, 9, 13, 151, 157,
181, 190–2; **6.III**, 119, 134, 135,
150, 160, 189, 281, 288, 292; **7.I**,
254, 272, 273; **7.III**, 77, 179; **8.I**, 47,
48, 128, 150–4, 201, 204, 209, 327,
344, 356, 357, 377, 426, 428, 432–6,
438, 440, 445, 449, 454; **8.II**, 5, 6,
25, 32, 88, 169, 227, 324, 325; **8.III**,
9, 12–21 passim, 43, 47, 51, 53, 57,
58, 60, 65–74 passim, 109, 111, 115,
117, 232, 240, 243, 322; **9**, ix, 8, 9,
13, 15, 24–8, 77, 78, 88, 90, 101,
102, 105–14 passim, 137, 140–9
passim, 180, 228, 323, 327, 328,
329, 332–9 passim, 343,345, 346,
361, 365, 366, 384; **10.I**, xii, 18,
33, 69, 85, 208, 213, 217, 252, 253,
256, 257, 258, 260, 263, 266, 269,
338–40, 343–51 passim, 362, 368,
369; **10.II**, 15, 16, 39, 50, 53, 116,

120, 122, 123, 137, 148, 149; **10.III**, 7–9, 29, 32, 35, 38, 68, 123–5, 198, 202; **11.I**, 31, 39, 96, 110, 182, 222, 281–3, 299; **11.II**, 48, 65, 67, 93, 182, 193, 218, 227, 235–7, 240–3, 249, 251, 252; **11.III**, 34, 35, 75, 104, 111, 112, 223; **12.I**, xii, 33, 36, 73, 75, 76, 146, 148, 153, 196; **12.II**, 60, 61, 70, 72, 90, 94, 159; **12.III**, 39, 60, 98, 125, 127, 162, 163, 183–9 passim; **12.IV**, 11–13, 15, 17, 54, 60, 68, 124, 145, 146, 148, 150, 151, 181, 204, 205, 214, 215, 221, 225, 226; **12.V**, 13, 31, 40, 85, 92, 95–7, 99, 151, 162, 164, 181; **13**, xi, xii, 19, 21–5, 43, 47, 49, 70, 87, 92, 97, 107, 109, 127, 129, 130, 132, 134, 135, 157, 163, 184, 185, 196, 204–13 passim, 218, 221–8 passim, 231–5, 276, 277, 282–6, 290, 292, 300, 313–16; **14**, 43, 63, 94, 100–4, 127, 128, 191, 218–27 passim, 233, 234, 236, 238, 240–3, 262–4, 267–9; **15.I**, *59–64*; **16.I**, 59, 75, 143–5, 151, 179, 239; **16.II**, 29, 60, 166, 207, 219, 231, 259, 265; **17**, 22, 57, 145, 148, 155, 259, 261, 262, 265, 269–78 passim, 287

aparté,
 11.II, 8–10
apathy,
 2.II, 195, 197, 200, 203
 8.III, 6
aphorism,
 11.III, 25
apocalypticism,
 10.I, 200, 224, 226, 228, 243, 245
apologetics,
 10.I, 98, 168; **10.III**, 109; **15.I**, *71–6*
aporia,
 2.I, 31, 32, 41, 44, 86, 98, 100, 116–22 passim, 131–4, 141, 145, 146; **2.II**, 189
apostle,
 12.IV, 74, 75, 181, 185, 188; **15.I**, *77–82*; **17**, 91–5, 211, 219, 293–7

Apostles' Creed,
 7.II, 98, 99, 106, 111–15, 121–5, 154, 193, 197, 212, 215, 222, 223, 308; **10.I**, 283, 285, 286, 388
appropriation,
 1.II, 108, 114, 120, 156, 157, 244, 256, 262, 267, 269–74, 275, 285, 322; **2.I**, 121, 124, 131, 218, 304; **2.II**, 176; **4**, xii, 62, 108, 111, 115, 116, 135; **5.I**, 89, 100, 105; **5.III**, 129; **6.I**, 32, 33; **7.II**, 119, 156, 169, 171, 347; **8.I**, 6, 22, 23, 66, 78, 317, 436; **9**, 83, 105, 203, 206, 207, 208, 210, 383, 384, 385; **10.I**, x, 21, 22, 67, 86, 127, 324, 329; **10.II**, 32, 152, 161, 183, 185; **10.III**, 84, 120, 182, 183; **11.I**, 22, 32, 39, 41, 81, 111, 113–15, 275, 300; **11.II**, 149, 226, 227, 229; **11.III**, 38, 172; **12.I**, 204; **12.II**, 8; **12.V**, 99; **13**, 246, 247, 251, 305; **14**, 198; **15.I**, *83–8*; **16.I**, 134; **17**, 264
approximation,
 1.II, 264, 292, 314, 317; **2.II**, 175; **7.II**, 42, 119, 120, 122, 124, 133, 225; **10.I**, 325; **11.I**, 276; **11.III**, 77; **12.I**, 20
Arabian Nights,
 16.I, 83
Archimedean Point,
 5.I, 14, 39; **5.III**, 103; **7.I**, 220; **10.I**, 148; **15.I**, *95–8*; **16.II**, 150, 151
Das Ärgerliche Leben und schreckliche Ende Johannes Fausti,
 20, M 1636
arguments for God's existence,
 12.V, 29
Arianism,
 4, 3
art. *See also* aesthetics
 8.I, 69, 79, 244; **11.II**, 1, 30, 31, 35, 75, 79, 105; **11.III**, 142, 150, 152, 153; **15.I**, *99–104*
"art is an anticipation of eternal life,"
 7.I, 153–9; **7.II**, 244
Ascension,
 1.II, 18, 22, 308; **4**, 115; **7.I**, 224; **10.I**, 284; **10.III**, 69

ascetism/asceticism,
  4, 52, 56, 63, 132, 251, 262, 278,
  279, 281, 283, 284; **5.II**, 12, 18, 136,
  206, 249; **10.III**, 85, 86, 93; **15.I**,
  105–8
assistant professor. *See Privatdocent*
Astraea juridical society,
  7.I, 15, 88
ataraxia,
  2.II, 166–7, 177, 179
atheism,
  5.I, 34, 149, 167; **5.III**, 47; **6.III**,
  166; **7.I**, 292, 293; **8.II**, 166, 170;
  8.III, 12; **10.I**, xii, 199, 200, 233,
  357; **10.II**, 12; **10.III**, 98, 100;
  11.I, 95; **11.II**, 26, 27, 71, 107, 177;
  11.III, 72, 74, 75, 184; **12.II**, 22, 27,
  105, 109, 113, 115, 116; **12.V**, 131,
  134, 143; **13**, 9, 18, 20, 179, 195,
  232; **14**, 37, 49, 82, 83, 115,
  124, 130
Athenæum reading society,
  5.III, 129; **7.I**, 4, 15, 20, 25, 27, 251
atonement,
  1.I, 29, 35, 38, 39, 70–2, 172; **1.II**,
  85, 133, 134, 144, 145, 151–7
  passim, 164, 289, 301; **4**, 168–71,
  176, 177; **5.II**, 27, 96, 107, 178, 189;
  6.III, 262, 263; **9**, 149; **10.I**, 24, 133,
  135; **11.II**, 93, 217; **11.III**, 7; **14**,
  242; **15.I**, *109–16*; **17**, 91, 269,
  270, 278
Attack on the Church,
  2.I, 3–25 passim; **5.I**, 139; **5.II**, 220;
  5.III, 89, 256, 262; **7.I**, 209, 298,
  303, 311; **7.II**, 43, 131–3, 166–9,
  172, 182, 184, 202, 236, 251–3, 269,
  270, 282, 298, 299, 320, 323, 327,
  330, 351, 352; **7.III**, 33, 68, 114,
  142, 146, 209; **8.I**, ix, 15, 20, 44, 47,
  61, 64, 67, 71, 74, 81, 82, 84, 85, 95,
  121, 125–9, 140, 165, 173–9 passim,
  206, 220, 238, 244, 252, 253, 312,
  313, 338, 378, 423, 425, 444; **10.I**,
  14, 17, 20, 21, 23, 53, 96, 167, 202,
  213, 232, 234, 235, 237, 238; **10.II**,

  30, 52, 64, 69, 71, 73, 78, 79, 94,
  122, 195, 196, 199, 200; **10.III**, 90,
  131; **12.I**, 62, 152, 153, 189; **12.II**,
  18, 28, 30, 35, 128, 129, 158, 160,
  162, 173, 174, 176; **12.III**, 125, 131;
  16.I, 159, 162; **16.II**, 36, 46, 149
Aufhebung. See also mediation,
  2.I, 56, 142; **4**, 172; **6.I**, 4, 5, 10, 11;
  7.II, 243; **8.III**, 52, 64; **11.II**, 116,
  126, 128, 129, 251, 252; **11.III**, 43;
  14, 60; **15.IV**, 131–6
Augsburg Confession,
  1.I, 6; **5.II**, 88, 99, 100, 160, 181,
  185, 193; **6.I**, 8; **7.II**, 44, 214, 312;
  17, 270
Den Augsburgske Confession,
  20, M 386–387
aut/aut. See also either/or
  2.II, 8–12; **7.I**, 63; **7.III**, 43
authenticity,
  2.I, 88, 104, 202, 208, 235, 242, 249,
  289; **4**, 13, 267, 162; **5.III**, 126, 129;
  8.I, 339, 432, 436; **8.III**, 30, 33, 70;
  9, 63, 87, 105, 107, 113, 202, 208,
  301, 303, 330, 331, 340, 342, 345,
  380, 384, 405, 407; **10.I**, 17–19, 133,
  199, 330, 387; **10.II**, 15; **10.III**, 15,
  64, 112, 118, 119, 122–4, 126, 165;
  11.I, 28, 33, 299, 300; **11.II**, 27, 29,
  98, 160; **11.III**, 16–18, 21, 37, 49,
  51, 56–8, 150, 225, 227; **12.I**, 123,
  199, 208, 223, 232; **12.III**, 140;
  12.V, 16, 69, 71, 144, 151, 152; **13**,
  41, 102, 147, 232, 247, 254, 255,
  277; **14**, 149, 154, 155, 219
authentic self,
  12.V, 143, 153, 154
authorial intention,
  11.II, 23, 34, 113, 114, 131
authority,
  1.II, 30, 35, 50, 65, 72, 103, 110,
  129, 180, 190–8 passim, 205, 252,
  261, 301, 308, 313, 314, 320–3; **4**,
  13, 14, 34, 42, 54, 76, 78, 92, 104,
  105, 157; **7.II**, 15, 16, 19, 42, 58,
  251, 328; **8.III**, 20; **9**, 179, 186, 284;

10.I, 79, 81, 167, 171, 172, 348;
10.III, 37, 59, 77, 79, 102, 116, 119,
145, 158; **11.I**, 109, 111, 168, 177,
178, 182; **11.II**, 7, 31, 69, 131, 132,
160, 216; **11.III**, 19, 20, 105–10,
113, 160, 207–12; **12.I**, x, 99, 106;
12.II, 84–6; **12.IV**, 19, 32, 59, 86,
181, 184; **12.V**, 154; **13**, 39, 85,
116, 203, 210, 211, 240–2, 253, 300,
305–8; **14**, 66, 128, 148, 202, 204,
237; **15.I**, *117–22*; **17**, xi, 60, 92,
94, 95, 137, 215–20, 224, 250, 263,
264, 266
authorship,
　15.I, *123–8*
autonomy,
　1.II, 58; **5.I**, ix, 12; **6.III**, 59, 60,
61, 226; **7.II**, 231, 238, 244, 276;
8.III, 14; **9**, 4, 49, 284, 396; **10.I**,
78, 172, 249, 342; **10.III**, 70, 71;
11.I, 29, 119; **11.II**, 121, 152, 177,
220; **11.III**, 101–3, 113, 182; **13**, 88,
89, 154, 262, 263; **16.II**, 17
autopsy,
　10.I, 85
awe,
　10.III, 185, 186
axiology,
　10.III, 46, 58, 60, 61, 65, 71

B
bad faith,
　9, 323, 330, 334, 340, 341, 345; **10.
III**, 118
bad infinity,
　6.I, 81, 100, 104, 123, 124, 352; **7.I**,
66, 120; **11.I**, 276
Bakkehuset,
　7.III, 258, 287
ballad,
　16.I, 15–19, 22, 23, 25, 27, 28
ballet,
　7.III, 67–82, 173; **16.II**, 123, 130
baptism/Baptists,
　1.II, 176; **4**, 79, 80, 83, 84, 98,
124, 135; **7.II**, 6, 7, 55–7, 98, 99,

103–7, 110–15, 122, 125, 130,
143, 194, 195, 198, 200, 204, 212,
215 17, 219, 222, 223, 233, 240,
241, 245, 313, 336; **8.I**, 127, 129,
130, 135; **10.I**, 283, 284; **11.I**, 247;
11.III, 169, 171; **12.V**, 39; **15.I**,
129–32
Baroque,
　5.III, 148, 157
beatific vision,
　4, 168
Beatitudes, the,
　1.II, 33, 36, 37, 39, 42–5
beauty,
　2.I, 47, 106, 108; **3**, 42; **8.II**, 228,
229; **17**, 9
becoming,
　2.I, 59, 62, 69, 70, 127; **12.V**, 144,
151
becoming oneself,
　10.I, 21, 50; **10.II**, 8
beginning,
　7.I, 44; **15.I**, *133–6*
beginning, absolute,
　7.I, 55
beginning, presuppositionless,
　7.I, 52–4, 57, 68
beginning of philosophy,
　2.II, 132; **5.I**, ix, 13; **6.I**, 101, 102,
262, 316, 321, 329, 336; **7.I**, 42, 43,
52, 53, 57, 68; **9**, 399; **11.II**, 241,
242, 244
behaviorism,
　9, 240; **13**, 154, 218
being/becoming,
　15.I, *137–44*
being and nothing,
　6.I, 10, 11; **7.I**, 43, 47, 52, 253; **7.II**,
6; **8.II**, 46
belief. *See* faith
Berlin,
　9, 23, 34, 38, 299, 328; **11.I**, 6, 25,
68, 85, 89, 109, 131, 187, 215; **11.II**,
9, 72, 78
Berlingske Tidende,
　7.III, 90, 92, 109, 126

Bible,
7.I, 181, 235, 241, 244, 283, 298, 315; **7.II**, 25–7, 37, 41–8, 50–7 passim, 66–70, 97–100, 105, 113–15, 119, 120, 122, 124, 135, 138, 155, 161, 162, 165, 168, 185, 212, 213, 215, 218, 223–5, 230, 305, 335; **7.III**, 108; **8.III**, 213; **9**, 35, 150, 300, 358, 359, 361–5; **10.I**, 3, 4, 44, 47, 58, 131–3, 146, 164, 167, 187, 224, 245, 271, 277, 278, 286, 326, 388; **10.II**, 9, 13, 48, 53, 93, 131, 179–85 passim, 191, 194, 195, 198, 210, 212; **10.III**, 13, 14, 32, 69, 75, 76, 121, 165; **11.I**, 225, 269 271; **11.II**, 8, 106, 142, 144, 146, 150, 152, 153, 188, 191, 212; **11.III**, 3–8, 170; **12.I**, 123, 127, 150, 160, 181, 209; **12.III**, 41, 161, 182; **12.V**, 41, 173, 184; **13**, 65, 70, 85, 86, 105, 141, 146–8, 166, 170, 210, 211; **14**, 9, 22, 23, 25, 95, 98, 197, 217, 236, 242, 258; **15.VI**, *9–16*

Old Testament, **6.III**, 84

   Genesis, **1.I**, *3–42*, *43–80*, 160, 185, 207, 209, 212, 237, 241; **1.II**, 7, 261, 274, 296 **6.I**, 6; **6.II**, 2–9 passim; **9**, 138, 140; **10.I**, 44, 270, 363; **10.II**, 121, 123; **10.III**, 166, 167, 199, 203, 204; **11.III**, 9, 107, 108, 143; **12.IV**, 129, 167, 168, 206; **12.V**, 191; **16.I**, 2

   Exodus, **1.I**, 4, 168; **1.II**, 231, 288

   Leviticus, **1.II**, 5

   Ruth, **1.I**, 238; **7.II**, 177

   Samuel, **1.I**, 102–8 passim, 111, 218; **1.II**, 231, 243

   Kings, **1.I**, 101, 110, 168, 197; **1.II**, 141

   Chronicles, **1.I**, 101, 102, 197, 238

   Ezra, **1.I**, 238; **7.II**, 161, 162

   Nehemiah, **1.I**, 197, 238

   Esther, **1.I**, 238; **16.II**, 250, 251, 253, 255

Job, **1.I**, ix, xi, 4, 38, 74, 75, *115–140*, 222, 234, 238, 240, 247, 261; **2.II**, 219, 320; **5.III**, 35, 36; **7.III**, 59; **9**, 304, 314, 315, 360, 362–4, 369; **10.I**, 13; **10.II**, 73, 126; **10.III**, 156; **11.I**, 293; **12.II**, 83, 145; **12.IV**, 63, 66, 67, 116, 203; **12.V**, 8; **13**, 65, 69, 73, 148, 166, 171, 203; **14**, 236, 242, 248; **16.II**, 122

Psalms, **1.I**, ix, xi, 101, 104, 105, *141–77*, 232, 238; **1.II**, 118, 233; **5.II**, 230; **6.I**, 171; **14**, 9, 10

Proverbs, **1.I**, 101, 108, 151, 238, 244; **2.I**, 293

Ecclesiastes, **1.I**, 101, 108, 161, *179–92*, 238, 257, 262; **1.II**, 278; **5.II**, 139, 182, 206; **5.III**, 279; **11.II**, 146, 147; **12.V**, 19; **13**, 65

Song of Solomon (or Song of Songs), **1.I**, 101, 108; **5.II**, 71; **9**, 307; **11.III**, 214

Isaiah, **1.I**, 160; **1.II**, 116; **9**, 312; **11.II**, 190, 192; **12.IV**, 65; **13**, 65, 148; **14**, 23

Jeremiah, **5.II**, 233; **10.I**, 8; **14**, 93

Ezekiel, **1.I**, 197

Daniel, **1.I**, 105, 195–200; **1.II**, 289

Apocrypha, **1.I**, 253–62

   Tobit, **1.I**, 257–60; **5.II**, 139; **9**, 300; **12.V**, 133; **16.I**, 19

   Wisdom of Solomon, **1.I**, 256, 257, 258, 261, 262

   Ecclesiasticus (or Book of Sirach), **1.I**, 253, 256, 257, 261; **2.II**, 253

   Maccabees, **1.I**, 7, 253, 254

   Esdras, **1.I**, 254, 256

New Testament, **7.II**, 41; **11.III**, 8; **12.II**, 52–4, 81, 82, 122, 138; **16.I**, 163

   Matthew, **1.I**, 24, 28, 94, 151, 152, 176; **1.II**, 5, 11, 12, 20–4, 27,

28, *33–50*, *55–76*, 95, 96, 103,
107, 110, 113, 124, 141, 153–64
passim, 169, 175 81 passim,
238, 268, 292, 293, 309, 310;
5.II, 15, 25, 94, 189, 242; **7.II**,
280, 281; **10.I**, 45, 53, 122, 283;
10.II, 136; **10.III**, 33, 34, 37,
38; **11.I**, 191; **12.II**, 143; **12.III**,
179; **16.II**, 253, 254; **17**, 73

Mark, **1.I**, 149; **1.II**, 28, 124, 152,
156–64 passim, 169, 182, 292,
293, 309; **2.I**, 302; **7.II**, 117;
10.I, 45, 122, 130; **11.I**, 191

Luke, **1.I**, 28, 93, 94, 107, 145,
164; **1.II**, 3–7, 10, 11, 13, 22,
27, 28, 33–5, 42, *55–76*, 94, 98,
100–2, 107–16 passim, 119,
123–35, 139, 152–64 passim,
169, 180, 182, 238, 243, 249,
292, 293, 299, 309, 310; **5.II**,
15; **6.II**, 62, 72; **7.II**, 69, 324;
10.I, 45, 122; **10.III**, 18, 167;
11.I, 191

John, **1.I**, 145, 156, 170, 174,
209; **1.II**, 19–21, 26, 94, 139,
152, 154, 155, 158–64 passim,
169, 174, 176, 177, 182, 191,
194, 255, 276, 292, 293, 299,
300, 304, 305, 308–10; **5.II**,
149, 165; **6.II**, 40; **10.I**, 122,
127, 128, 194; **10.II**, 209, 210;
10.III, 34; **11.II**, 222; **14**, 187;
16.I, 138

Acts of the Apostles, **1.I**, 177;
1.II, 175, 181, 191, 223, 227,
229, 233, 259, 260, 296, 299,
300; **7.II**, 106, 197, 319, 351;
10.I, 248

Paul, **6.II**, 25; **12.II**, 127

Romans, **1.I**, 46, 48, 54, 72, 74,
79, 111, 153; **1.II**, 192, 195,
202, 203, 238, 255, 276, 308,
311; **2.I**, 306; **5.II**, 85, 90, 94,
180, 187; **6.I**, 55; **10.I**, 11, 195,
198; **10.II**, 198; **10.III**, 10;
11.II, 250; **14**, 21

Corinthians, **1.I**, 165, 168; **1.II**,
140, 154, 160, 189, 190, 192,
193, 198, 200–2, 308, 311; **2.I**,
50, 60; **5.II**, 115, 123, 152; **6.I**,
57; **7.II**, 199, 202, 323; **14**, 104

Galatians, **1.II**, 174, 190, 205,
212, 224, 255, 308; **2.I**, 64; **5.II**,
92, 182; **7.II**, 11; **10.III**, 37

Ephesians, **1.II**, 6, 183, 195, 197,
224, 255; **7.II**, 31

Philippians, **1.I**, 48, 66, 72, 79;
1.II, 163, 178, 180, 223, 224,
230, 234; **5.II**, 256; **9**, 300;
10.III, 146

Colossians, **1.II**, 223, 224,
229, 232

Thessalonians, **1.II**, 223, 224, 229,
230; **6.I**, 263, 264; **7.II**, 81

Timothy, **1.I**, 148, 167; **1.II**, 223,
224, 229, 230, 232, 234, 299

Titus, **1.II**, 223, 224, 230, 231

Philemon, **1.II**, 223, 224

Hebrews, **1.I**, 46–8, 54, 66, 72, 79,
160; **1.II**, 113, 192, 194, 223,
224, 229–32, 234, 238, 255,
299, 300, 308; **2.II**, 63; **5.II**,
122; **11.III**, 4

James, **1.I**, 24, 29, 48, 66, 72,
79, 104, 107, 157, 160, 161,
167, 174, 217, 255, 260; **1.II**,
189, 190, 193, 194, 196, 201,
209–15, 223, 224, 231, 237,
255, 256, 269, 270, 273, 300,
308, 311; **5.II**, 90, 199, 202,
234–8; **6.I**, 6; **9**, 305; **11.II**,
147; **12.II**, 127

Peter, **1.I**, 151; **1.II**, 124, 189, 190,
212, 237, 255, 300, 308

John, **1.II**, 255, 300, 303; **2.I**, 303

Jude, **1.II**, 212, 255, 300, 311

Revelation, **1.I**, 260; **7.II**, 230;
14, 197

Bible editions (in Søren Kierkegaard's
library),
20, M 1–33, 86–91, 2193; A I 1–17,
43–44; U 86

biblical criticism,
   7.I, 1–10
Bibliotheca Kierkegaardiana,
   8.I, 58, 273
Bibliothek for det smukke Kiøn,
   20, A II 143–144, 153–157
Bildung. See culture
Bildungsroman,
   6.III, 199, 202; **7.III**, 19, 21, 23,
   105, 115–19, 144–6, 212
biography,
   3, 76–8, 125, 141, 163, 164
blood witnesses,
   1.II, 163; **4**, 92
body,
   13, 10, 11, 19, 20, 23, 123, 154, 167,
   300, 318
Bogkataloger (that is, in Søren
   Kierkegaard's library),
   20, M 981–987; U 28
Bolshevism,
   11.I, 119; **13**, 268, 270, 271
Borch's College,
   5.III, 80; **7.I**, 2; **7.II**, 104
boredom,
   1.I, 236; **3**, 43; **5.III**, 267; **7.I**, 146;
   7.III, 179; **8.II**, 227; **8.III**, 110,
   112, 117, 129; **9**, 110, 113; **11.I**, 55,
   177, 182, 293; **11.II**, 153; **11.III**,
   58–60; **12.I**, 24, 25, 82; **12.III**,
   130, 170; **12.IV**, 9, 125; **13**, xi, 58,
   90; **16.II**, 70, 71, 129, 192, 202; **17**,
   17, 135
Borgerdyd School in Christianshavn,
   7.II, 213
Borgerdyd School in Copenhagen,
   1.II, 222; **2.I**, 220, 222; **2.II**, 48; **3,**
   ix, xi, 3, 13, 15, 41, 57–9, 78, 79,
   106, 149, 167, 168
   7.I, 2, 86, 102, 104; **7.II**, 2, 29, 190,
   213, 335; **10.II**, 110
Borgervennen,
   7.III, 85
bourgeois,
   6.III, 145, 146; **12.III**, 167, 168;
   12.IV, 117–19, 164, 186

bourgeois-philistinism,
   4, 292, 294, 295
Der Brenner,
   8.I, 328–31, 347, 349, 351, 355, 358,
   363, 367; **9**, 39, 40, 159, 160, 164;
   10.III, 49; **11.I**, 108, 109, 111, 112,
   114, 115, 119, 179, 216, 217, 228;
   12.I, xi, 31, 33, 93, 96, 101, 117, 141,
   158, 159, 163, 175, 214, 229; **14**, 183,
   190, 191
Buddhism,
   8.III, 151; **13**, 167
bull of Phalaris,
   14, 128
Burgtheater,
   9, 34
Buridan's ass,
   5.I, 64, 65

C
caesura,
   11.II, 13, 121, 127
calling,
   15.I, *145–8*
Calvinism,
   13, 115, 151, 163, 165, 259; **16.II**,
   86
capitalism,
   11.I, 163; **12.III**, 168; **12.V**, 78,
   80, 82; **13**, 20, 95, 96, 98, 107, 114,
   115, 123, 206, 262, 269; **14**, 74,
   125, 246
care/concern,
   9, 101; **10.II**, 116; **11.I**, 56, 59; **11.II**,
   252; **11.III**, 34; **12.I**, 223, 224; **13**,
   47, 90, 109, 239; **15.I**, *149–56*
Carlsbad Decrees,
   6.I, 51
*Catalogus Librorum quos reliquit
   N.[iels] B.[ygom] Krarup,*
   20, U 28
categorical imperative,
   10.I, 74; **12.V**, 153; **14**, 82, 104;
   16.II, 118
category,
   15.I, *157–60*

catharsis,
 1.II, 25
Catholicism,
 1.II, 259; **4**, 36, 40, 193, 202, 193;
 5.I, x, 1, 135, 136, 159; **5.II**, 10, 178,
 194, 250; **5.III**, 43, 95; **7.II**, 100,
 315; **8.I**, 97, 429; **8.II**, 7, 17, 29, 31,
 32; **9**, 209, 217–20, 228, 229, 380;
 10.I, xi; **10.II**, 26, 106, 107; **11.I**,
 4, 272; **11.II**, 207, 229; **11.III**, 121,
 127, 129; **12.I**, 94, 98, 109, 166;
 12.II, 27; **12.IV**, 102, 111, 135, 144,
 158, 159, 170, 175, 176, 188; **12.V**,
 33–43, 126, 139, 153; **13**, 164, 177,
 195, 239, 298; **14**, 179, 185, 193,
 203, 204; **15.I**, *161–6*
causality,
 5.I, 24, 36
cause/effect,
 15.I, *167–74*
Cave, Allegory of the,
 2.I, 119, 284
certainty,
 15.I, *175–80*
change,
 2.II, 17, 27, 28–34
Chanson de Roland,
 16.II, 39
charity,
 11.II, 208, 219–22, 224–6
chatter,
 1.I, 188–90; **11.I**, 54; **14**, 190; **15.I**,
 181–4
childhood,
 15.I, *185–92*
children's literature,
 7.I, 141, 271
*China. historisch, romantisch,
 malerisch*,
 20, M 2036
Chladni figure,
 7.I, 217, 220
choice. *See also* decision
 8.II, 290, 308; **9**, 11, 13–15, 174,
 227, 287, 333, 336, 338, 339, 344,
 345, 400, 405, 407; **10.I**, 218; **10.II**,
 116, 145; **11.I**, 111, 132, 136, 281,
 282; **11.II**, 79, 85, 97–100, 103,
 125, 249; **11.III**, 58–61, 63, 101,
 102, 104–6, 110, 111, 113, 117, 122–9
 passim, 139, 214, 222–4, 227; **12.I**,
 7, 10, 11, 67, 71, 76, 80, 81, 83, 84,
 129,188, 241; **12.II**, 71; **12.III**, 10, 31,
 72, 78, 83, 135, 184; **12.V**, 46, 131;
 13, 116, 124, 146, 153, 219, 220, 227,
 242, 259–61, 263, 265–71 passim,
 280, 282, 292, 302, 312; **14**, 45, 47,
 77, 96, 148, 155, 165; **15.I**, *193–200*;
 17, 183, 184, 189, 275, 277
choice, radical,
 17, 181, 182
choosing oneself,
 12.V, 52; **17**, 8, 184
Christendom,
 1.I, 44, 72, 74, 96, 97, 148, 149, 154,
 155, 157, 161, 232, 245–7; **1.II**, 21,
 48, 79, 80, 83, 84, 95, 96, 97, 108,
 111, 120, 181, 203, 210, 214, 215,
 237, 241, 243, 272, 276, 277; **2.I**, 6,
 10–12, 21, 138, 142; **2.II**, 96, 202;
 3, 154, 157, 158; **5.I**, 102, 104, 119,
 120, 139, 160; **5.II**, 13, 17, 31–41
 passim, 82, 83, 101, 123, 174, 177,
 190, 198, 200, 201, 205, 206, 232;
 5.III, 17, 23, 197; **8.I**, 16, 134, 315;
 9, 271, 378; **10.I**, 9, 10, 14, 26, 28,
 32, 33, 235, 237, 341, 367, 380; **10.II**,
 26, 27, 30, 64, 69, 71, 79, 117, 122;
 10.III, 122, 131; **11.I**, 28, 37, 172,
 175, 256, 260, 262, 268, 270, 280;
 11.II, 58, 144–6, 163; **11.III**, 148,
 163, 168, 184; **12.I**, 62, 106, 108,
 143, 152, 164, 167, 189; **12.II**, 32, 53,
 82, 102, 117, 126, 129, 131, 158, 176;
 13, 251; **14**, x, 33, 108, 233, 250;
 15.I, *207–10*; **16.I**, 147, 164, 167,
 168, 197, 267, 269, 272, 275; **16.II**,
 45–7, 112; **17**, 47, 273, 277
Christianity,
 1.I, 49, 50, 60, 74–9 passim, 89, 92,
 95, 98, 102, 145, 149, 152, 155, 157,
 159, 163, 167, 175, 181, 211, 239,

245, 246; **2.I**, 5, 6, 10, 17, 19, 23, 28, 34, 37, 41–6 passim, 51–3, 64–71 passim, 74, 76, 77, 79, 82–6, 123, 124, 129, 132–8 passim, 141, 142, 145, 271, 272, 274–6, 290–2, 306; **2.II**, 61, 78, 88, 93–4, 96–7, 140–1, 177, 201, 283; **3,** 3, 27–31, 63, 65, 84, 95, 134, 135, 140, 141, 147, 151–9 passim, 171, 174, 179, 189, 203, 205, 210; **5.I**, ix, x, 5, 23–7, 41, 55–9, 78, 82, 85, 95–7, 101, 102, 119, 132, 133, 135, 138, 139, 149–52, 156–60, 188; **5.II**, 12, 14–16, 21, 25–9, 31, 38, 43, 69, 82–4, 97, 101, 103–6, 112, 118, 124, 137, 140, 142, 151–4, 159, 162–4, 174, 179, 190, 194–206 passim, 220–34 passim, 239, 241, 242, 247, 252, 252; **5.III**, 17, 21–3, 26, 45, 47, 99, 100, 103, 107, 197, 205, 206, 256, 274, 279; **6.I**, 2–4, 9–11, 28, 34, 37, 40–2, 172, 173, 213, 278, 279, 286, 287, 299, 300, 370, 371; **6.II**, 1, 2, 5, 8, 10–12, 15–17, 25–8, 31–4, 40–3, 46, 47, 55, 59, 61–3, 65, 75, 91, 92, 102, 103, 108, 110, 130, 134, 136, 138, 145–8, 151, 152, 164, 171–3, 175, 193, 199, 200, 204, 207–9, 217, 218, 220, 221, 233–53 passim; **6.III**, 2, 9, 17, 19, 28, 39, 46, 47, 66, 82, 83, 85, 161, 165, 171, 221, 224, 236, 263, 295, 298, 302–5, 308–10; **7.I**, xii, 2, 5, 6, 9, 10, 32, 63, 66, 86, 91, 115, 132, 160, 169, 172–6, 188, 205, 206, 208, 222, 224, 225, 234, 241–4, 249, 251, 253, 274, 282, 289, 290, 293, 295, 299, 300, 303–13 passim; **7.II**, 3–8, 17, 19, 24, 26, 29–37 passim, 43, 44, 56, 60, 67, 69, 70, 76, 79, 80–3, 96–102 passim, 105–12 passim, 117–19, 126, 127, 130–3, 138, 157, 162, 165–8, 175–9, 183–5, 189, 191, 198, 199, 202, 204, 206, 211, 217, 221–6, 234, 243–53 passim, 257, 267, 270–3, 277–82, 294, 295, 298, 300, 311, 313, 317–30

passim, 335–52 passim; **7.III**, 56, 88, 101, 107, 113, 127, 137, 140, 209, 216, 220, 222; **8.I**, 6, 8, 12, 15–20, 22, 23, 31–9 passim, 50, 62–6, 74, 82, 86, 91, 94, 95, 97, 128, 131, 134, 135, 138–45 passim, 156, 159, 177, 179, 180, 203, 207–9, 213, 221, 222, 240, 241, 244, 246, 247, 252, 255, 260, 263, 283, 313, 315, 329, 330, 333, 340, 343, 346, 352, 354, 361, 362, 368, 424, 426, 427, 442–4, 447, 454; **8.III**, 176, 182, 184, 213, 214, 218, 234, 237–46 passim, 254–8, 273; **9**, 48, 49, 67, 78, 80, 87, 99, 128, 138, 139, 145, 149, 165–7, 170–89 passim, 190, 209, 248, 252, 255, 271–83 passim, 309, 367, 368, 369, 378, 380, 382, 395, 396, 400; **10.II**, 3–23, 25–44, 46, 48, 49, 50, 52, 55, 56, 58, 59, 64, 71, 72, 74, 76–9, 81, 95, 97, 98, 107, 108, 117, 125, 126, 131, 138, 145–9, 152, 153, 161, 167, 173, 175, 180–5, 193, 198, 200, 206–15 passim; **11.I**, x, 16, 27, 28, 30, 36, 37, 95, 114, 115, 117, 118, 157–60, 167, 168, 172, 176, 180, 232, 246, 247, 250, 254–6, 258, 261, 262, 267, 268, 270, 274, 275, 278, 279, 291, 298, 301; **11.II**, 11, 30, 48, 52, 56, 58, 59, 67, 71, 77, 118, 126, 142, 143, 145, 146, 150, 152, 153, 162, 165, 216, 224–6, 249; **11.III**, 2–7, 20, 23, 64, 67, 71, 76, 77, 79, 80, 82, 94, 105, 109, 113, 118, 121, 123, 124, 126, 144, 148, 162, 165–74 passim, 179, 188, 192, 203, 206, 211, 215, 225; **12.I**, 21, 23, 24, 39, 51, 53, 82, 94, 95, 103, 105, 107, 123, 143, 144, 146, 148, 152, 166, 167, 187, 188, 230; **12.II**, 5, 17, 22, 26, 27, 30, 32, 52–4, 73, 82, 87, 88, 92–4, 102, 105, 108, 109, 111, 114, 127, 128, 130, 138, 141, 145, 149, 153–63 passim, 174; **12.III**, 3, 4, 9, 19, 57–9, 70, 72, 73, 77, 80, 112, 113, 122, 124, 127–9, 135–8, 140, 156,

159–61, 167, 171, 189; **12.IV**, 1,
3–5, 9, 17, 18, 20, 22, 32, 33, 56, 57,
68, 70, 75, 104, 106, 121, 143, 154,
162, 170, 172, 179, 180, 182–4, 186,
205, 206, 208, 217, 218, 225; **12.V**,
15, 18, 28, 33–43, 69, 70, 97, 98,
126, 151, 152; **13**, 24, 58, 60, 61, 66,
67, 71–4, 76, 83, 105, 135, 138, 140,
141, 146, 148, 160, 161, 164–7, 172,
195, 208, 209, 211, 219, 221, 226,
233, 235, 250, 251, 298, 299, 301,
303–5, 308, 309, 315, 317–19; **14**,
ix, x, 14, 15, 33, 34, 36, 45, 83, 90,
96, 98, 112, 115, 124, 130, 139, 143,
151, 184, 213, 214, 222, 238; **16.I**,
22, 27, 28, 98, 151, 159, 161, 163–8
passim, 193, 194, 198, 215–17, 230,
231, 233, 254, 257, 260, 263, 264,
268, 269, 271–3, 275; **16.II**, 28, 30,
35, 46, 47, 67–9, 92, 99, 116, 134,
135, 136, 158, 165, 194, 210, 219,
220, 225, 229–32, 235–47; **17**, xi,
xiii, 9, 11, 12, 18, 21, 40, 41, 44, 45,
47, 48, 53, 89–90, 121, 123, 125–7,
131–7 passim, 148, 186, 219, 255

Christianity, Biblical,
  10.II, 27, 29
Christianity, New Testament,
  5.II, 197, 202; **7.I**, 172; **10.I**, 232–8
  passim; **10.II**, 38; **11.I**, 280, 299;
  11.II, 226; **11.III**, 223; **12.II**, 160,
  162; **12.III**, 76, 161; **16.I**, 165, 223
Christianity, official,
  12.II, 53, 61, 126, 129, 131, 137
Christology,
  1.II, 113, 293, 305; **4**, 5, 11, 28, 51,
  62; **6.II**, 235–53 passim; **8.I**, 8, 268,
  275, 276, 278; **8.II**, 225; **8.III**, 244,
  246, 255; **9**, 149, 150, 276, 277,
  278; **10.I**, 83, 128, 135, 136, 148,
  188, 189, 192, 244, 245, 263, 264,
  325–30, 347, 349, 359; **10.II**, 86, 93,
  94, 107, 131, 132–7, 146; **10.III**, 21,
  25, 35; **11.I**, 16, 40; **11.II**, 213, 214,
  218, 221, 229, 250; **12.I**, 52; **13**, 71,
  307, 308, 316, 319

Church, the,
  10.II, 17, 27, 38, 111, 195, 196, 202;
  15.I, *211–14*
cinema,
  11.II, 94, 99, 101, 102
civil marriage,
  7.II, 313–17, 320, 323, 324
Clara Raphael controversy,
  7.III, 84–92 passim, 142–4
Classicism,
  1.II, 193; **5.III**, 137, 145, 157, 246;
  15.II, *1–4*
cogito,
  6.I, 70; **9**, 241, 244, 250, 397; **11.I**,
  116; **11.II**, 130, 132, 133
collateral, the,
  7.I, 236, 239, 240, 252–5
colonialism,
  14, 257, 259
comedy/comic,
  2.I, 167–98, 228, 251, 252; **2.II**, 61,
  62, 75, 293; **5.III**, 16–26 passim, 77,
  81, 83–7, 97, 125–33, 171, 179, 198,
  200, 241, 245–70 passim; **6.II**, 27,
  29; **6.III**, 4, 6, 7, 20, 67, 118, 191,
  23, 215, 250, 264, 309; **7.II**, 232,
  238, 245; **7.III**, 281; **10.II**, 34, 35;
  10.III, 16; **12.I**, 20–2, 49, 51; **12.II**,
  80; **12.IV**, 6, 137; **15.II**, *5–10*; **16.I**,
  52, 53, 55, 56, 58, 61, 89–95, 159,
  164–7, 175, 201–8, 284; **16.II**, 7, 8,
  22, 24, 43–8, 151, 181–6; **17**, 129,
  188, 235
commitment,
  10.II, 110, 117, 125; **11.III**, 36, 51,
  53, 56–61, 63, 64, 66, 67, 78–80, 82,
  101, 111, 113, 122, 125, 189, 204,
  221
common man,
  7.III, 122; **15.II**, *11–16*
communication,
  2.I, 24, 82, 115, 116, 122, 124, 127,
  131, 133, 134, 139, 142, 144, 145,
  259, 304; **6.III**, 105, 156; **7.II**, 159,
  176, 249; **8.I**, 78, 79, 353, 354,
  381, 432, 450, 454; **8.II**, 46, 221–7

passim, 305, 309; **8.III**, 70; **9**, 26, 35, 164, 185, 206, 302, 303, 307, 385, 407; **10.I**, 174; **10.II**, 42; **11.I**, 78, 89, 126, 168, 172, 181, 258, 283; **11.II**, 56–8, 66, 70, 105, 142, 146, 170, 239; **11.III**, 39, 204; **12.I**, 20, 25, 103, 105, 106, 143, 241; **12.II**, 65–99; **12.V**, 57, 71, 94, 117; **13**, 125, 126, 182, 246, 247, 260; **14**, 66, 68, 74; **15.II**, *17–24*; **16.I**, 126, 127; **17**, xi, 236

communication, direct, **1.II**, 22, 25, 108, 320–2; **2.I**, 129, 138; **7.I**, 129, 191, 193–5, 199, 205, 299; **7.II**, 250; **10.I**, 8, 10, 12; **10.III**, 34; **12.III**, 5; **12.IV**, 76

communication, indirect, **1.I**, 180, 181; **1.II**, 25–9, 108, 114–20 passim, 190, 237–45; **2.I**, 115, 124, 137–8, 142, 204, 205, 305; **2.II**, 84–5, 92, 97; **5.II**, 101, 139; **5.III**, 78, 88, 90, 196, 197; **6.I**, 20, 21, 83, 84, 213, 221, 222; **6.II**, 206, 222; **6.III**, 106, 186, 190; **7.I**, 1, 200, 205, 199; **7.II**, 89, 251; **7.III**, 292; **8.I**, 49, 78, 182, 260, 457; **8.II**, 45, 92, 219–27 passim, 249, 269, 270, 272, 302; **8.III**, 6, 51, 65, 75, 81, 105, 107, 114, 236, 248, 249, 253; **9**, 101, 170–7 passim, 182, 188, 189, 202, 205, 271, 302, 319, 378, 379, 384, 386, 400, 403, 406; **10.I**, 9, 12, 95, 165, 172, 362; **10. II**, 55, 73, 77, 136; **11.I**, 168, 172, 189, 214, 231, 232, 234; **11.II**, 4, 6, 64, 77, 147, 150, 159, 160, 163, 164; **11.III**, 31, 225; **12.I**, 21, 55, 126, 237, 238, 240, 243; **12.II**, 8, 30, 72–4, 94; **12.III**, 6, 9; **12.IV**, 58, 181; **12.V**, 51, 69, 71, 113, 114, 117; **13**, xii, 57, 74, 181, 183, 203, 204, 206, 232; **15.II**, *17–24*; **16.I**, 128, 263, 267, 270; **17**, 78, 79, 98, 137, 148, 172

communicative action, **14**, 73, 75

communion, **4**, 68, 74–9, 82, 84, 86; **7.II**, 103, 105, 106, 110–12, 125, 215, 222, 350; **15.II**, *25–8*

communism, **10.III**, 102, 116, 136; **12.V**, 34, 40; **14**, 18, 108, 117, 197, 209, 220, 257

community, **6.I**, 17–24; **9**, 35, 43, 48, 49, 51, 53, 318; **10.I**, 25, 43, 53, 70, 75, 76, 79, 80, 82, 85, 160, 162, 193–6, 213, 215, 216, 245, 329; **10.III**, 38, 48, 50, 71, 92, 112, 114, 118, 119, 121–3, 128, 199, 206, 207; **11.I**, 172; **11.II**, 55, 64, 72, 218; **12.I**, 104 n, 184; **12.III**, 112; **12.IV**, 166; **13**, 140, 141, 239, 310; **14**, ix, x, xiv, 18, 82, 129, 139–42, 144, 161, 184, 221, 233

comprehension. *See* understanding

Concept, the, **6.III**, 58, 61; **7.II**, 3, 4; **15.II**, *29–34*

concrete/abstract, **15.II**, *35–42*

Confessing Church, **10.I**, 43–5, 105, 145

Confessio Augustana invariata, **20**, M 469

confession, **15.II**, *43–6*

confinium, **10.III**, 17

conformism, **11.I**, 298, 300

conformity, **13**, 100–2, 105, 108, 153, 179, 232

Confucianism, **8.III**, 114

conscience, **2.I**, 277, 291; **2.II**, 69, 70, 78, 283; **4**, 115, 148; **5.I**, 118, 149, 150, 153, 160; **6.III**, 37, 38, 79, 250; **7.II**, 268, 269, 272, 277, 281, 319, 320, 324, 325; **9**, 101, 202, 227, 229, 266, 267, 283, 284, 285; **10.I**, 166, 169, 171, 206; **10.II**, 119, 120, 147; **11.I**, 23,

30, 132; **11.II**, 122; **12.I**, 38, 106,
159, 178; **12.II**, 151; **12.IV**, 12, 153;
12.V, 31, 80, 93, 97; **13**, 91, 159,
166, 261; **14**, 17, 37, 64, 79; **15.II**,
47–54

consciousness,
15.II, *55–60*

consumerism,
13, 3, 5, 89, 123

contemporaneity,
1.II, 316, 319, 322; **2.I**, 304; **5.I**, 95;
6.II, 49; **7.II**, 111, 121, 124, 223,
224; **8.I**, 97, 311, 343, 439; **8.II**,
291; **8.III**, 88, 280; **9**, 133, 305, 400,
405; **10.I**, xii, 59, 60, 71, 84, 96,
149, 233, 234, 323, 359, 360; **10.III**,
14, 17, 22, 29, 32, 36, 38, 53, 54, 68,
69, 71; **11.I**, 14, 132, 134, 192; **12.II**,
5; **12.IV**, 71; **14**, 82; **15.II**, *61–6*

content and form,
2.II, 294

contingency,
7.I, 41; **10.I**, 80; **12.IV**, 168; **14**, 65,
66, 166, 232, 240, 245; **15.II**, *67–72*

contradiction,
1.I, 187; **2.I**, 57, 62, 135, 136, 138,
191; **2.II**, 3–20 passim, 23, 75, 78,
134; **5.I**, 17, 55, 56, 175, 176; **6.I**,
85, 134, 322, 325, 326, 329, 337,
355; **6.II**, 4, 113; **7.I**, 44, 61–3;
8.I, 203; **10.I**, 29, 80, 94, 205, 253,
254, 324, 355, 356, 357; **10.II**, 6, 7;
10.III, 10, 14, 16, 19, 88; **12.I**, 21–5,
46, 103, 145, 190, 206; **12.V**, 83,
84; **15.II**, *73–80*; **16.I**, 94, 128, 129,
167, 177, 178; **16.II**, 5, 6, 33

Copenhagen Flying Post. See Heiberg,
Johan Ludvig, *Kjøbenhavns*
Flyvende Post

corrective,
15.II, *81–6*

The Corsair,
1.I, 150; **2.I**, 137, 191–4 passim,
241, 284; **2.II**, 288; **3**, 153; **5.III**,
20, 86, 88, 175, 252, 254; **6.I**, 262;
6.II, 68, 217, 221, 240; **6.III**, 179,

265; **7.I**, ix, 24, 29, 31, 247; **7.II**,
18, 162, 182, 183, 199, 200, 327;
7.III, 26, 105–14 passim, 123–41
passim, 144–7, 163, 213, 214,
247–53 passim, 278; **8.I**, 11, 13, 15,
16, 71, 422; **8.II**, 255, 307; **10.II**,
69, 94; **11.III**, 144; **12.I**, 69, 102,
159, 161–4; **12.II**, 25, 32, 34, 36, 50;
12.III, 134; **12.IV**, 120; **13**, x, 58,
59; **16.I**, 36, 206, 207, 256; **16.II**,
51, 54, 184; **17**, 36, 67, 80, 82, 84,
85, 101, 167, 202, 203

Council of Nicaea,
7.II, 70

Counter-Reformation,
5.II, 44

courage,
15.II, *87–92*

Court Theater in Copenhagen,
5.III, 143

creatio ex nihilo,
1.I, 4, 7, 8, 10, 16, 26, 33, 35, 39

creation,
1.I, 13–15, 39; **4**, 4; **6.II**, 2–8 passim, 102, 103, 108–11, 113, 132;
6.III, 262, 263; **9**, 43, 53, 54, 65,
149, 150, 307, 308, 310, 317, 368;
10.I, 4, 6, 26, 44, 72, 75, 76, 85, 93,
168, 192–4, 248; **10.II**, 151; **10.III**,
11, 57, 71, 144, 146; **11.I**, 61, 153,
280; **11.II**, 145, 250, 251; **11.III**,
5, 7; **12.I**, 51; **13**, 24, 74, 189, 190,
315; **14**, 214; **15.II**, *93–100*

Creator,
10.I, 92

credo quia absurdum,
12.I, 50; **12.III**, 29

Criminelsager,
20, M 926–931

crisis,
13, xii, 167, 81, 90, 121–5, 128, 129,
135, 140, 141, 146, 148, 165, 188,
231, 260, 261, 265, 271; **14**, 21, 154,
202; **15.II**, *101–6*; **17**, 107–15

critical theory,
11.I, x; **11.III**, 203

criticism,
12.V, 87–101
crowd,
1.I, 180, 190, 191; **1.II**, 241; **2.I**,
128; **5.III**, 88, 100, 107; **8.III**, 68,
75, 133, 142; **9**, 45, 48, 51, 52, 105,
111, 112; **10.I**, 268; **10.II**, 110; **10.
III**, 118; **11.II**, 152; **12.I**, 149, 150;
12.IV, 10–13; **12.V**, 40; **13**, 41, 102,
146–8, 152, 288; **14**, 14, 16, 25, 154,
188; **15.II**, *107–14*; 204, 205, 266,
267
crucifixion,
1.II, 6, 20, 30, 80, 84, 86, 151–65,
180, 289; **4**, 51, 54, 57, 115; **9**, 360,
368; **10.I**, 190; **13**, 318; **16.I**, 266
cultural radicalism,
8.I, 17, 33, 82–4, 126, 137, 142, 165
culture,
6.III, 175; **7.III**, 157, 158, 218, 226;
15.II, *115–20*
culture Protestantism,
10.I, 116, 120, 232, 238, 378
cura pastoralis,
5.II, 39
Cynicism/Cynics,
3, 26; **11.II**, 167
Cÿprianús,
20, M 1462

D

daimon,
2.II, 63, 78, 306; **3**, 7, 15, 16; **6.I**,
106–8, 115; **16.II**, 78
daimonic, the,
8.II, 268; **8.III**, 6, 18, 19, 21, 45
dance,
15.II, *121–8*; **16.I**, 194; **16.II**, 99,
123–5
Danish Church,
16.I, 264, 267; **16.II**, 264
Danish Constitution of 1849,
7.I, 170, 173, 242, 243, 248; **7.II**,
103, 126, 155, 195, 313, 314, 336,
350; **7.III**, 95, 106, 114, 115, 133,
138, 226

Danish Historical Society, the,
7.III, 234
Danish Society for Language and
Literature, the,
8.I, 56
Danish State Church,
7.I, 169, 173–6; **8.I**, 82
Danmark,
7.II, 156
Dannebroge,
7.II, 217
Danne-Virke,
7.II, 106, 155, 168
Danskeren,
7.II, 109; **7.III**, 92
Dansk Folkeblad,
7.I, 170
Dansk Folkekalender for 1841–42,
20, A II 314–315
Dansk Kirketidende,
7.II, 102, 124–6, 166, 168, 196, 200
Dansk Literaturtidende,
7.I, 15
Dansk-Norsk Forlagscatalog,
20, M 981
*Dansk Ordbog udgiven under
Videnskabernes Selskabs Bestyrelse*,
20, A II 5–8
*Dansk-Tydsk og Tydsk-Dansk Lomme-
Ordbog*,
20, M 1025
Dansk Ugeskrift,
7.I, 16
Darwinism,
12.II, 103, 112; **12.III**, 109, 130,
168, 170
das Man (the they) *See* also crowd
9, 48, 105, 110–12
death,
1.I, 9, 13, 25, 27, 48, 52, 67, 73, 79,
94, 101, 158, 167, 169, 171, 173,
201, 240, 257; **1.II**, 4, 84, 85, 135,
139–47 passim, 152–4, 158, 159,
163, 175, 176, 181; **2.I**, 116, 117,
120–1, 123, 127, 136–40 passim,
143, 145, 203; **2.II**, 113; **5.II**, 24;

5.III, 266; **8.I**, 164; **8.III**, 3, 10, 12,
13, 18, 21, 49–53, 61, 233; **9**, 7, 65,
71, 91, 101, 105, 108, 114, 148, 156,
207, 210, 303, 304, 318, 362, 381,
383; **10.I**, 10, 28, 47, 198, 201, 205,
248, 344; **11.I**, 31, 96, 110, 111, 128,
189, 190, 217, 218, 263, 269, 290,
299; **11.II**, 26, 28, 29, 33–5, 74–8,
111, 117–20, 128, 129, 131, 246,
249, 250, 252; **11.III**, 73, 74, 144;
12.I, 15, 17, 18, 24, 177, 179, 181,
188, 213, 230, 231; **12.III**, 46, 90,
92, 94, 99, 182, 188; **12.IV**, 19, 31,
32, 72, 74, 75, 81–3, 88–96, 110,
117, 128, 133, 200, 201, 205; **12.V**,
11; **13**, 18, 20–5 passim, 63, 75, 90,
91, 130, 131, 163, 177, 188, 189,
202, 235, 254, 280, 282, 284–6, 290,
293, 309; **14**, 33, 105, 151, 191, 216,
218, 222, 236, 245; **15.II**, *129–34*;
16.I, 117, 255

death of God. *See* God, death of
death of the author,
11.II, 23, 24, 33; **12.I**, ix; **17**, xiii,
246
deception,
2.I, 86, 122–4, 131, 138, 144–6, 281;
12.I, 24, 149, 150; **16.I**, 2, 21, 73,
75, 84, 108, 129, 152, 154, 260–3;
17, 227, 229–32, 235–40
decision. *See also* choice
9, 14, 17, 171, 174, 179, 229, 287,
333, 335, 337, 339, 341; **10.I**, 18, 22,
50, 52, 55, 59, 60, 85, 86, 88, 267,
326, 350, 366, 382; **10.II**, 10, 13, 14,
16, 18, 32, 36, 40, 51, 116, 117, 126,
134, 138, 184; **10.III**, 61, 70; **11.I**,
31, 33, 34, 39, 55, 114, 117, 119,
131, 133, 165, 170, 177, 195, 196,
198, 282, 283; **11.II**, 103, 112, 118,
120, 121, 131, 132, 142, 160; **11.III**,
128; **12.I**, 6–11, 21, 26, 46, 49, 54,
86, 106–8, 123, 205; **12.IV**, 11, 17;
13, 103, 124, 130, 219, 220, 234,
261, 262, 266, 270, 303, 312; **14**, 6,
16, 25, 35, 36, 45, 62, 76, 139, 184,

186, 187, 192, 194–6, 202, 204, 233;
15.II, *135–8*; **17**, 178, 189, 190
decisionism,
11.I, 114
deconstruction,
8.I, 98; **8.III**, 229, 252, 256; **11.I**, xi;
11.II, 129–31, 208; **11.III**, 209, 211,
214; **12.IV**, 193, 202, 208; **13**, 139;
14, 41, 54
Deer Park,
5.III, 41
defiance,
1.II, 103; **4**, 90, 124, 230; **6.III**, 226;
9, 72, 180, 287, 342; **10.I**, 93; **10.III**,
127; **11.I**, 195, 197–9, 201; **11.II**, 12;
12.III, 160; **13**, xii, 143, 227, 289;
14, 248; **15.II**, *139–46*; **17**, 17, 43
deism,
1.I, xii; **1.II**, 286, 288, 290; **2.I**,
271; **5.I**, 84, 149, 151, 152, 156;
5.III, 276
Delphi, oracle at,
2.I, 9, 17, 75, 77, 80, 119, 273; **2.II**,
159
demand of the age,
6.III, 86; **7.I**, 48, 49, 234; **16.I**, 271;
17, 200
demands of the time. *See* demand of
the age
democracy,
7.II, 201, 219, 313, 319, 323; **12.I**,
64; **12.IV**, 120; **14**, xi–xiii, 18, 24,
75, 120, 125, 148, 178, 190, 195,
196, 200, 232
demon, demonic, the,
1.I, 36, 257, 259; **5.III**, 8, 9, 192,
193, 215–19; **6.II**, 11, 12, 18; **6.III**,
59, 79, 134, 164, 246; **7.III**, 77–81,
179, 294; **8.I**, 47, 368; **9**, 66, 84–6,
89, 90, 147, 180, 340; **10.I**, 364,
368; **10.III**, 147, 148; **11.I**, 23, 38,
174; **11.II**, 66, 67, 72, 74, 117, 225;
11.III, 35; **12.I**, 148, 185–8, 208,
209; **12.II**, 5, 11, 81, 94, 111; **12.III**,
35, 165, 183; **12.IV**, 183; **12.V**, 41,
81, 180; **13**, 44, 146, 170, 243, 255,

261, 304; **14**, 67, 128, 189, 204, 216,
241, 243, 263, 268; **15.II**, *147–52*;
16.I, 19, 22, 25, 26, 28, 43, 82, 86,
143–5, 191, 192, 215; **16.II**, 22–7,
91, 123, 124, 145, 158, 199–213,
242; **17**, 254, 273
demonism,
  12.V, 15
demythologization,
  10.I, 98, 133, 190
Den i den gandske Verden bekiendte
  Ertz-Sort-Kunstner og Trold-Karl
  Doctor Johan Faust
  20, U 35
de omnibus dubitandum est,
  7.I, 198; **7.II**, 243
depression,
  12.II, 140; **13**, 23, 39, 64, 111, 133,
  155, 178, 185; **16.II**, 7
desire,
  9, 110, 144, 148, 286, 378; **11.I**,
  17, 70, 76, 112, 171, 202, 263, 271;
  11.II, 76, 178–80, 194, 196; **12.I**,
  187; **12.III**, 90; **13**, 97, 103, 112,
  113, 138, 140, 144, 145, 181, 183,
  188, 203, 208, 210, 211, 225, 315;
  14, 56; **15.II**, *153–8*; **16.II**, 176
despair,
  1.I, 58, 110, 116, 183, 192, 213;
  1.II, 9, 13, 74, 87, 116, 146, 147,
  175; **2.I**, 21, 122, 128, 136, 139–46
  passim, 188; **2.II**, 62, 201; **3**, 6,
  44, 48, 141; **4**, 31, 54, 58, 59, 90,
  223–36, 127, 128, 230–2, 277; **5.I**,
  14, 15, 181; **5.II**, 73, 105, 106, 198;
  5.III, 4, 5, 9, 126, 149, 216–22
  passim; **6.I**, 74, 75, 78, 80, 86, 133;
  6.II, 151, 187, 217; **6.III**, 37, 133,
  164–6, 186, 200, 214, 225, 226,
  282; **7.I**, 133, 159, 299; **7.II**, 85,
  119, 120, 122, 171, 225; **7.III**, 78,
  83, 94, 95, 133, 134; **8.I**, 153, 161,
  201, 206, 254, 338, 358, 372, 428,
  432, 442, 443, 445, 449; **8.II**, 6,
  25, 166, 169, 216, 223, 226, 229,
  262, 292, 307, 324, 325; **8.III**, 15,

16, 47, 60, 65–70, 110–12, 115,
117, 129, 131, 138, 183, 240, 243,
291, 320; **9**, ix, 65, 76, 78, 81, 84,
87, 90, 105, 114, 132, 135–7, 140,
146–9, 172, 210, 223, 264, 283,
284, 285, 301, 318, 340, 341, 360,
364, 370, 399, 407; **10.I**, xii, 3,
15, 18, 20, 26, 33, 91–4, 133, 169,
253, 260, 262, 265, 269, 303, 304,
339, 346, 351–3, 357, 362, 364,
369; **10.II**, 50, 97, 149, 151, 159,
177, 179, 181, 184; **10.III**, 30, 68,
117, 126, 127; **11.I**, 17, 31, 39, 60,
111, 113, 115, 118, 167, 168, 182,
193–203 passim, 215, 220, 225,
271, 292, 296, 297; **11.II**, 18, 27,
75, 76, 126–8, 131, 132, 182, 184,
227, 240, 241–3, 251; **11.III**, 6, 35,
51, 61, 63, 67, 111, 112, 148, 149,
221, 223; **12.I**, 11, 15–18, 22, 24,
49, 74, 82–5, 122, 128; **12.II**, 11,
79, 92, 94, 110, 111, 116, 128, 155,
156, 159; **12.III**, 8, 10, 46, 47, 75,
80, 125, 160, 165, 166, 180, 190;
12.IV, 3, 13, 32, 33, 36, 56, 58,
61, 83, 116, 123, 127, 151, 153,
164, 179, 181, 184–6, 189, 213–22
passim, 225, 226; **12.V**, 8, 10, 12,
16–19, 46, 52, 69, 78, 82–5, 134,
151, 153, 160, 162, 163, 166, 167;
13, xi, xii, 22, 23, 36, 44, 68, 70,
85, 88, 90, 92, 97, 101, 102, 110,
121, 128, 133, 135, 143, 144, 152,
154, 156–8, 178, 185, 228–31, 233,
235, 248, 252–5, 278, 287–9, 292,
302, 304, 314, 316; **14**, 3, 4, 45, 48,
61, 62, 65, 67, 94, 104, 113, 115,
116, 124, 125, 128, 130, 154, 187,
192, 214, 221, 233, 234, 236–8,
240, 242–9 passim, 258, 261, 263,
265–7, 269; **15.II**, *159–64*; **16.I**,
19, 72, 75, 98–9. 116. 153. 176,
178, 182, 192–3, 218–24, 227, 239;
16.II, 7, 8, 29, 116, 124, 193, 207,
208, 210, 231, 237, 239–45; **17**, 3,
11–15, 17–19, 43–6, 48, 113, 119,

127, 161, 180, 181, 183, 184, 187,
191, 210, 231, 233, 253, 255, 306
detachment,
  5.II, 255, 256
determinism,
  2.II, 17, 18; **5.I**, 37, 43; **10.I**, 79
devil,
  1.II, 38; **7.II**, 11, 19, 167, 215; **12.I**,
  174, 185–8
Devotio Moderna,
  5.II, 39
dialectic,
  2.I, 296, 300; **4**, 126, 158, 161; **6.III**,
  40, 57, 78, 193, 241, 243, 248, 252,
  260, 266, 273; **7.I**, 185, 253, 254,
  291, 292; **8.I**, 144, 211, 336, 337;
  8.III, 51, 52, 64, 110, 113–16, 139,
  275, 291, 292, 299; **10.I**, 3, 12, 14,
  16, 20–3, 33, 74, 80, 88, 90, 98, 99,
  112, 133, 148, 164, 169, 193, 198,
  200, 201, 217, 218, 323, 327, 345,
  347, 350, 352, 353, 356, 357, 360,
  362, 363, 365, 366, 369, 370, 381,
  385; **10.II**, 89, 128; **10.III**, 17, 198,
  200, 201; **12.III**, 5, 29; **12.IV**, 6,
  37, 47, 62, 70, 73, 121, 122, 205;
  12.V, 83, 84, 144; **13**, 3, 11–13, 57,
  81, 82, 88, 125–7, 197–9, 204, 227,
  286, 289, 297, 299, 300, 312, 315;
  14, xiv, 1, 7, 14, 16, 21, 44, 46, 48,
  92, 93, 104, 110, 123–5, 233, 238,
  243–5; **15.II**, *165–70*
dialectic, negative,
  8.I, 366
dialectic, qualitative,
  10.III, 55, 70
dialectical method,
  2.II, 6, 7, 12, 84; **6.I**, 104; **8.I**, 62;
  10.I, 323; **10.II**, 124, 178; **11.III**,
  205; **17**, 7, 13
dialectical theism,
  10.II, 107, 127, 128, 138
dialogical philosophy,
  9, 33, 35, 40, 41, 50–4; **10.III**, 18,
  27; **11.I**, x, 107, 140, 198, 199, 230,
  259, 262, 270, 271, 274

dialectical theology. *See* theology,
  dialectical
dialogue,
  15.II, *171–8*
Dies irae,
  20, A I 92
Diet of Worms,
  5.II, 117, 173–6, 188
difference,
  11.II, 92, 113, 114, 130
difference, absolute,
  2.I, 82, 133; **7.I**, 185; **17**, 44, 46
difference, qualitative,
  10.I, xii, 9, 14, 17, 20, 27, 30, 31,
  58, 78, 328; **10.II**, 31, 52, 55, 79, 89,
  96, 134, 135, 151; **10.III**, 9, 10, 56,
  57, 61, 71, 79, 83, 84, 86, 87, 90, 91,
  94, 179; **11.II**, 229; **12.I**, 206; **13**,
  254, 307, 313, 317; **14**, 61, 99; **15.V**,
  179–84; **17**, 73, 91, 92, 216
dilettantism,
  7.III, 171
disciple at second hand,
  10.III, 32
discipleship,
  10.I, 54–7, 60
dizziness. *See* vertigo
Docetism,
  1.I, 158, 159
dogma/doctrine,
  15.II, *179–86*
dogmatics,
  10.I, 6, 12, 13, 15, 75, 76, 132, 133,
  148, 161, 162, 166, 170, 171, 173,
  378; **10.III**, 8
Donatism,
  4, 11; **10.III**, 56
Don Giovanni. See Mozart, *Don
  Giovanni*
Don Quixote,
  16.I, 285
double-mindedness,
  1.I, 184, 191; **1.II**, 108, 111, 116, 213
double movement,
  11.I, 190, 191, 296; **11.II**, 71, 116,
  117; **12.II**, 155; **15.II**, *187–94*

double-reflection,
  6.I, 83, 84, 221; **7.II**, 159; **9**, 205,
  206, 207, 208; **10.I**, 88; **11.II**, 111,
  126; **12.I**, 21; **15.II**, *195–8*; **17**, 78,
  97, 98
doubt. *See also* skepticism
  1.I, 11, 25, 26, 28, 29, 37, 64, 116,
  147, 213; **1.II**, 8, 20, 49, 79, 80,
  82, 90, 257, 261; **2.II**, 172–4, 190;
  4, 14, 172; **5.I**, ix, 11–17 passim,
  43, 62, 149, 150, 174, 175; **5.II**,
  54; **5.III**, 117, 202, 204; **6.II**, 86;
  6.III, 60, 61, 63, 67, 73, 75, 206,
  256; **7.I**, 224, 297; **7.II**, 83, 240,
  243, 346; **8.II**, 4; **8.III**, 129; **9**, 3,
  228, 380, 400; **10.I**, 69, 94, 336,
  340; **11.I**, 195, 198, 262, 271;
  11.II, 132, 144; **12.II**, 144; **12.III**,
  147, 152; **12.V**, 78, 84, 93, 180; **13**,
  70, 85, 87–9, 92, 97, 104, 123, 133,
  218, 314, 318; **14**, 35–7, 154, 200,
  246, 249; **15.VI**, *53–8*; **16.I**, 75–6,
  81–2, 107, 116, 143, 173, 209–28;
  16.II, 7, 9, 19, 21, 24–6, 102, 106,
  116, 126, 128, 130, 145, 230; **17**,
  119, 253
doxology,
  1.I, 115
drama, Greek,
  8.II, 156
drama/theater,
  2.II, 313–25; **3**, 163–83; **5.III**,
  77, 82, 83, 86, 110, 121, 125–33,
  169–82 passim, 185–207 passim,
  225–42 passim, 245–70 passim;
  6.III, 4, 125, 126, 172–7, 244; **7.I**,
  39; **7.III**, 39, 67, 70, 76–8, 119,
  170–8 passim, 189–208, 209–11,
  215–22 passim, 235, 258, 267,
  269, 275–83; **7.III**, 169–87,
  189–208, 235, 275–83; **11.II**, 33,
  88–90, 101; **12.I**, x, 17, 21, 44–54,
  71, 82, 143, 144, 150, 152–4;
  12.III, *109–44, 145–76*; **12.V**,
  130; **13**, 64, 122, 126–8, 135; **15.
  VI**, *151–6*; **16.I**, 50; **16.II**, 181–6,

199–213; **17**, 107–15; **17**, 58,
  107–15, 305
dread. *See* anxiety
dream,
  12.V, 90, 95, 96, 97; **13**, 34, 37, 38,
  133, 187, 315; **15.II**, *199–206*
dualism,
  5.I, 42, 167; **10.I**, 30, 200, 213–16,
  361, 369, 370, 379, 387–90
duty,
  7.II, 34–6; **9**, 17, 338; **10.II**, 9, 15,
  17, 36, 48, 49, 120, 147, 148, 162–4,
  168; **11.I**, 219, 248, 252, 274; **11.II**,
  100, 119–21, 131, 216, 217; **12.I**, 10,
  11, 72, 74, 219; **12.III**, 39, 71, 72,
  160, 166; **13**, 68, 103, 106, 112, 157,
  262; **14**, 149, 194; **15.II**, *207–12*; **17**,
  177, 178, 187, 263
dying from the world,
  12.II, 127
dying to/renunciation,
  15.II, *213–18*

E
earnestness,
  2.II, 83; **4**, 56; **6.II**, 178–80; **7.III**,
  38; **8.III**, 70; **9**, 66, 182, 342; **10.I**,
  34; **11.I**, 38, 172; **11.II**, 147, 148;
  12.I, 205, 231; **12.II**, 80; **14**, 17,
  249; **17**, 135, 146, 148, 184, 217,
  236, 237, 239, 265
earthquake, the,
  8.I, 30
ecclesiology,
  4, 11, 54, 62, 73; **10.III**, 68, 70
echo,
  12.III, 149
economics,
  11.II, 6, 43–5, 55
Edict of Nantes,
  5.II, 130
edification,
  1.I, 123, 128
edifying discourse/deliberation/
  sermon,
  15.II, *229–34*; **17**, 188

education,
  7.III, 88, 101, 114, 115, 157, 194,
  226, 231; **10.I**, 67
either/or. *See also aut/aut*
  2.II, 13–15, 23, 35, 140; **10.I**,
  379–81, 385–7; **10.II**, 17; **10.III**,
  69, 144, 147; **11.I**, 130, 136, 283;
  11.II, 97; **12.I**, 176, 205; **12.III**,
  113, 128, 129, 134, 137, 154, 189;
  17, 191
Eleatics,
  2.I, xi; **2.II**, 113, *123–45*, 152, 154;
  7.I, 67, 187; **11.II**, 86, 159; **12.IV**,
  125; **13**, 41; **17**, 54
elenchus or *elenctic* method. *See also*
  Socrates, method
  2.I, 116–18, 121, 124–9, 143–6;
  16.I, 265, 273
Elers College,
  7.III, 248, 258
elves, trolles, and nisses,
  12.II, 151, 152; **16.I**, *187–99*
emancipation of women,
  5.III, 83; **7.III**, *83–103*, 142, 143,
  194, 195; **12.III**, 17, 67; **14**, xii; **17**,
  28
emotion. *See also* mood *and* feeling
  11.I, 76; **15.IV**, 197–204
empathy. *See* sympathy/empathy
empiricism, radical,
  11.III, 87–95 passim
Enlightenment,
  1.I, x, 179, 232, 233; **1.II**, 170,
  256, 257, 286, 296, 313; **2.I**, 271–6
  passim; **5.I**, ix, 2, 11, 12, 24, 33,
  34, 77, 80–9 passim, 101, 104,
  149; **5.II**, 68, 150, 163, 164; **5.III**,
  70, 126, 195, 203, 246, 270–6 passim; **6.III**, 98, 103, 106, 107, 118,
  129, 176; **7.I**, 36; **7.II**, 24–6, 30,
  96, 108, 120; **7.III**, 158; **10.I**, 78,
  148, 210, 214; **10.II**, 51, 85; **10.III**,
  104, 136; **11.III**, 71, 124–6; **12.III**,
  118, 119; **12.V**, 34, 82; **13**, 206,
  232; **14**, 34, 79, 226; **16.I**, 105; **17**,
  163, 181

ennui,
  17, 15
enthusiasm,
  15.II, *235–41*
envy,
  12.I, 206; **15.III**, *1–8*
epic,
  7.III, 19, 23, 36, 37, 45, 171–6,
  258–60, 265, 266, 289; **15.III**, *9–12*;
  16.I, 49–62 passim
Epicureanism,
  2.II, 166; **5.II**, 206; **12.V**, 70
epigram,
  15.III, *13–20*
epistemology,
  2.I, 100, 115–19 passim, 132, 133, 145
equality,
  5.III, 102, 103; **10.II**, 157, 159, 160,
  168; **14**, xi, xii, 14, 15, 24, 90, 104,
  200, 216, 245, 259
Erlangen School,
  7.II, 153–5; **10.I**, 243
eros. *See* love, *eros*
erotic. *See* love, erotic
eroticism,
  16.I, 151, 247; **17**, 55, 185, 189
eschatology,
  10.I, 125, 128, 134–6, 185, 224, 226,
  228, 232, 238, 239, 244, 248, 264,
  345, 369; **10.III**, 5, 11
essence,
  6.III, 71, 203
established order, the,
  1.II, 110; **7.II**, 38, 130, 167, 172,
  175, 176, 182, 246, 250, 295, 297,
  317–27 passim; **16.I**, 268, 269, 376;
  16.II, 111, 113, 116, 117
estrangement,
  10.I, 344–6, 350–3, 360, 362, 368, 369
eternal, the,
  7.I, 121; **7.II**, 59; **11.III**, 53, 83;
  12.III, 166; **12.V**, 9, 19, 27, 28
eternal and temporal,
  1.II, 146; **2.I**, 46, 49, 54–7, 63, 69,
  72; **11.II**, 127; **11.III**, 57, 192; **12.V**,
  144; **17**, 12, 42, 186

eternal happiness. *See* happiness, eternal

eternal life,
  1.II, 176

eternal return,
  11.II, 47, 100, 101

eternity,
  1.I, 77, 78, 156–9, 182, 186, 187, 192, 231; **1.II**, 12, 45, 66, 76, 141, 146, 147, 164, 176, 178, 179; **2.I**, 45–72; **5.I**, 167, 172, 182, 184; **5.II**, 55; **7.II**, 16, 33, 118, 127, 129, 244, 300, 345; **8.I**, 211, 357, 382, 442, 446; **8.II**, 48, 296, 308; **8.III**, 20, 53, 54, 57, 58, 61, 65, 70, 135, 239, 291; **11.I**, 160, 168, 191, 262; **11.II**, 88; **12.I**, 25, 179, 181–3, 188, 228, 231; **12.IV**, 82

eternity and time. *See* time and eternity

ethical life,
  6.III, 201, 215; **16.I**, 5, 6

ethics, the ethical. *See also* morality
  2.I, 16, 54, 137, 145; **2.II**, 47–58, 73, 75, 78–9, 83, 155, 157, 195, 242; **5.I**, 23, 28, 29, 41, 43; **6.I**, 35, 81–3, 116, 118, 135, 136, 138, 179, 181, 186–90, 194, 217, 224, 281, 283, 287, 326, 330; **6.II**, 184, 185, 202, 214, 215, 220, 250; **7.I**, 56, 120, 187, 230, 274, 282, 299; **8.I**, 15, 19, 20, 81, 203, 336, 433, 434, 441, 450, 452, 457; **8.III**, 251; **9**, 1, 2, 5, 9, 14, 17, 19, 28, 35, 43, 46, 47, 49, 50, 52, 64, 77, 78, 82, 83, 88, 90, 133, 145, 172, 176, 187, 201, 224, 226–9, 264, 266, 270–6 passim, 280, 282, 284, 287, 300, 304, 309, 310, 312, 315, 331–8 passim, 344, 359, 360, 364, 366, 367–9, 383, 399, 404; **10.I**, xii, 6, 30, 45, 49, 50, 59, 68, 81, 82, 86, 87, 123, 125, 128–36 passim, 150, 157, 161, 162, 165, 168, 202, 237, 278, 301, 322, 329, 330, 363, 378, 380, 381; **10.II**, 8–10, 13–18, 27, 38, 39, 47–9, 51, 57, 70, 120, 122, 144, 145, 147, 148, 157, 159, 162–8, 184, 205–11, 215; **10.III**, 15, 86, 92, 179, 183, 184; **11.I**, xi, 40, 52, 56, 89, 91, 105, 110, 126, 130, 132, 138, 139, 147, 189, 210, 212–15, 218–23, 226–8, 230, 231, 234, 235, 252, 253, 257, 259–63, 272, 276, 279–83, 295; **11.II**, 24, 30–2, 38, 48, 58, 59, 67, 72, 73, 85, 86, 103, 111, 115–17, 119, 120, 122, 126, 131–3, 143, 162, 173–205, 219, 223, 250; **11.III**, 42, 55–61, 66, 110, 123, 125, 127–9; **12.I**, 2, 9–12, 21, 34, 35, 38, 48, 69, 71–6, 82–7, 101, 103, 105, 123, 130, 147, 166, 180 189, 209, 210, 241; **12.III**, 17, 23, 58, 130, 134; **12.IV**, 167; **12.V**, 39, 41, 107, 134, 160, 180; **13**, 35, 36, 41, 60–2, 66, 76, 81, 96, 102, 109, 121, 128, 143, 147, 159, 160, 166, 167, 170, 226, 232, 259–71, 297, 299, 301–6, 309–14, 317; **14**, ix, xi, 12, 13, 25, 35, 47, 49, 57, 58, 63–5, 75, 78, 81, 82, 93, 108, 114, 115, 117, 118, 121, 124–6, 139, 143, 161, 166, 187, 199, 250, 267, 268; **15.III**, *21–8*; **16.I**, 4, 6, 7, 10, 19; **16.II**, 5, 77, 79, 209; **17**, 11, 171, 172, 177–92, 262, 269, 270, 277

ethics, Christian,
  5.II, 9; **10.II**, 14, 207, 208; **10.III**, 92; **12.III**, 72

ethics, existential,
  12.III, 62

ethics, suspension of. *See* teleological suspension of the ethical

Eucharist,
  12.V, 39

eudaimonism,
  13, 106

evangelicalism,
  10.II, 45, 48

Evangelisk-christelig Psalmebog,
  20, M 197

Evangelisk-kristelig Psalmebog,
  20, M 195–196

Every Good Gift,
  1.I, 26, 27, 29, 32, 37, 39
evil,
  1.I, 4, 8, 9, 12, 17–23, 36, 40, 60,
  115, 118, 119, 127, 169, 175, 201;
  2.I, 66, 75, 77, 78; **3**, 17; **5.I**, 3, 58,
  59, 68, 95, 149; **5.II**, 45, 49, 50, 57,
  167; **5.III**, 4; **6.I**, 4, 7, 8–11, 50,
  51, 56, 57, 60, 87, 135, 180, 186,
  188, 189, 194, 226, 287; **6.II**, 8, 9,
  32, 55, 69, 106, 108, 147, 149–51,
  155–7, 185; **7.I**, 130, 135, 243,
  272–5, 282, 296; **7.II**, 3–6, 10, 11,
  19; **9**, 25, 29, 84, 86, 90, 133, 146,
  147, 304, 310, 311, 316–18, 361,
  362, 365, 366, 405; **10.I**, 48, 81,
  134, 218, 248, 266, 363; **10.II**, 5,
  77, 148, 149; **10.III**, 9, 82, 179;
  11.I, 26, 54, 126, 218–20, 281, 282,
  284; **11.II**, 56, 57, 59, 86, 89, 98,
  100, 106, 117, 132, 218, 234, 236,
  240–4, 248; **12.I**, 35, 36, 76, 185;
  13, 147, 166, 169–72, 235, 252,
  301; **14**, 17, 100, 201, 210, 217,
  218, 225, 232, 233, 236, 239–42,
  249; **15.III**, *29–36*; **16.II**, 23, 27,
  40, 91, 130, 207, 208, 209, 211,
  215, 219, 228; **17**, 11, 57, 182, 183,
  207, 271
evil, radical,
  10.II, 149
exception,
  1.I, 136; **9**, 165, 174–6, 178, 181,
  182; **11.II**, 10, 70, 121, 236–9; **12.I**,
  104, 200, 209; **13**, 168, 300; **14**,
  1–4, 6, 7, 13, 14, 16, 21–3, 25, 26,
  33, 178, 181, 184, 185, 187, 188,
  191, 194–6, 198–205 passim; **15.III**,
  37–44
excluded middle, the law of,
  2.II, 3–16 passim, 23; **6.II**, 3, 4, 6,
  7, 17, 213; **7.I**, 44, 59–62; **7.II**, 276;
  8.III, 16; **16.II**, 33
exegesis,
  10.I, 122, 135, 146, 148, 150, 157,
  162, 165, 196, 243, 244, 246, 252

existence,
  2.II, 30–3, 36, 39, 41, 78, 95, 134,
  139, 141, 155, 156, 159, 307; **5.I**,
  ix, 28, 41, 61, 68; **6.I**, 67, 102, 104,
  115, 192–4, 282, 287, 317, 325–9;
  7.II, 31, 33, 37, 108, 113, 159, 160,
  177, 178, 185, 243, 248, 256, 329,
  345; **8.I**, 344, 356, 382; **8.II**, 43,
  157, 220, 223, 225, 296, 304, 324,
  325; **8.III**, 4, 5, 70, 108, 111, 115; **9**,
  23, 25, 27, 48, 56, 65, 68, 72, 85–91
  passim, 102, 107, 135, 136, 138,
  181, 184, 199, 200–2, 205, 207–9,
  224–6, 238, 239, 252, 381, 394, 397,
  401, 402, 406, 407; **10.I**, 2, 20, 80,
  93, 134, 164, 323, 342, 346, 348,
  350–2, 361–3, 366, 368; **10.II**, 16,
  76, 78, 112, 113, 116, 148, 193, 198,
  200; **10.III**, 61, 62; **11.I**, ix, 9, 15,
  17, 22, 30–5, 39, 52, 55, 56, 59, 61,
  62, 70–81 passim, 87, 97, 99, 105,
  110, 111, 113–17, 119, 125, 128,
  129, 131–5, 140, 150, 151, 157–9,
  166–9, 172, 174, 178–80, 188, 189,
  192, 201, 222, 226, 227, 229, 234,
  250–2, 254, 257–63, 268, 270, 274,
  275, 277, 279, 281, 284, 285, 290,
  296, 298–300; **11.II**, 8, 9, 10, 13, 14,
  17, 26, 47, 49–54, 59, 70, 97, 111,
  112, 128, 150, 153, 169, 170, 181–3,
  185, 193, 236, 238, 240, 245, 246,
  248; **11.III**, 19, 80, 93; **12.I**, 2, 7,
  8, 16–25, 71, 72, 76, 79, 82, 86, 87,
  106, 130, 143, 150, 151, 154, 177,
  201, 213, 239–41; **12.IV**, 187; **12.V**,
  83, 85, 107–9, 112, 151, 153; **13**, 24,
  29, 34, 37, 39–49, 58, 60, 61, 106,
  115, 121, 129–30, 133, 134, 143,
  177, 199, 211, 218–20, 223, 261,
  263, 268, 277, 278, 280–3, 288–92,
  298, 303, 314, 317; **14**, 34, 35, 45,
  47–9, 59, 61, 62, 96, 102, 124, 138,
  139, 153, 164, 186, 203, 212, 215,
  217, 219–27 passim; **15.III**, *45–52*
existence, poetic-artistic,
  6.III, 116

existence, spheres of,
  10.II, 69; **11.III**, 51, 53, 55, 58;
  12.II, 26, 32
existentialism,
  8.I, 41, 80, 98, 162, 183, 209, 211,
  225, 238, 251, 254, 257, 287, 339,
  379, 421, 428, 431–50; **8.II**, 3, 6,
  7, 10, 17, 29–31, 39, 44, 85–95
  passim, 164, 168–73, 205, 207, 213,
  215–7, 223–9 passim, 262–4, 267,
  268, 289–91, 295, 306, 318, 319,
  324; **8.III**, 4–9, 13–15, 19, 33, 46,
  49–51, 54–60, 63, 64, 67, 70–4, 77,
  85, 86, 104, 107–13 passim, 116,
  118, 127, 132–9 passim, 149–52,
  179, 184, 187, 188, 205, 229, 231–5,
  251, 252, 269, 270, 273–5, 285,
  290, 320, 322; **10.I**, x, 13, 15, 16,
  33, 44, 65, 68, 72, 77–96, 135, 195,
  269, 338, 344, 346, 349–53, 359–61,
  363, 368; **10.II**, 10, 55, 74, 96–8,
  106, 108, 111–18 passim, 130, 131,
  137, 138, 151, 152, 174, 178–82,
  198, 211; **10.III**, 8, 10, 15, 115, 118,
  142, 177, 190, 202; **11.I**, x, 10, 18,
  23, 24, 28, 32–4, 39, 55, 61, 79, 88,
  105, 123, 133, 136, 138, 150, 167,
  182, 234, 289, 297, 301; **11.II**, 3,
  8, 26–9, 31, 50, 52–4, 58, 112, 150,
  236, 237, 238, 246; **11.III**, 13–15,
  18, 24–6, 34, 74–6, 80, 100–6 passim, 121, 135–44 passim, 148, 153;
  12.I, 81, 87, 115, 129, 154, 176;
  12.II, 19, 115; **12.III**, 3, 5, 28, 29,
  35, 36; **12.IV**, 20, 21, 27–9, 33, 148,
  165, 166, 170, 171, 175, 222, 224;
  12.V, 7, 10, 28, 41, 52, 68, 80, 81,
  106, 125, 140, 143, 146; **13**, 30, 99,
  207, 217–22, 228, 229, 231, 232,
  235, 240, 242–4, 248–50, 273, 274,
  276–87 passim, 291, 292; **14**, 24, 53,
  92, 96, 98, 99, 102, 127, 129, 131,
  138, 142, 147, 152, 161, 162, 211,
  226, 231, 234, 257, 259, 261, 269
existentialism, atheistic,
  8.III, 85, 113, 138

existentialism, religious,
  8.III, 9, 52, 78, 82, 84, 113, 138,
  177, 178
existing order, the. *See* established
  order, the
expectancy,
  1.II, 3–14
experience,
  15.III, *53–60*
expressionism,
  11.II, 97, 98
exterior and interior. *See* outer and
  inner, the

F
Die Fackel,
  12.I, 31, *157–67*
facticity,
  11.I, 98, 129, 135, 138, 140; **11.III**,
  53–8, 60, 63
Fædrelandet,
  5.III, 20; **7.I**, ix, xi, 16, 20–8 passim,
  31–3, 88, 95, 97, 170, 182, 186, 209,
  292, 298, 312; **7.II**, 244, 251, 269,
  270, 275, 299, 311, 320, 326, 351;
  7.III, 24, 109, 112, 123, 130, 136,
  190, 201, 202, 214, 251–3; **12.I**, 62;
  17, 27, 32, 36, 67, 81, 84–6, 107,
  108, 195, 243, 244; **20**, U 39
fairy-tale,
  6.III, 117, 118; **7.I**, 142–4, 216, 271;
  7.III, 1–5, 11, 12, 21, 45, 174, 262,
  264; **10.I**, 204; **12.IV**, 128, 129; **13**,
  56, 188; **15.III**, *61–6*; **16.I**, 21, 23,
  42, 83, 135, 148, 187–9, 198, 241;
  16.II, 66, 135, 207
faith. *See also* πίστις/pistis
  1.I, xii, 26, 29, 36, 37, 39, 40, 44–53
  passim, 58, 64–80 passim, 93, 94,
  97, 116, 130, 148–55 passim, 177,
  213–17, 234, 240–2, 246, 247, 259,
  260, 262; **1.II**, 17–30, 79–82, 85, 86,
  87, 90, 110, 126, 147, 153, 157, 175,
  180, 192–4, 196, 199–205, 210, 211,
  214, 241, 249, 261–70 passim, 285,
  291, 292, 301, 303, 312, 314–24

passim; **2.I**, 28, 29, 33, 34, 37, 39, 41–4, 64, 65, 67, 69, 71, 72, 74, 80, 83–6, 91, 136, 141, 142, 144, 204, 209, 271, 283, 286, 290, 305, 306; **2.II**, 22, 38, 66, 82, 88–97 passim, 113, 174–5, 178, 240–3, 304; **3**, 45, 46, 61–5, 84, 99, 189, 190; **4**, 5, 6, 14–16, 23, 24, 32, 33, 38, 40–3, 47, 54, 57, 58, 62, 63, 68, 72–9, 84–6, 90, 99, 100, 104, 116, 117, 123, 124, 126, 127, 131, 133–8, 148, 150, 151, 159–63, 167–82, 185, 191, 192, 198, 199, 202, 231, 232, 243, 270, 273, 294; **5.I**, ix, 5, 7, 12, 15, 16, 23–7 passim, 38, 43, 66, 69, 77, 93, 95, 100, 102, 104, 133, 149, 150, 157, 158, 167, 184, 188; **5.II**, 22, 24, 26, 27, 29, 82–4, 87–96 passim, 101–7 passim, 123, 124, 152, 154, 176, 179, 180, 187, 189, 193, 194, 205, 206, 219, 239, 240, 246, 247, 255; **5.III**, 17, 45, 192, 193, 206; **6.I**, 52, 59, 61, 68, 69, 82, 83, 135–8, 182–8 passim, 195, 224, 263; **6.II**, 12, 24, 26, 49, 59, 63, 70, 71, 80, 84–90 passim, 96, 97, 125, 131, 136–8, 144, 207–9, 214, 215, 217, 222, 233, 242, 243, 246, 251, 252; **6.III**, 13, 16, 19, 36, 61, 73, 98–100, 105, 106, 108, 124, 166, 171, 174, 177, 224, 227, 310; **7.I**, 188, 195, 206, 207, 222, 231, 234, 241, 253, 294, 296, 305, 311; **7.II**, 7, 8, 19, 42, 54, 58–60, 62, 65, 69, 75–85 passim, 90–2, 108, 113, 127, 156, 166, 169, 202, 222, 223, 225, 242, 244, 245, 257, 258, 268, 269, 277–9; 72–5, 137; **8.I**, 14, 17, 19, 22, 23, 35, 37, 39, 40, 49, 59–61, 65–7, 78, 128, 155, 177, 179, 180, 182, 184, 201, 204–7, 211, 221, 222, 244, 250, 254, 255, 311, 333, 340–6 passim, 352–4, 361, 362, 440–3, 453–5; **8.II**, 8, 21, 87, 90–2, 165, 216–8, 222, 223, 226, 259, 260, 262, 272, 273, 290, 291–6, 318, 324, 325; **8.III**, 9, 44, 45, 47,

48, 53, 69, 74, 77, 80, 115, 181–3, 214, 215, 218, 232–41 passim, 244, 246, 254–7, 290; **9**, 48, 49, 81, 85, 86, 90, 100, 146, 149, 164, 166, 171, 179, 180, 184–6, 188, 190, 207, 209, 210, 211, 217, 218, 223–8, 247–9, 264–7, 273–82 passim, 305, 306, 308, 310–18 passim, 338, 360–9 passim, 380, 384, 399, 400; **10.I**, x, xi, 5, 8, 17–19, 23, 26, 27, 32, 33, 55, 68, 69, 71, 77, 80–6 passim, 90, 92, 95, 98, 123–5, 127, 132, 133, 135, 136, 146, 147, 149, 167, 171, 188, 202, 206, 214, 228, 246–8, 250, 262, 267, 268, 324, 327, 328, 336, 340, 347, 348, 350, 358, 359, 361, 389; **10.II**, 3–8, 11–14, 18–21, 30–3, 36, 39, 42, 46, 49, 50, 56, 93, 95, 97, 115, 119, 121, 122, 124, 126, 127, 129, 130, 131, 134, 136, 147, 152, 153, 161, 165, 166, 174, 176–85 passim, 193, 198, 200, 201; **10.III**, 18, 20, 32, 35, 38, 54, 64, 69, 80, 100, 107–9, 120, 125–7, 146, 159–65, 171, 176–81, 186, 200, 202, 209; **11.I**, x, 37, 61, 95, 96, 106, 131, 132, 150, 156–9, 167, 168, 171, 189, 191, 192, 195, 198, 200, 201, 215, 217, 226–32 passim, 248, 249, 252, 258–63, 268–71, 274, 275, 279, 284, 285, 291, 294, 296–8, 301; **11.II**, 4, 6, 9, 14–18, 27, 32, 39, 56, 70, 72, 89, 95, 97, 99, 101, 102, 106, 118, 125, 132, 142–4, 145, 147, 153, 184, 185, 187, 195, 213, 216, 222, 224, 225, 243, 245, 248, 250, 251; **11.III**, 4, 7, 15, 16, 21, 22, 37–9, 64, 67, 78, 88, 108, 109, 113, 124, 128, 129, 158, 173, 185, 206, 209, 210, 212; **12.I**, 22–26, 44, 53, 54, 69, 72–4, 83, 94, 103, 106–8, 124, 127, 131, 147, 151–4, 202, 240, 244; **12.II**, 4, 90, 91, 93, 94, 126, 144, 146, 154, 155, 162; **12.III**, 8, 33–5, 37, 55, 135, 166, 167; **12.IV**, 16, 17, 20–2, 32, 33, 103, 104, 130, 151, 164, 167,

169, 179, 180, 198; **12.V**, 9, 31, 39, 84, 85, 129, 135, 160, 172, 180, 184, 194; **13**, 24, 25, 59, 62, 66, 70, 72–4, 85, 100, 109, 112, 113, 121, 128, 129, 135, 138, 145, 160, 164, 170, 187, 189, 209, 217, 218, 226, 253, 270, 304–6, 313, 314, 317–19; **14**, ix, x, 31, 32, 36, 37, 42, 59, 61–3, 65, 66, 79, 81, 83, 91, 98, 103, 115, 124, 126, 129, 130, 191, 192, 198, 222, 233, 234, 237, 238, 240–3, 245, 248, 249, 264; **15.III**, *67–72*; **16.I**, 9, 26, 43, 45, 98, 117, 118, 124, 192, 270; **17**, xiii, 42, 44–6, 48, 53, 121, 131, 132, 137, 143–56 passim, 181, 188–90, 278, 307–9

faith and knowledge,
   7.I, 290–5, 304, 305, 307, 311; **7.II**, 90, 341; **8.I**, 4–9, 12, 18, 32, 203

faith and works,
   1.II, 200, 205, 211, 213; **5.II**, 88, 89, 97, 193, 194, 196, 202, 237

Fall, the,
   1.I, 5–15 passim, 18, 19, 23–5, 29, 30, 33, 36, 39, 119, 152, 213; **2.I**, 43, 64, 65; **6.II**, 6–9, 50, 106, 108, 149, 150, 152, 157; **7.I**, 254; **8.I**, 344; **8.III**, 58; **9**, 24, 25, 28, 65, 105, 107–12, 114, 317, 357, 361–6; **10.I**, 48, 72, 85, 92, 93, 257, 270, 340, 344, 363; **10.II**, 39, 121, 123; **11.I**, 282, 283; **11.II**, 235, 241; **11.III**, 5; **12.I**, 150; **12.II**, 170; **12.III**, 39, 183, 185; **12.V**, 96, 113; **13**, 313, 314, 316; **14**, 92

fanaticism,
   11.III, 83, 109; **14**, 153

farce,
   15.VI, *215–20*

Fascism. *See* National Socialism

fatalism,
   17, 16

fate,
   2.II, 64, 66, 72, 217, 219, 258, 272, 305; **3**, 18; **16.II**, 5, 16, 17, 28, 51, 58, 60–3, 90, 156, 158, 160, 161,

201, 203, 207, 227, 235, 239–41, 243, 245, 251, 254

The Fatherland. See Fædrelandet

fear,
   5.II, 12; **9**, 6, 14, 24–6, 28, 108, 109, 111, 299, 330, 335; **11.II**, 193, 249; **12.I**, 17, 32, 73–6, 85; **12.IV**, 81; **12.V**, 30, 31, 96; **13**, 23, 25, 87, 96, 102, 113, 121, 162, 163, 188, 222, 225, 227, 281–5, 292; **14**, 63, 64, 101, 103, 200, 205, 215–19, 222, 242, 258, 269

fear and trembling
   10.I, 33, 203, 213; **10.II**, 16, 49, 164, 215; **10.III**, 18, 146; **11.II**, 116, 144, 195, 209, 237; **11.III**, 9, 35, 172

feeling. *See also* mood *and* emotion,
   15.IV, *197–204*

felix culpa,
   1.I, 4, 7, 8, 11, 12, 16, 19, 21, 27, 33, 36, 37, 39, 40

feminism. *See also* emancipation of women
   8.I, 457; **9**, 1–21; **11.I**, xi; **11.II**, 2; **13**, 9, 10, 111, 177, 179; **14**, 54

fideism,
   4, 15; **5.I**, 2, 27; **10.I**, 23; **10.II**, 6, 178, 181; **11.III**, 76, 83

Figaro,
   7.III, 252

finite/finitude,
   1.II, 146; **9**, 1, 105, 210, 341, 407; **11.II**, 14, 18, 30; **11.III**, 53; **12.I**, 21, 25–7, 50–2, 75, 124, 179, 183, 225, 232; **12.V**, 83; **13**, 19, 22, 23, 42, 73, 130, 131, 184–6, 209, 260, 281, 284, 288, 289, 290, 292, 293; **14**, 4, 46, 59–61, 63, 65, 96, 101, 102, 110, 184, 219, 265; **15.III**, *73–80*

finite and infinite,
   2.II, 264; **4**, 225; **6.III**, 56, 57, 165, 166, 195, 198, 201, 203, 207, 217, 219, 220, 241, 251, 252, 261, 262; **8.III**, 51, 54; **10.I**, 3, 20, 256, 261, 265, 338, 344, 347, 348, 350, 356, 359–62, 367–9, 380; **10.II**, 11, 94,

127; **10.III**, 61, 64–6, 117, 160;
11.I, 94–6, 131, 135, 139, 152, 167,
168, 252, 259, 279, 282, 284, **11.II**,
15, 17, 76, 88, 89, 92–5, 116, 127,
148, 177, 179, 192, 234, 242; **11.III**,
57; **12.III**, 90; **12.V**, 144; **15.III**,
73–80; **16.II**, 28, 82; **17**, 12, 42,
130, 134, 151, 211, 307, 309; **17**,
128, 129, 307

Flood, the,
   1.I, 4

folklore,
   13, 56

folk tales,
   16.I, 23, 31, 83, 187, 188; **16.II**, 66,
139, 215–21

foreknowledge,
   4, 114, 123, 208–16 passim

forgetfulness,
   17, 6

forgiveness,
   15.III, *81–8*

form and content,
   7.III, 241, 251

Formula of Concord,
   5.II, 21; **10.III**, 159

foundation,
   11.III, 24, 35, 43, 125, 126, 147,
152, 158, 159, 161, 162, 167, 173,
178, 180–2, 196, 222, 223

foundationalism,
   10.II, 45; **11.III**, 180, 181

Frankfurt am Main,
   9, 35, 161, 178, 356

Frankfurt School,
   8.III, 252; **10.I**, 339; **11.II**, 44; **13**, 3,
95; **14**, 53, 74, 137

Frederiksberg Castle,
   7.III, 258

freedom,
   1.I, 4–8 passim, 11–21 passim,
28–40 passim, 133, 164; **1.II**, 24, 26,
58, 60, 64, 74, 141; **2.I**, 64, 125, 145;
2.II, 17, 26, 35–6, 39, 42–5, 62, 64,
113, 174, 189, 199, 217; **3**, 42, 44,
83, 98, 107, 140; **4**, 15, 27, 29, 30,

31, 32, 34, 99, 114, 123–7, 192, 194,
195, 208–10, 213, 214, 280; **5.I**, 15,
16, 34–42 passim, 53, 59, 60, 63–6,
69, 71, 95, 105, 167, 169, 173; **5.II**,
43, 47, 56, 114, 167, 179; **5.III**, 126,
129; **6.I**, 8, 12, 82–4, 107, 112–14,
121, 131, 180, 186, 194, 226, 256,
293, 302, 304, 326, 327, 330, 370;
6.II, 1, 2, 8, 9, 13, 14, 16–18, 41,
44, 45, 60, 61, 65, 67, 104, 106, 108,
109, 132, 147–50, 153, 155–7, 178,
179, 181, 184, 190; **6.III**, 78, 175;
7.I, 17, 19, 24, 25, 37, 40, 41, 53, 62,
86–8, 91–5, 140, 148, 152, 174, 175,
235, 242, 248, 277, 278, 294, 308,
309; **7.II**, 102–4, 107, 109, 127, 131,
132, 134, 175, 176, 185, 195, 216,
217, 233, 235, 242, 250, 313, 317,
321; **7.III**, 77, 88; **8.I**, 23, 71, 139,
144, 145, 161, 182, 376, 423, 425,
427, 431–40 passim, 445, 449; **8.II**,
43, 46, 87, 91, 220, 223, 226, 227,
259, 261, 263, 269, 290, 325; **8.III**,
8, 13, 14, 47, 48, 51, 53, 60, 65, 67,
70–7 passim, 111, 112, 243, 244,
251, 292; **9**, 11–14, 18, 23, 72, 76,
88, 108–12, 140, 141, 157, 206, 207,
210, 267, 276, 279, 283, 284, 285,
307, 317, 323, 327, 328–35 passim,
341, 359, 361, 363, 366, 367, 404,
405; **10.I**, 21, 22, 27, 28, 31, 48, 72,
79, 81, 85, 87, 92, 203, 204, 206,
210, 213, 214, 216, 217, 246, 257,
261–3, 267, 269, 271, 344, 347, 363,
368, 380; **10.II**, 10, 13, 16, 29, 30,
31, 35, 46, 49, 116, 121–3, 143–50
passim; **10.III**, 8, 9, 59, 67, 68, 72,
125, 126, 136, 146, 180, 181; **11.I**,
117, 128, 138, 154, 192, 194, 203,
253, 256, 262, 272, 282, 283; **11.II**,
17, 27, 74, 85, 86, 127, 142–4, 148,
151–3, 159, 210, 212, 236, 249–51;
11.III, 7, 53–5, 58, 60, 63, 101–6,
112, 113, 221; **12.I**, 2–11, 64, 75,
76, 80–4, 120, 148, 154, 208; **12.II**,
23, 28, 79, 80, 90, 111, 125; **12.III**,

10, 39, 184, 185; **12.IV**, 12, 27, 168,
225; **12.V**, 8, 39, 42, 96, 127, 129,
132, 134, 135, 151, 157–60, 164,
165, 167, 183; **13**, xi, 1, 12, 20–4, 42,
60, 72, 100–2, 105, 107, 115, 129,
132, 146, 155, 163, 188, 189, 209,
213, 220–3, 226–8, 230, 233–5, 248,
260, 269, 277, 280, 282, 284, 286,
292, 300, 301; **14**, xiv, 4, 30, 63, 64,
78, 90, 100, 102–4, 148, 160, 162,
164, 165, 167, 186, 214–19, 223,
240–4, 248, 258, 262, 263, 265–7,
269; **15.III**, *89–92*; **16.I**, 56, 60, 144,
145, 152; **17**, 10, 15–17, 42, 46, 183,
184, 189, 229, 271, 272, 274, 275
freedom, human,
   4, 208; **5.I**, ix
freedom, sphere of,
   2.I, 55–7; **7.I**, 62
freedom and necessity,
   11.II, 127; **17**, 12, 42
freedom of press,
   7.II, 28
free will,
   2.II, 6, 201; **5.I**, 15, 16, 51, 53, 54,
   61, 65, 72, 170
French Revolution (1789),
   5.I, 147, 148, 153, 154; **5.II**, 124;
   6.III, 18, 19; **7.I**, 36, 306; **7.II**, 28;
   7.III, 44, 151, 156, 157; **8.I**, 71;
   12.V, 34, 40; **14**, 14, 15, 193, 213
French Revolution of July 1830,
   5.III, 114; **7.I**, 15, 88; **7.II**, 191;
   7.III, 108
French Revolution (1848),
   5.III, 94, 96, 104, 116; **7.I**, 78, 80
friendship,
   2.II, 55, 56, 157; **5.I**, 117
Den Frisindede,
   7.I, 24, 221; **16.II**, 51
Frue Kirke in Copenhagen,
   1.II, 145
fullness of time,
   1.II, 174; **2.I**, 64, 67, 69
fundamentalism,
   10.I, x, 6; **10.II**, 4, 5, 17, 26, 39, 40

G
gadfly,
   10.II, 137; **12.I**, 199, 202, 204; **13**,
   244; **14**, 201, 233, 245
Gæa,
   7.III, 111, 112, 120, 214, 248, 250,
   251, 252
Geistlig Kalender,
   20, M 378
Generalkort over Danmark,
   20, U 40
genius,
   7.II, 1, 15–19, 136, 168, 177, 178,
   182, 191, 225, 344, 349; **7.III**, 20,
   21, 24, 25; **10.I**, 81; **12.II**, 84, 85;
   13, 31, 58, 59, 66, 88, 213, 231, 270,
   305–7; **15.III**, *93–8*; **16.II**, 35; **17**,
   91–5, 113, 209
genre,
   7.III, 171, 173, 265, 266
German Christian Movement,
   10.I, 156
gift,
   1.II, 123, 127, 134, 212, 214; **5.II**,
   193, 194, 196; **11.II**, 19, 68, 101,
   112, 117–19, 127, 131–3, 209, 210,
   214, 215, 217, 226, 228, 229, 250,
   252
gnoseology,
   4, 53, 57
gnosis,
   10.III, 14
Gnosticism,
   1.I, 118, 157; **4**, 51, 104, 105, 111,
   132; **5.II**, 44, 46, 47; **6.II**, 24;
   11.III, 215; **12.IV**, 75; **12.V**, 173;
   14, 210, 225–7
God,
   3, 25–8, 30, 32, 61, 64, 96, 98, 115,
   118, 127, 130, 136, 157, 174–9, 189,
   191, 205, 207; **5.I**, 2, 3, 6, 7, 11, 23,
   24, 42, 52–61 passim, 67, 68, 70,
   83, 87, 88, 97, 98, 100–5, 116, 122,
   131, 135, 150, 160, 167–87 passim;
   6.III, 10, 14, 17, 37–46 passim,
   56–61, 83, 84, 102, 104, 106–8, 119,

131, 134, 140, 145, 147, 166, 174, 178–80, 189, 198, 201, 215, 226, 227, 242, 245, 249–51, 256, 262, 263, 272, 275, 295, 303–10 passim; **8.I**, 6, 10, 23, 38, 39, 49, 65, 66, 74, 87, 128, 134, 177, 204, 206, 207, 211, 220, 238, 240, 245–50, 252, 317, 327, 332, 337, 340, 348, 353, 354, 441, 453; **9**, 8, 14, 23, 25, 26, 34, 42–54 passim, 66, 78, 81, 84, 85, 86, 87, 90, 110, 111, 133, 137–40, 145–9, 151, 165, 170, 210, 224, 225, 227–9, 248, 249, 252, 266, 274, 280–3, 300–19 passim, 331, 336–9, 342, 359–70 passim, 378, 381–5, 396, 400, 404, 405; **10.I**, 31; **11.I**, 15–17, 28, 30, 40, 96, 107, 108, 112, 116–18, 137, 155, 157–9, 168, 170, 191–8, 200–3, 217, 218, 232, 233, 247, 253, 269, 276, 280, 293, 296–8, 300; **11.II**, 10, 14–17, 27, 36, 48, 51–3, 59, 71–9 passim, 88, 100, 107, 112, 119–33 passim, 141–53 passim, 177, 184–95 passim, 212–14, 216, 220–9 passim, 237, 240, 243, 244, 250, 252; **12.I**, 24, 27, 32, 34, 38, 39, 49, 51, 54, 74, 76, 95, 103, 104, 107, 120, 124, 125, 145, 151, 152, 159, 166, 179, 181–4, 188, 190, 224, 224; **12.IV**, 11, 16–18, 20, 21, 32, 46, 59, 66, 94–8, 126, 167–9, 182, 196, 203, 205–7; **13**, 20, 21, 24, 57, 58, 61, 66, 67, 70, 71, 92, 98, 99, 101, 106, 108, 115–17, 130, 131, 135, 147, 148, 152, 155, 160–2, 164–6, 168–72, 186–90, 206, 210, 211, 213, 221, 226, 230, 247, 251, 253–5, 266, 267, 270, 288, 289, 293, 299, 303, 304, 306, 307, 311, 313–16, 318; **14**, ix, xiv, 16, 20, 23–5, 33–5, 45, 47, 48, 63, 65, 79, 80, 91–3, 96–9, 101–4, 112, 118, 119, 124, 129, 130, 184, 186, 195, 196, 198–201, 204, 210, 220, 221, 224, 225, 237, 242, 243, 248, 249, 252; **15.III**, *99–106*

God, death of, **9**, 48, 252; **10.I**, 200, 202, 213; **10.III**, 131; **11.II**, 18, 71, 90, 237; **12.II**, 102; **12.IV**, 120; **12.V**, 17, 52; **13**, 160, 230, 251, 253, 255; **14**, 44, 45
God, existence of, **10.I**, 343
God, kingdom of, **10.I**, 2, 67, 131, 193, 206, 218, 224, 226, 229, 247–9, 283, 345, 383, 386
God, proof of, **10.I**, 89, 90, 199, 201, 255, 264, 343
God is dead. *See* God, death of
God-man, **1.II**, 23, 26, 29, 30, 82, 85, 87, 90, 113, 151, 180, 215, 240, 253, 263, 270, 305; **2.I**, 43, 48, 67, 81, 136, 142; **2.II**, 92–5; **7.II**, 62; **7.III**, 220; **8.I**, 22, 59, 247, 276, 350, 354, 362; **9**, 66, 78, 85, 89, 174, 400, 405; **10.I**, 9, 82, 95, 127, 323, 325, 326; **10.II**, 19, 131, 132, 161; **10.III**, 120; **11.I**, 30, 279; **11.II**, 128, 147, 214, 229, 237; **11.III**, 67, 225; **12.I**, 50, 147, 151, 152; **12.II**, 7, 161; **12.IV**, 121; **13**, 77, 303, 305, 307, 318, 319; **14**, 25, 139, 140, 239
going further (or beyond), **2.II**, 135, 152; **7.I**, 70; **7.II**, 241, 242, 252; **16.II**, 146
good, absolute, **17**, 124, 125, 134, 135
good, highest, **17**, 123–5, 133, 134
good, the, **2.I**, 47, 106; **2.II**, 185, 186, 192; **15.III**, *107–12*
good Samaritan, the, **1.I**, 219, 220; **1.II**, 142, 237, 243
good works, **10.I**, 55
Governance, **1.I**, 96, 97; **5.II**, 141; **6.III**, 68; **7.I**, 190, 192, 203, 313; **7.II**, 182; **15.III**, *113–18*; **16.I**, 260, 261; **16.II**, 153

Grace,
  1.I, xi, 4, 15, 27, 67, 95, 111, 136, 150, 170, 173, 177, 214, 215, 232; **1.II**, 4, 5, 36–9, 43, 47, 70, 73, 81, 82, 89, 126, 127, 131, 134, 135, 140, 147, 156, 157, 191–3, 199–205 passim, 209, 210, 214, 215, 269, 276, 277; **2.I**, 43, 74, 79, 83–6; **2.II**, 69, 73, 78; **3**, 45, 63, 87, 98, 191, 203; **4**, 11, 14, 15, 24, 27, 29, 30, 41, 72, 84, 97, 103–8, 114–17, 123, 124, 126, 132, 135, 150, 154, 168, 189, 193, 228, 291, 295; **5.I**, 58, 160, 186; **5.II**, 22, 27, 28, 77, 82, 83, 88–90, 93–107 passim, 150, 176, 179–83, 187, 193–202, 237, 241; **6.I**, 181, 182, 189–93; **6.II**, 32, 33, 45, 49, 204, 210, 216; **7.II**, 27, 34, 110, 273, 281; **7.III**, 63, 222; **8.I**, 35, 180; **8.III**, 29, 216, 244, 245, 250, 255, 256; **9**, 113, 148, 311; **10.I**, 1, 3, 15, 17–19, 22, 24–6, 30, 31, 33, 34, 45, 54, 55, 69, 71, 168, 214, 350; **10.II**, 30, 51, 53, 89, 93, 98, 146, 159, 166, 208, 215, 216; **10.III**, 56, 57, 101, 102, 126, 146, 148, 149, 182; **11.I**, 16, 157, 158, 171; **11.II**, 52, 57, 58, 79, 93, 142, 217, 229, 250, 251; **11.III**, 128, 188, 212, 214, 215; **12.I**, 52, 53; **12.II**, 130, 153, 154, 176; **12.III**, 4; **12.IV**, 21, 164, 165, 172, 182; **12.V**, 39, 97; **13**, 99, 172, 208, 221; **14**, 23, 65, 243, 250–2; **15.III**, *119–24*; **16.II**, 47, 124, 231; **17**, 46, 131, 278
grace, election by,
  5.II, 197–9
gratitude,
  15.III, *125–30*
great earthquake,
  5.III, 220; **7.III**, 285; **12.IV**, 115, 116,
Greeks, the,
  6.I, 9, 10, 103–27, 131, 132, 315, 316, 319; **8.I**, 49, 227

Grib Forest,
  3, 133
grief,
  1.I, 25, 123, 137, 151, *179–94*
Grundtvig Academy (Copenhagen),
  8.I, 97
Grundtvigianism,
  10.II, 194; **12.II**, 66, 138, 144; **12.III**, 113, 126, 129
Guadalquivir river,
  16.I, xi, *279–95*
guilt,
  1.I, 30, 31, 37, 101–13 passim, 123, 136, 147, 148, 152, 153, 201, 222, 255, 258; **1.II**, 28, 39, 43, 58, 84, 87, 99, 102, 116, 118, 126, 144, 146, 152, 155, 156, 160, 163, 195; **2.II**, 79, 215–17, 227, 230, 313, 319, 321; **9**, 101, 107, 108, 111, 114, 170, 228, 266, 267, 273, 281–3, 287, 334; **10.I**, 18, 32, 33, 78, 79, 80, 89, 214, 263, 265, 266, 327, 337, 344, 348, 351–3, 356, 357, 363, 364, 368, 369; **10.II**, 123, 148, 149; **10.III**, 85, 147, 161; **11.I**, 128, 199, 212, 252, 282, 283; **11.II**, 120, 132, 227, 229, 241, 249; **11.III**, 34, 75, 112; **12.I**, 3, 6, 76, 85, 86, 128, 144, 146, 184; **12.III**, 150, 170, 181, 182, 185; **12.IV**, 14, 118, 151, 153, 216, 225; **12.V**, 111, 112; **13**, 88, 89, 92, 130, 147, 213, 223, 225, 227, 277, 286, 287, 292, 315; **14**, 112, 113, 240, 262–5, 269; **15.III**, *131–6*; **16.I**, 52, 57, 58, 60, 105, 108, 109; **16.II**, 25, 58, 61–3, 66, 92, 93, 96, 99, 101, 147, 158–60, 208, 210, 211, 219, 220; **17**, 74, 91, 125–7, 130, 131, 151, 225, 232–6, 270, 272–8
guilty/not guilty,
  17, 74
Gyldendal Publishing House,
  7.III, 234

H
Hamlet,
  16.I, 128

ἁμαρτία. *See also* apathy
  2.II, 59, 63–6, 215–19
ἀπάθεια,
  2.II, 195
happiness,
  2.II, 50, 57, 62; **12.I**, 69, 76, 84,
  187; **15.III**, *137–44*
happiness, eternal. *See also* salvation
  1.II, 21, 178, 181, 201, 202, 264,
  265, 315, 318; **2.I**, 43; **9**, 317, 383;
  10.II, 31, 161, 183; **12.II**, 162; **12.V**,
  112; **15.VI**, *1–8*; **17**, 123, 124, 131–4
Hasidism,
  9, 34, 46; **10.I**, xii; **10.III**, 155, 157,
  171, 192
Hegelianism,
  1.I, 22, 58, 62, 64, 92; **2.I**, 48, 51,
  56, 71, 139; **2.II**, 4, 19, 20, 25,
  36, 45, 131, 139, 165; **7.I**, xi, 2–6,
  9, 50, 51, 71, 98, 119, 120, 133,
  137, 145, 151–4, 186, 235, 238,
  255, 292, 293, 307, 309; **7.II**, 2–12
  passim, 19, 63, 87, 90, 92, 159,
  161–72 passim, 231, 233, 240–6,
  276, 278, 337–52 passim; **7.III**, 81,
  170, 175, 181, 182; **8.I**, 67, 155,
  178, 203, 278; **9**, 103, 204, 236,
  247, 393, 397, 401, 402; **10.II**, 15;
  10.III, 10, 55, 62, 70; **11.I**, 170,
  250, 251, 259; **11.II**, 49, 116, 183,
  236; **11.III**, 169, 171, 173, 174;
  12.I, 19, 101, 196, 205; **12.II**, 32;
  12.IV, 69, 179, 180, 185; **14**, 31,
  163, 210; **16.I**, 26, 270
Hegelianism, Danish,
  17, 201
Die Heilige Schrift des Neuen Bundes,
  20, A I 43–44
Hellenism,
  10.III, 76
hereditary sin. *See* sin, original
hermeneutics,
  7.II, 41–6; **8.III**, 15; **10.I**, 135,
  145, 146, 151, 197, 210, 213, 246,
  247; **10.III**, 32; **11.I**, x, xi, 92, 99,
  123–45; **11.II**, 233

hero,
  12.I, 16–18, 25, 27, 48, 50, 131, 153;
  12.IV, 9, 18, 19, 35; **12.V**, 114–16,
  180; **15.III**, *145–50*; **16.II**, 15, 17,
  19, 22–4, 27, 31, 35, 36, 40, 41, 51,
  62, 111, 117, 145, 209; **17**, 150, 307
hero, aesthetic,
  16.II, 22, 61
hero, religious,
  16.II, 59, 60, 61, 63
hero, tragic,
  16.II, 22, 61, 62
heroism,
  11.I, 58
Herrnhutism,
  5.II, 23, 67, 151, 163, 252
hiddenness,
  16.I, 43
higher lunacy,
  2.II, 14; **7.III**, 39
higher unity,
  2.II, 140, 155
High Priest,
  1.II, 113, 130, 145, 159, 238
hiin Enkelte. See single individual, the
Hinduism,
  13, 167
Historians Dispute, the,
  14, 74, 76, 77, 80
historicity, historicism,
  10.I, xii, 111, 133, 135, 145, 146,
  151, 156, 164, 196, 197, 210, 213,
  243, 245–7, 267, 322, 384, 388, 389;
  10.III, 6, 104, 106, 109; **11.I**, 137,
  138, 149, 150; **11.III**, 3, 186, 191
Historisk Tidsskrift,
  7.III, 234
history,
  1.II, 266–9, 308, 312; **2.II**, 4, 12, 44,
  74, 247, 248, 301–11; **3**, xiii, 15, 23,
  53–65 passim, 75–8, 90, 105, 125,
  138–9, 148–9, 153, 155, 181, 185–8,
  198, 202, 207, 210; **5.I**, 66, 67, 102;
  5.III, 112, 115, 116; **6.I**, 171, 172;
  6.III, 71, 175 178, 179; **7.II**, 107,
  113, 116, 119, 122–6, 133, 159, 161,

175, 185, 186, 323; **8.I**, 382; **9**, 3,
161, 164, 178, 179, 244, 245, 272,
310, 314, 316, 317, 319; **10.I**, 9, 59,
85, 87, 88, 149, 170, 171, 186, 189,
190, 196, 197, 199, 207, 210–16,
224–7, 229, 231, 234, 239, 243–50
passim, 252, 254, 255, 271, 323–6,
336, 342, 344, 345, 350, 360, 362,
363, 365, 377, 380, 382, 383, 386,
388, 389; **10.III**, 32, 62, 107, 120;
11.I, 14, 18, 25, 28, 49, 50, 70, 74,
78, 85, 91, 96, 99, 123, 132, 134,
149, 150, 152, 159, 166, 167, 173,
173, 179, 218, 248, 251, 253, 254,
268; **11.II**, 5, 10, 11–14, 71, 96, 104,
117, 118, 141, 148, 252; **11.III**, 5,
29, 43, 83, 118, 137, 192, 205; **12.I**,
6, 50, 152, 185, 200, 202, 237; **12.II**,
168; **12.III**, 89, 146, 169; **12.IV**, 7,
69, 118, 120–3, 222, 223; **12.V**, 29,
42, 47, 49, 51, 53, 54, 83, 88–90,
116, 121–3, 129, 159, 164, 167, 183;
13, 8, 9, 34, 41, 61, 63, 69, 71, 86,
91, 99, 114, 137, 145, 205, 219, 223,
231, 299, 303–5; **14**, 4, 7, 32, 34,
36, 97, 102, 119, 123, 124, 126, 149,
150, 153, 160, 164–6, 192, 213, 220,
240; **15.III**, *151–6*; **16.II**, 159, 160;
17, 127, 178, 187

history, end of,
    10.I, 244, 248, 249, 272; **14**, 164,
    165

Hochland,
    10.I, xi; **10.III**, 31, 48–50; **11.I**, 10;
    12.I, 93

Holocaust,
    11.II, 119, 122, 175; **12.IV**, 85, 205,
    215, 225, 226; **12.V**, 171, 173, 174

Holy Spirit,
    1.I, 9, 28, 29, 43; **10.I**, 3, 4, 32, 47,
    51, 69, 70, 76, 84, 86, 149, 188, 190,
    191, 194, 206, 215, 216, 328, 264,
    265, 328, 345, 347; **11.III**, 170, 171;
    15.III, *157–62*

homiletics,
    10.I, 47, 163, 165

Hong Kierkegaard Library at St. Olaf
    College,
    8.I, xi, 258; **8.II**, 48, 49, 53, 195, 310;
    8.III, 236, 278, 279, 298, 299, 323,
    324

hope,
    1.I, 8, 37, 46, 52, 54, 102, 139, 140,
    161, 177, 180, 184, 186, 187, 192,
    201, 231, 246; **2.I**, 5, 8, 10, 12, 14,
    87; **5.II**, 12; **9**, 65, 71, 76, 81, 85, 86,
    91, 210, 310–18 passim; **10.I**, 17,
    149, 188, 189, 193, 198, 201, 204,
    205, 208, 217, 218, 241, 246, 251;
    11.I, 5, 15, 17, 74, 75, 192, 198, 203,
    284; **11.II**, 26, 27, 48, 127, 142, 143,
    151, 153, 222, 225, 236, 240, 248–52;
    11.III, 6, 182, 194; **12.I**, 23, 25, 51,
    129; **12.III**, 171; **12.IV**, 74, 152;
    12.V, 68, 83, 85; **13**, 70, 85, 87, 88,
    92, 143, 177, 187, 189, 221, 235, 302;
    14, 232, 238, 240, 248, 252; **15.III**,
    163–8; **17**, 130, 131, 186, 306, 307

horror,
    13, 170, 181, 184, 185, 187

hubris,
    16.II, 60, 155, 157–9

Huguenots,
    5.II, 130; **5.III**, 111, 112

humanism,
    5.II, 111–14, 177; **12.II**, 18, 23, 30;
    12.V, 78; **13**, 76, 99, 116, 179, 180,
    218, 232, 243, 248, 251, 292; **14**, 48,
    49, 97, 231

humility/humiliation,
    1.I, 13, 14, 24, 28, 29, 37, 39, 96,
    130, 163, 164, 259, 262; **1.II**, 30,
    41, 114, 115, 158, 160, 163, 180,
    184, 202, 212, 215, 289; **5.II**, 11, 76,
    77, 82, 103, 170, 241, 256; **7.I**, 218,
    312; **15.III**, *169–74*

humor,
    1.II, 96; **2.I**, 38, 205, 261, 284, 285,
    287; **4**, 133, 136, 137, 230; **5.I**, x;
    5.II, 7, 8, 17, 140; **5.III**, 268; **6.I**,
    300, 301; **6.II**, 27, 34, 64, 65; **6.III**,
    31, 32, 69, 103, 107, 116, 125–9,

132, 134, 144, 156–65 passim, 271,
275; **7.I**, 117, 131, 132, 159; **7.II**,
175, 239; **7.III**, 44, 55, 177, 266;
8.I, 50, 201, 205, 323, 430, 439;
8.II, 5, 222, 271; **8.III**, 89, 117, 218;
9, 399; **10.III**, 106; **11.I**, 254, 263,
283–5; **11.II**, 83, 89, 116; **11.III**, 25,
197; **12.I**, 21–3, 27, 39, 48–50, 145,
189, 207; **12.III**, 3, 5, 6, 9; **12.IV**,
101, 110, 126; **13**, 316–18; **15.III**,
175–82; **16.I**, 166, 167; **16.II**, 8, 115,
117, 127–30, 135, 145, 147, 193,
199, 203, 230, 262; **17**, xiii, 40, 117,
128–30, 132, 187, 188, 211

Humoristiske Intelligensblade,
20, U 71
hypocrisy,
15.III, *183–8*

I
Idea, the,
6.III, 57, 71, 242, 252, 255; **7.I**, 239,
240, 294
idealism,
4, 186, 227, 265; **5.I**, 41, 88; **5.III**,
187, 207; **6.I**, 3, 4, 9, 11; **6.II**, 47,
102, 108, 112, 144, 200, 207, 213;
6.III, 55, 298; **7.I**, 47, 58; **8.I**, 162;
8.II, 90; **8.III**, 5, 14, 51, 108, 110;
9, 51, 52, 101, 202, 302; **10.I**, xii,
44, 48, 49, 68, 79, 97, 195, 243,
341, 346, 379, 383; **10.II**, 86, 144,
145, 147, 148; **10.III**, 19, 61; **11.I**,
13–15, 18, 21, 31, 35, 57, 59, 60, 99,
109, 112, 127, 136–8, 147, 250, 259;
11.II, 122, 141, 181, 182; **11.III**,
1–3, 35, 187; **12.II**, 28; **12.III**, 154,
155, 158, 159; **12.IV**, 166, 195; **13**,
312, 313; **14**, 96
idealism, German,
7.II, 258; **8.III**, 67, 97, 127, 176; **9**,
ix, 23, 47, 200, 201, 250, 395; **10.I**,
88, 156, 162, 173, 247, 272, 345;
10.III, 9, 67, 68, 70, 71; **11.I**, 6, 28,
39, 70, 127–30, 250; **11.II**, 236–8;

12.I, 37; **13**, 297, 311; **14**, 53, 61, 91,
216; **16.II**, 176
idealism, speculative. *See* speculative
idealism
idealism, transcendental,
5.I, 35, 36; **7.I**, 17
ideality,
5.I, 17, 56, 71, 103, 174, 175, 179,
180, 184–6
ideas and forms, the doctrine of,
2.I, 46, 108
identity,
2.II, 4; **11.I**, xi; **11.III**, 119; **15.III**,
189–94
identity and difference,
2.II, 3, 5, 20–3; **15.III**, *189–94*
identity crisis,
13, 81, 84
identity of indiscernibles,
2.II, 5, 21
illness. *See* sickness
illuminism,
5.II, 47
illusion, acoustical,
12.I, 26
imaginary construction,
17, 74, 76
imagination,
8.II, 38; **10.III**, 182, 183; **15.III**,
195–202
imago Dei,
10.I, 71; **10.II**, 58; **10.III**, 100
imitatio Christi. *See* imitation of Christ
imitation,
1.I, 15, 79, 148, 261; **1.II**, 49, 76,
118, 128, 151, 163, 164, 178, 184,
195, 215, 244, 251–4, 261, 266, 267,
275, 277, 303; **4**, xii, 36, 57, 114–16,
200; **5.III**, 22; **7.II**, 111, 126, 130,
176, 183, 251, 279, 293, 297; **10.I**,
24, 60, 149; **10.II**, 30; **10.III**, 131,
146; **11.I**, 37, 280; **11.II**, 125, 230;
11.III, 143, 144, 149; **12.I**, 151;
12.II, 4, 126, 127, 130, 149, 154,
161; **12.V**, 18; **13**, 72, 76, 138, 140,
145, 146, 288; **15.III**, *203–8*

imitation of Christ,
  5.II, 9, 18, 28, 29, 76, 77, 83, 97,
  101–7 passim, 153, 170, 179, 193,
  197, 199, 220, 221, 230, 239, 240,
  247, 256; **7.I**, 223, 224, 289, 313;
  8.III, 245; **9**, 85, 89, 150, 174, 274,
  368; **16.I**, 162; **17**, 46–8
immanence. *See also* transcendence
  and transcendence and immanence
  1.II, 75, 76, 197; **2.I**, 28, 33–44
  passim, 56, 80, 84; **4**, 63; **8.I**, 364,
  374; **8.II**, 227; **10.I**, 66, 70, 71, 88,
  89, 370, 380; **10.III**, 57, 87, 90, 91,
  95, 147; **11.I**, 253; **15.III**, *209–14*;
  16.II, 59
immanentism,
  10.III, 75, 90, 94, 98, 109
immediacy,
  2.II, 9, 66, 73, 82, 158; **6.I**, 5, 107,
  134, 316–18; **6.II**, 137, 207, 215;
  7.III, 18, 112, 161, 173, 177, 178,
  221, 226, 267, 269, 270; **9**, 17, 83,
  141, 405; **10.II**, 47, 53; **11.I**, 29, 73,
  76, 134, 155; **11.II**, 65, 75, 76, 216,
  217, 228; **12.I**, 11, 72, 106, 152, 224,
  225, 232; **12.IV**, 151, 152; **12.V**, 16,
  17; **14**, 94, 184, 186, 267; **15.III**,
  215–22; **16.I**, 10–11, 19, 34–8, 107–8,
  124, 126, 134, 141–3, 147–53, 191,
  210, 216, 224–7, 238; **16.II**, 9, 19,
  22–5, 31, 40, 53, 96, 98, 99, 103, 105,
  106, 125, 175, 205, 207, 243; **17**, 4, 5,
  113, 125, 163, 180, 183, 187, 190
immediacy and reflection,
  7.III, 177, 178, 265, 266, 279;
  15.III, *215–22*
immortality,
  1.II, 172, 175, 180–3; **2.I**, 47, 48,
  54, 98, 106, 121, 122, 273, 279; **2.II**,
  265, 290; **3**, 24; **4**, 4, 6, 124; **5.I**,
  180; **5.III**, 47; **6.II**, 29, 41, 43, 235,
  247–53 passim; **6.III**, 178; **7.I**, 66,
  107, 112, 117, 123, 145, 149–58 passim, 185, 239, 244, 255, 293, 294,
  297; **7.II**, 28, 34, 35, 345; **7.III**, 40,
  41; **8.II**, 21; **9**, 170, 211, 377, 380–4;

10.II, 5; **11.II**, 19; **11.III**, 160; **12.I**,
  153; **15.III**, *223–30*
immortality of soul,
  2.I, 47, 48
inauthenticity. *See also* authenticity
  9, 105, 342; **11.I**, 33, 300; **11.III**, 16,
  18; **12.I**, 200, 208; **12.V**, 69
incarnation,
  1.I, 8, 15, 92, 136, 158, 159, 163,
  164; **1.II**, 7, 158, 241, 242, 249, 252,
  265, 269, 300; **2.I**, 37, 80; **2.II**, 9,
  39, 40, 172; **4**, 4–6, 16, 28, 57, 104,
  107, 111, 132, 168–71, 194, 195,
  197, 198, 202; **5.I**, 57, 177; **5.III**,
  140, 251; **6.I**, 351, 366, 370; **6.II**, 4,
  8, 12, 13, 16, 17, 61, 62, 102, 103,
  111, 112, 136, 138, 173, 241; **6.III**,
  38, 262; **7.I**, 63, 297; **7.II**, 69, 76,
  79, 80, 91, 92, 186, 275–7; **8.I**, 221,
  340; **8.II**, 92, 225; **8.III**, 68, 70, 234,
  240, 244, 246; **9**, 139, 148, 150, 179,
  202, 248; **10.I**, 5, 6, 27, 29, 31, 32,
  81, 83, 135, 148, 195, 244, 254, 326,
  359, 360, 366, 370; **10.II**, 11, 12,
  16, 17, 77, 86, 93, 97, 107, 128, 131,
  132, 134; **10.III**, 21, 22, 107, 146;
  11.II, 191, 192; **11.III**, 5, 75–80,
  168; **12.I**, 24, 148; **12.II**, 4, 7; **12.IV**,
  172; **12.V**, 29; **13**, 303, 311, 316,
  318; **14**, 155, 186; **16.I**, 151, 269;
  16.II, 35; **17**, 122
inclosing reserve,
  7.III, 77; **9**, 101, 113; **11.I**, 172;
  12.II, 111; **13**, 158; **14**, 189, 268;
  16.I, 145; **16.II**, 124; **17**, 71, 227,
  254, 255
incognito,
  1.II, 26, 30, 159, 162, 319; **10.I**, 9,
  12, 28, 29, 84, 95, 127, 132, 136,
  167, 172, 217, 325, 328; **10.II**,
  134–6, 139; **10.III**, 14, 34; **11.II**, 4,
  160, 184, 187, 192, 217, 218, 252;
  12.I, 52, 242; **14**, 108, 115, 124, 128;
  15.III, *231–6*; **16.I**, 167; **17**, 131, 132
indesluttethed,
  1.II, 76

indifferentism,
   10.I, 214, 216
indirect communication. *See*
   communication, indirect
individual, the. *See* also single
   individual, the
   5.III, 107, 131; **8.I**, 6, 15, 17, 94, 139,
   240, 431, 438, 454; **8.II**, 8, 20, 27, 33,
   46, 207, 256, 275, 303, 304, 308, 324;
   9, 11, 34, 35, 39, 42–5, 48–54 passim,
   64, 105, 137, 139, 145, 147, 173,
   210, 223, 227, 267, 272, 275, 276,
   282, 285, 286, 287, 302, 323, 325,
   334–9, 342–4, 384, 396, 397, 403,
   404, 407; **10.I**, 60, 79, 195; **10.II**, 8,
   56; **10.III**, 16; **11.II**, 9, 16, 28, 38, 51,
   54, 70, 144, 145, 151, 152, 166, 170,
   187, 216, 224, 246, 250; **11.III**, 106,
   110; **12.I**, 4–10, 48, 54, 145–8, 166,
   199, 208; **12.IV**, 166; **13**, 24, 35, 36,
   38, 39, 41, 46, 66, 98, 115, 125, 133,
   146, 147, 152, 153, 182, 219, 222,
   230, 231, 269, 270, 280, 310; **14**, ix,
   xi–xiv, 2, 14–16, 18, 19, 23–6, 32, 34,
   42, 48, 59, 63, 76–8, 80, 82, 138–40,
   142–4, 161, 165, 239; **15.IV**, *1–8*
individualism, individuality,
   8.I, 248, 333, 334; **8.II**, 293; **9**, 4,
   44, 57, 83, 89, 112, 131, 207, 263,
   266, 272, 274, 275, 277, 283, 286,
   287, 344, 399; **10.I**, 51, 52, 215;
   10.II, 114–16; **10.III**, 16; **11.II**, 18,
   37, 51, 57, 64, 74, 90, 152, 169, 223;
   12.I, 53; **12.IV**, 177; **13**, 19, 21, 36,
   37, 60, 62, 67, 98–105, 115, 123,
   125, 134, 152, 153, 179, 230, 265,
   269; **14**, xiv, 63, 98, 138, 139, 141,
   143, 144, 155, 186, 245, 246
indulgences,
   4, 200, 201, 295
infinite. *See* finite/infinite
infinite and finite. *See* finite and infinite
infinity,
   1.II, 24, 146; **7.II**, 33, 59; **8.I**, 211;
   10.III, 18; **11.I**, 157, 252; **11.II**, 88, 94;
   12.II, 10; **12.V**, 83, 130; **16.II**, 80, 150

innate ideas,
   2.I, 119, 132, 133
Inner Mission,
   12.II, 66
inner/outer,
   2.I, 52, 200; **2.II**, 227; **4**, 211; **5.III**,
   155, 179; **6.I**, 137; **6.III**, 11, 21,
   43, 130, 179, 199, 203, 204, 208;
   7.II, 320, 322; **7.III**, 80, 120, 263;
   8.I, 80, 83, 87, 200; **8.III**, 75, 241;
   10.III, 62; **11.II**, 113, 183; **12.I**, 26,
   34, 147, 148, 240; **12.II**, 172; **14**, 2,
   19, 187; **15.IV**, *9–16*; **16.I**, 58, 75,
   183, 255; **16.II**, 7, 82, 146, 160; **17**,
   250, 251, 253–5
innocence,
   1.I, 18, 23, 24, 27, 30–3, 36–9, 107,
   126, 136, 138, 259; **9**, 109, 141, 361,
   362, 365; **10.I**, 363; **10.II**, 121–3;
   11.I, 272, 281, 282; **11.II**, 56, 241;
   12.I, 73; **12.V**, 96; **13**, 38, 130, 148,
   208, 222, 223, 313, 315; **14**, 11, 120,
   223, 263–5; **16.I**, 20, 21, 46, 59–60,
   75, 82, 84, 122, 126, 129, 168, 226,
   227; **16.II**, 99, 219, 220, 261
inspiration,
   7.III, 199
instant. *See* moment, the
intellectualism,
   11.III, 94
Intelligensblade. See Heiberg, Johan
   Ludvig, *Intelligensblade*
intensity/extensity,
   15.IV, *17–24*
intentionality,
   9, 110, 130–2, 140, 142, 149, 151;
   11.I, 150, 151, 157; **11.II**, 113, 114,
   130, 132, 215; **14**, 225
inter-esse,
   2.II, 36–7; **5.I**, 44; **9**, 175
interest,
   12.V, 110
interesting, the,
   9, 113; **11.I**, 72; **11.II**, 59, 141, 152;
   11.III, 60, 143; **12.IV**, 6, 14; **15.IV**,
   25–32; **16.I**, 225; **17**, 166

International Kierkegaard Commentary,
8.I, xi, 258; **8.III**, 185, 236
International Kierkegaard Newsletter,
8.III, 185
internet,
11.III, 49, 58, 63, 64
intersubjectivity,
8.I, 348, 452
intratextuality,
1.II, 238–40
introversion/extraversion,
13, 151, 156–8
inward deepening,
5.I, 100; **5.II**, 197, 232, 240; **8.I**, 22;
15.IV, *33–8*; **17**, 48, 126, 260
inwardness,
1.I, 32, 73, 169, 188, 190, 200, 201,
244; **1.II**, 95, 98, 102, 107–20, 142,
202, 214, 256; **2.I**, 33, 34, 36, 41,
42, 135, 184, 232; **3**, 63, 132; **5.I**,
40, 95, 100, 119, 175; **5.III**, 23, 48,
178, 192–5, 204, 205, 279; **7.I**, 5, 82,
120, 158, 206, 223, 224, 242, 305;
7.II, 111, 169, 225, 318, 320, 321;
7.III, 161, 162, 203, 263, 269; **8.I**,
14, 15, 23, 245, 329, 336, 364–6,
452; **9**, 128, 206, 207, 264, 265, 274,
277, 379, 383–6; **10.I**, 16, 86, 213,
324, 327, 355; **10.II**, 10, 11, 13, 15,
19, 21, 32, 40, 42, 89, 92, 114, 119,
184; **10.III**, 20, 37, 106, 107, 120,
159, 160; **11.I**, 13–15, 19, 21, 25–7,
29, 32, 33, 39, 40, 53, 55, 60, 67,
72, 78, 80, 110, 118, 160, 228, 263,
269, 275; **11.II**, 38, 228, 245; **11.III**,
35, 43, 79, 80, 150, 171–3; **12.I**,
105, 130, 175, 189; **12.II**, 147, 148,
154; **12.IV**, 16, 72, 177; **12.V**, 99,
151, 196; **13**, 38, 70, 157, 182, 226,
230; **14**, 15, 46, 61, 140, 143, 185,
192; **15.IV**, *33–8*; **16.I**, 35, 43, 265,
270–2; **16.II**, 209; **17**, 136, 250, 254,
255, 260, 265, 266
Irische Elfenmärchen,
16.II, 125

irony,
1.I, 51, 162, 164; **1.II**, 96, 254; **2.I**,
23–5, 37, 38, 41, 51, 121, 124–7,
137, 169, 183–8, 256–9, 262, 284,
287, 293, 296, 301, 302; **2.II**, 82,
190; **3**, 16, 60, 65, 208; **4**, 133, 136,
230, 278; **5.I**, x, 175; **5.II**, 17, 119,
140; **5.III**, 3, 78, 186, 187, 190, 241,
255, 267, 268; **6.I**, 71, 104, 108,
112–14, 117–27 passim, 170, 293,
294, 298–301, 304, 305; **6.II**, 5, 27,
28, 35, 86, 90, 96, 211–13; **6.III**, 19,
38, 69, 103, 107, 116, 118, 123–34
passim, 144, 145, 147, 151, 162, 164,
235–69, 271–6 passim, 293, 299–308
passim; **7.I**, 1, 6, 9, 10, 117, 122,
123, 129, 132, 135, 152, 159, 229,
245; **7.II**, 160, 170, 171, 175, 232,
233, 239; **7.III**, 38–41, 44, 67, 68,
122, 129, 130, 174, 176, 177, 179,
218, 225, 228, 231, 250, 266; **8.I**,
49, 81, 164, 205, 209, 212, 382, 430,
437, 439, 442, 450; **8.II**, 6, 221, 222,
268, 269, 271, 275, 290, 295, 307;
8.III, 5, 6, 15, 16, 117, 119, 136, 188,
216–18, 236, 248, 255; **9**, 7, 8, 223,
341, 342, 399; **10.I**, 21, 203, 213,
232, 367, 379; **10.II**, 9, 34–6; **10.III**,
106; **11.I**, 213, 231; **11.II**, 83, 120,
126, 160; **11.III**, 25, 29, 32, 37–43
passim, 183, 196, 197, 204, 205, 208;
12.I, 16, 38, 39, 48, 50, 126, 127,
130, 149, 197, 200, 204–10, 237–40;
12.II, 52; **12.III**, 6, 9, 28, 33, 90, 91,
93, 100, 121; **12.IV**, 16, 55, 59, 60,
69, 70, 101, 110, 123, 126; **12.V**, 27,
30, 70, 71, 122, 123, 127, 163, 177;
13, 5, 9, 58, 70, 74, 75, 92, 200, 206;
14, 61, 184, 185, 223; **15.IV**, *39–44*;
16.I, 133–5, 138, 166, 174, 196, 198,
262–4, 275; **16.II**, 2–9 passim, 75–82
passim, 135, 143, 146, 160–1, 202,
204–6, 210; **17**, xiii, 33, 35, 120,
128, 129, 131, 132, 166, 211
irony, Christian,
6.III, 129, 130, 185–233

irony, controlled,
  6.I, 122; **6.III**, 70, 131, 147, 306,
  307; **16.II**, 5, 9
irony, philosophical,
  6.III, 193
irony, Romantic,
  2.I, 171, 172, 259, 288, 299, 301,
  308; **2.II**, 172; **4**, 319; **5.II**, 54; **6.III**,
  70, 127, 139–53, 159, 187, 208–10,
  217, 219, 221–3, 240, 243, 249,
  251, 253, 255, 256, 258, 260, 264,
  272; **7.I**, 130, 131, 133, 140; **8.III**,
  249; **10.II**, 35; **12.I**, 190, 239; **12.II**,
  57–60; **12.V**, 128
irony, Socratic,
  2.I, 6, 23–5, 37, 38, 41, 49–53, 70,
  74, 87–104, 119, 124–7, 137, 138,
  143, 169, 171, 172, 183–8, 199–209
  passim, 221, 224, 237, 239, 240,
  248, 250, 253, 256–65 passim,
  279–81, 284–302 passim, 308; **2.II**,
  114, 117, 172, 186, 191, 192; **5.III**,
  88; **6.III**, 70, 106, 147, 148, 194,
  248, 253; **8.III**, 45, 46, 89, 276; **11.**
  II, 160–3, 170; **11.III**, 43; **12.I**, 203,
  204, 239; **16.II**, 9
irrational, the,
  8.I, 19; **15.IV**, *45–8*
irrationalism, irrationality,
  4, 57; **8.II**, 19, 36, 87, 166, 169,
  207, 225, 291, 293; **8.II**, 294;
  8.III, 113, 117, 181 213, 232, 233;
  9, 71, 78–81, 86, 88, 226, 227,
  228, 355, 378, 380; **10.I**, 23, 87,
  247, 359, 370, 382, 388; **10.II**,
  112, 175; **11.I**, 24, 133, 148–50,
  154, 155, 159, 171; **11.II**, 27, 32,
  50, 211, 238; **11.III**, 117, 122,
  126, 158, 166, 172; **12.I**, 102, 107;
  12.V, 83–5; **13**, 101, 313; **14**, 37,
  69, 97, 120–3, 125, 130, 152, 222;
  17, 122, 182
Islam,
  1.I, 90–2
isolated individual,
  14, xiii, 123, 138, 166, 264

isolation,
  1.I, 57, 66, 103; **2.I**, 21, 54, 101,
  303; **4**, 245, 246, 276, 279–81, 283,
  289–98; **6.III**, 130, 131, 199–208
  passim, 215, 220, 221, 224; **8.III**,
  53; **9**, 54, 88, 173, 265, 302, 304;
  11.I, 8, 272; **11.II**, 72; **11.III**, 141;
  12.I, 10, 84, 94, 199; **12.V**, 30; **13**,
  81, 90, 115, 121, 122, 158, 277, 280,
  288, 317; **14**, xiii, 140

J
Jansenism,
  5.I, 130, 139; **5.II**, 133
jest,
  9, 105; **11.I**, 263; **11.II**, 147, 148;
  12.I, 190
Jesuits,
  5.I, 130, 139
Jewish emancipation,
  6.I, 18
Jews,
  10.II, 11, 38; **11.I**, 36
journalism. *See also* press, the
  15.V, *121–8*
joy,
  9, 66, 68, 73, 77, 82, 91, 135, 137,
  143, 145, 266, 268, 274–8, 282, 287;
  11.I, 219, 255, 280, 284; **11.II**, 67;
  12.I, 73, 75, 184; **12.II**, 6, 12; **13**,
  68, 70, 72, 73, 126, 130, 309; **14**,
  240; **15.IV**, *49–54*; **16.I**, 75, 149,
  190, 227
Judaism,
  1.II, 93, 97, 118, 172, 191, 192, 194,
  289, 297, 305, 323; **2.I**, 64, 65; **3**, 26,
  127, 153; **4**, 51, 53, 59, 60, 63, 107,
  150; **6.II**, 1, 59, 171, 172, 174–6,
  193, 243–6; **6.III**, 2, 19, 20, 100,
  107; **7.I**, 132, 253; **7.II**, 69, 70, 122,
  130, 161, 162; **9**, 33–61, 299–321,
  355, 396; **10.I**, xi, xii, 259; **10.III**,
  134; **11.I**, 50, 253; **11.II**, 174, 190–2;
  11.III, 99, 203, 215; **12.I**, 123, 206,
  207; **12.II**, 20, 21, 147; **12.IV**, 18,
  206; **13**, 67, 71, 72, 301; **14**, xii, xiii,

1, 22, 25, 32, 58, 181, 198; **15.IV**,
  55–8; **16.II**, 46, 243, 245
justice,
  2.I, 47; **2.II**, 56
justification,
  5.II, 22, 27, 28, 85–90 passim, 93,
  102, 176, 177, 180, 187; **10.I**, 30,
  189, 203, 214, 336, 348, 351

K
Kabbala,
  10.III, 171, 174, 175
kabbalism,
  5.II, 43, 44, 46
kabbalism, Christian,
  5.II, 51
κάθαρσις,
  2.II, 59, 62, 68–78 passim, 212, 213
kairos,
  10.I, 209, 210, 338, 345, 346
Kantianism,
  9, 157, 158, 166, 179, 189, 395, 397,
  399; **11.I**, 123, 133, 137; **12.I**, 34,
  35, 37
kenosis,
  10.I, 254; **10.II**, 86, 97; **11.II**, 220
kerygma,
  1.II, 241; **10.I**, 120, 124, 126, 131,
  244, 328
Ketzer-Lexicon,
  20, M 597–599
Kierkegaard: special issue of *Kairos*,
  18.IV, *131–6*
Kierkegaard vivant,
  18.IV, *137–42*
Kierkegaardiana,
  8.I, x, 56, 58, 258
*Kierkegaard Studies. Monograph
  Series*,
  8.I, 92
Kierkegaard Studies. Yearbook,
  8.I, xi, 92, 258
kinesis,
  11.II, 86
kingdom of God,
  11.I, 191, 192

kingdom of heaven,
  1.II, 25, 37, 268
κίνησις. *See also* movement
  1.II, 6, 71, 74, 158; **2.I**, 55, 58;
  2.II, 26, 29–34, 37, 154; **5.I**, 66–71,
  92, 185
kitsch,
  12.I, 35
Kjøbenhavns flyvende Post. See
  Heiberg, Johan Ludvig, *Kjøbenhavns
  flyvende Post*
Kjøbenhavnsposten,
  7.I, 16, 17, 24, 26, 27, 88, 92–7, 184;
  7.III, 37, 92, 252; **16.II**, 51; **17**, 27,
  30, 31; **20**, U 75
knight,
  12.V, 130, 131
knight of faith,
  1.II, 268; **2.II**, 66, 67, 76, 238, 242;
  7.II, 73, 76, 78, 83, 90, 91; **9**, 91,
  227, 266, 279, 280, 360, 368; **10.I**,
  12; **10.II**, 112, 124, 163, 194; **10.III**,
  33, 178, 180–3, 184, 198, 199, 202,
  203; **11.I**, 61; **11.II**, 4, 33, 35, 36, 38,
  39, 89, 90, 92, 94, 95, 106; **11.III**, 9,
  19, 37, 39, 64, 113, 143, 144, 151,
  152, 171, 184, 189, 194, 214; **12.I**,
  73, 124; **12.IV**, 16, 22, 187; **13**, 73,
  304; **14**, 63, 66, 199, 223, 263; **16.I**,
  2, 7, 8, 10; **16.II**, 27; **17**, 144, 150,
  307, 308
knight of infinite resignation,
  7.III, 73, 74; **16.II**, 30
knowledge
  16.I, 21, 31, 66–8, 75, 129, 132–4,
  137–9, 205, 212, 215–19, 224–6,
  262–6, 271–6
knowledge, absolute,
  5.I, 36, 38
*Københavnsposten. See
  Kjøbenhavnsposten*
Königstädter Theater in Berlin,
  5.III, 41; **7.III**, 41, 81; **11.II**, 9
Koran, the,
  8.III, 7, 9, 13, 46, 47, 89; **11.III**, 9;
  20, M 603

Kristiania Bohemians,
  12.III, 177, 186, 189

L
language,
  2.I, 57; **5.III**, 278–80; **6.I**, 134, 296,
  297, 299; **6.III**, 152, 186; **7.I**, 270,
  271, 278–80; **7.III**, 79, 80, 227, 228,
  231, 234, 239, 263, 265; **8.I**, 348,
  360, 361, 381; **8.III**, 299; **9**, 106,
  305–9, 318, 319; **10.I**, 3, 5, 32, 146,
  147, 174, 243, 247, 248, 325, 369;
  10.II, 28, 110, 163, 214, 215; **11.I**,
  x, 10, 53, 54, 69, 78, 124, 126, 127,
  129, 136, 137, 168, 209, 213, 219,
  220, 222–5, 227, 232, 233, 234,
  260, 261, 273; **11.II**, 4, 6, 7, 17,
  26, 33, 35–9, 63, 64, 66, 67, 73, 78,
  79, 89, 113–16, 120, 131, 145, 160,
  214, 248, 252; **11.III**, 2–8 passim,
  14, 17, 18, 21, 37–9, 157, 166; **12.I**,
  20, 38, 100, 165, 240, 234, 244;
  12.III, 30, 32, 120, 121; **12.IV**, 16,
  86, 97, 110, 127–9, 201, 202; **12.V**,
  71, 125, 169; **13**, 9, 98, 138–40,
  161, 165, 179, 181, 182, 190, 198,
  203, 249, 298; **14**, 4, 5, 13, 56, 58,
  66–8, 82, 83, 96, 268; **15.IV**, *59–66*;
  16.I, 145, 150, 151, 214, 247; **16.II**,
  14, 59, 63, 76, 80, 82, 90, 91, 104,
  144, 210, 211
language, ordinary,
  11.III, 2, 3, 7, 15, 16, 18, 21, 22,
  157, 164, 170
language-games,
  11.III, 167
Last Judgment,
  9, 317; **11.II**, 222; **12.I**, 125; **13**, 6
laughter,
  16.II, 3, 6–9, 127, 200
law,
  1.I, 232; **5.II**, 82–106 passim,
  180–3, 197; **15.IV**, *67–70*
law and gospel,
  5.II, 86–94 passim, 102, 181–3, 190,
  193–6, 206

leap,
  1.I, 14, 31, 32, 37, 39, 52, 59; **1.II**,
  319; **2.I**, 66, 67; **2.II**, 22, 37, 38, 44;
  4, 12, 125, 127, 137, 175; **5.I**, ix,
  33–44 passim, 85, 88, 91–7 passim,
  182; **6.I**, 7, 82, 259, 261, 262, 309,
  310, 313, 325–31, 359, 360; **6.II**, 9,
  177, 192; **7.I**, 56, 65, 187, 274; **7.III**,
  72–81; **8.I**, 19, 20, 128; **8.II**, 2, 4, 19,
  158, 223, 225, 227, 305; **8.III**, 47,
  51–3, 68, 117, 118, 138, 218, 237,
  255, 257; **9**, 49, 80, 90, 147, 179,
  332, 333, 360, 380; **10.I**, xii, 85, 254,
  270, 358–61, 363, 365, 370, 380,
  382; **10.II**, 36, 39, 52, 93, 97, 112,
  114, 129, 130, 131, 134, 151, 178,
  179, 184; **10.III**, 38, 61, 64, 65, 70,
  159–62, 200, 202; **11.I**, 31, 59, 95,
  117, 118, 167, 168, 171, 177, 272,
  281–3, 294, 295, 298; **11.II**, 26, 27,
  33, 71, 89, 90, 93, 100, 106, 133, 241,
  247, 249; **11.III**, 33–9 passim, 43,
  76, 78, 82, 117, 128, 148, 214; **12.I**,
  74, 83, 103, 107, 127, 208; **12.II**,
  27; **12.III**, 46, 80, 125, 167; **12.IV**,
  22, 154; **12.V**, 149, 150, 151, 153,
  159; **13**, 61, 130, 152, 223; **14**, 16,
  31, 36, 37, 42, 47, 48, 110, 111, 154,
  222–4, 267, 268; **15.IV**, *71–8*; **16.II**,
  123, 130, 147; **17**, 272, 175
leap of faith,
  10.I, 18, 301, 302, 325–8; **10.II**, 9,
  69, 175, 176, 181
Lebensphilosophie,
  8.I, 342
legends,
  15.IV, *79–84*
Les Temps Modernes,
  9, 7, 8, 235; **14**, 159
Lethe River,
  2.I, 68
leveling,
  5.III, 100; **6.III**, 35; **7.I**, 173; **7.II**,
  242, 250, 252; **7.III**, 162, 163; **8.I**, 84,
  212; **9**, 104, 173, 272, 273; **10.I**, 160,
  268; **10.II**, 29; **10.III**, 112, 115–22

passim, 128; **11.I**, 109, 111, 116, 118, 169, 228, 229; **11.II**, 125; **11.III**, 51, 60–4, 222, 225; **12.I**, 102, 197, 200, 206, 208, 210; **12.II**, 79, 131, 173; **13**, 135, 152, 153; **14**, xi, xii, 14–16, 24, 148, 154, 155, 190, 245; **15.IV**, *85–8*

Lexicon philosophicum, **20**, M 623

liberalism, **10.II**, 29, 86; **10.III**, 16; **11.II**, 55; **11.III**, 118, 182, 183, 194; **12.V**, 34, 40

liberum arbitrium, **1.I**, 35; **6.I**, 8

Libri symbolici, **20**, M 624

life-view, **8.I**, 32; **12.I**, 10, 71, 72, 103, 174; **15.IV**, *89–96*; **16.I**, 117; **17**, 128, 147, 155, 205–12 passim

lilies of the field and the birds of the air, **1.I**, 4, 108, 176; **1.II**, 33, *55–76*, 141, 237; **7.I**, 224

linguistics, **13**, 138, 200

literary criticism, **7.III**, 169–87

literature, **7.III**, 1–31, 105–49, 151–67, 209–23, 233–45, 247–55; **8.II**, 156; **11.II**, 24, 26, 27, 29–32, 35, 38–40, 44, 46, 63, 67, 68, 70, 71–3, 75, 189; **13**, 8, 55, 56, 137, 138, 141, 143, 146, 179–81, 217, 220, 233, 264, 275

living poetically. *See* poetic living

logic, **2.I**, 56, 58, 60, 62, 118, 135, 140, 143, 144; **2.II**, 3–23, 25, 36, 174; **5.I**, 41, 42; **6.I**, 4, 129, 137, 255, 256, 258, 259, *312–31*, 335–73; **7.I**, 10, 38, 44, 47–50, 53–60 passim, 63, 105, 120, 152, 181, 186–8, 230–3, 240, 291–4; **7.II**, 6–10, 19, 163, 164, 231, 237, 341; **11.I**, 148; **11.III**, 91, 92, 94; **15.IV**, *97–104*

logic, Hegelian, **2.II**, 139–40

logic, speculative. *See* speculative logic

logos, **1.I**, 15; **1.II**, 143, 300; **4**, 51, 111, 113, 153; **6.III**, 56, 61; **8.III**, 12; **9**, 139, 140, 148, 150, 245; **11.I**, 35, 129, 136; **11.II**, 86, 96, 124, 127, 178, 183; **12.I**, 94; **14**, 5, 96

loneliness, **12.V**, 10, 53

look, the, **9**, 323

Lord's Prayer, **1.II**, 39, 40, 43

love, **1.I**, 44, 53, 54, 56, 58, 60, 63–72 passim, 115, 136, 139, 148, 151, 152, 158, 159, 162, 170, 174, 177, 207–12, 232, 261; **1.II**, 6, 11, 28, 30, 36–41, 48–50, 72, 73, 80, 82, 83, 87–9, 95, 97, 99, 100, 126, 127, 130–5, 142, 144, 145, 147, 151–62 passim, 179, 184, 192, 193, 194, 200–3, 205, 212, 213, 265, 314; **2.I**, 10, 12, 22, 74, 98, 105–14, 117, 122, 123, 124–9, 130, 143, 144–6, 171, 190, 205, 237, 263, 290; **2.II**, 40, 56–8, 68, 178–9, 204, 230, 265, 319–20; **3**, ix, 2–7, 21, 30, 43, 45, 47, 61, 72, 76, 88, 91–7 passim, 100, 126, 132–8 passim, 158–9, 164–77 passim, 186, 205, 206; **4**, 13, 29, 32, 33, 41, 50, 51, 80, 82, 107, 108, 145–66, 176, 223, 224, 228, 230, 245, 256–61, 279, 284, 302, 305, 308, 312, 319, 320; **5.I**, 172, 173; **5.II**, 11, 45, 50, 77, 95, 98, 124, 134, 135, 137, 143, 167, 169, 170, 176, 187, 188, 227, 239, 240; **5.III**, 6, 7, 23, 56, 103, 126, 127, 149–53 passim, 176–80 passim, 182; **6.II**, 49, 206, 209, 220; **6.III**, 74, 77–9, 83, 121–4, 174, 180, 197, 222; **7.II**, 69, 235, 236; **7.III**, 263, 289, 292–6; **8.I**, 64, 65, 72, 73,

90, 177, 246, 250; **8.III**, 77, 256; **9**,
12, 17, 149–51, 207, 210, 211, 274,
278, 283, 303–19 passim, 323, 368,
369, 370; **10.I**, xi, xii, 4, 6, 8, 11, 12,
17–34 passim, 52, 58, 68, 75, 76,
81, 82, 92, 97, 127, 131–6, 147, 171,
194, 202, 205, 206, 214–18, 248,
263, 326, 344, 349, 364, 387; **10.II**,
14–18, 29, 46, 48, 57–9, 71, 95, 110,
132, 143, 147, 148, 157–60, 165,
167, 168, 201, 205–16 passim; **10.III**,
18, 33–5, 63, 119, 126, 146, 147, 162,
167, 168, 175, 178, 180, 183–6, 206;
11.I, 25–7, 40, 152, 251, 300; **11.II**,
18, 19, 94, 118, 160, 218, 221, 222,
225, 252; **11.III**, 66, 78, 102, 109,
160, 161, 205, 207, 212, 215; **12.I**,
51, 52, 72, 106, 187, 227; **12.II**, 6,
13; **12.III**, 4, 9, 17, 21, 22, 58–60,
62, 95–9, 151–4, 160, 161, 171, 188;
12.IV, 9, 57, 64, 67, 72, 74, 110, 130;
12.V, 8, 13, 53, 96, 97, 99, 133, 144,
157, 169, 170, 177–81, 183, 193; **13**,
46, 71, 81, 86–91, 95–119 passim,
138, 169, 201, 211, 220, 235, 252,
265, 270, 292, 293, 303, 308–10; **14**,
30, 42, 49, 66, 91, 104, 110, 250–3;
15.IV, *105–10*; **16.I**, 7, 17, 19, 21,
25, 27, 34, 37–8, 41–8, 52, 60–1,
65–8, 72–6, 82–4, 90, 94, 103–5,
108–9, 121–6, 129, 132–9, 146, 154,
165–6, 176–83, 190, 226–7, 245–6,
274, 284, 293; **16.II**, 33, 45, 62, 70,
76–8, 81, 82, 101, 210, 226; **17**, 4,
46, 69, 98, 122, 132, 134, 178, 183,
185–90, 226, 231, 239, 240, 252,
263, 289, 304
love, *agape*,
　　10.I, 13, 25, 31, 51, 52, 76; **10.II**,
　　157, 205–15 passim; **10.III**, 12; **11.
　　II**, 209, 218, 221, 223, 224, 228;
　　12.V, 13; **13**, 70, 111, 22, 252, 292,
　　309, 310
love, Christian,
　　8.III, 250, 255, 257; **10.I**, 13; **11.I**, 26,
　　27, 40

love, *eros*,
　　2.I, 69, 70, 74, 126, 144; **10.I**, 25,
　　31, 51, 52, 81; **10.II**, 205–15 passim;
　　10.III, 12, 63, 65, 72; **11.II**, 219–21,
　　223, 224, 228; **12.III**, 3; **12.V**, 13, 19,
　　177; **16.II**, 226
love, erotic,
　　11.II, 46, 47, 59, 160, 161, 209,
　　218–25; **12.I**, 184; **12.II**, 106, 107,
　　111, 113, 123, 168; **12.III**, 147; **13**,
　　56, 60, 67, 105, 106, 109, 110, 113,
　　114, 128, 308; **14**, 198; **16.I**, 190–2;
　　17, 5, 7, 9, 13, 63, 163, 164, 171,
　　186–8
love, Platonic *eros*,
　　2.I, 105–14
love, preferential,
　　10.I, 130
love, reflective,
　　17, 9, 10
love, romantic,
　　10.III, 12; **17**, 9, 10
love of God,
　　10.I, 33, 130; **10.II**, 213; **12.I**, 125
love of neighbor,
　　9, 44, 46, 47, 48, 52, 85, 310, 313,
　　314; **10.I**, 11, 25, 33, 129–32, 206,
　　207, 213; **10.II**, 15, 59, 157–9, 167,
　　168, 210, 213; **10.III**, 38; **11.II**,
　　216, 217, 223, 224; **12.V**, 18; **13**,
　　85, 90, 105, 106, 109, 111, 114,
　　211, 310
love of oneself,
　　10.II, 158, 159, 168
Lukács School,
　　12.V, 172
Lutheranism,
　　2.I, 77; **10.II**, 15, 28, 30, 38, 39, 42,
　　135, 192, 194, 198, 200, 201, 208;
　　12.II, 54; **16.II**, 68
Lyceum (debate society in
　　Copenhagen),
　　7.II, 305
lyric,
　　7.III, 4, 19–23, 34, 59, 63, 172–6,
　　195, 209, 211, 215, 241, 258, 265,

266, 286, 290, 292, 295, 296; **15.IV**,
111–14; **16.I**, 50–62 passim
*lystig Historie om Uglspils Overmand,
En,*
20, M 1467

M
*Maanedsskrift for Christendom og
Historie,*
7.II, 102, 217
Maanedsskrift for Litteratur,
7.I, 107, 129, 136, 139, 150, 154,
155, 215, 251; **7.III**, 7, 85, 213
madness,
12.I, 15, 18, 27
Madrid School,
12.V, 87, 91
maieutics,
1.II, 27; **2.I**, 73, *115–46*, 206, 222,
291; **2.II**, 186, 187; **8.II**, 216, 272,
305; **9**, 146, 302, 378, 379, 384–6;
11.I, 231; **11.II**, 160, 164, 166; **12.II**,
5; **12.III**, 4, 9; **12.V**, 70, 115, 117;
13, 189, 190, 204, 247, 292; **16.I**,
259, 260, 265, 266, 272, 273, 275,
276; **17**, 2, 21, 59
majority, the,
14, xii, 14
Malantschuk Memorial Collection,
8.III, 178, 188, 209, 210
Manichaeism,
1.I, 8; **4**, 11; **5.I**, 5; **10.II**, 90, 93
Marburg School,
10.III, 195
Marcionism,
10.I, 195, 213–15
*Marcolfus, eller en lystig Sam
tale imellem Kong Salomon og
Marcolfus,*
20, M 1471; A II 227
marriage,
1.I, 103, 109, 165, 198, 237, 238;
1.II, 181, 182, 265; **2.I**, 110; **2.II**,
117; **4**, 61, 62; **5.III**, 6, 54, 153, 178,
180; **6.III**, 4, 9, 16, 21, 35, 44, 74,
79, 99, 100, 104, 123, 198, 222; **7.I**,
79; **7.III**, 83, 98, 99, 101, 263, 264,
269, 295, 296; **8.I**, 80; **8.II**, 3; **10.II**,
117, 120, 212; **10.III**, 18; **11.I**, 262,
271; **11.III**, 21, 22, 36; **12.I**, 69,
82, 119, 121, 123, 131; **12.II**, 32,
34; **12.III**, 16, 17, 21, 22, 154, 170;
12.IV, 7, 149, 152; **13**, 67, 103; **14**,
124; **15.IV**, *115–22*; **16.I**, 23, 32–4,
38, 41, 45, 46, 60, 65, 76, 83, 104,
105, 109, 145, 153, 154, 173, 231,
244, 245; **16.II**, 26; **17**, 9, 10, 78,
99, 170, 178, 185–90, 199, 228, 231,
251–3, 287, 288, 292
martyr/martyrdom. *See also*
persecution
1.I, 66, 79, 80; **2.I**, 21; **3**, 154, 159; **4**,
36, 42, 43, 68, 72, 73, 75, 78, 84, 86;
5.II, 12, 18, 178, 179, 199, 204–6,
219, 225, 228, 235, 241; **5.III**, 107;
6.III, 39; **7.I**, 82, 275; **7.II**, 127, 162,
200, 293, 319; **7.III**, 114; **8.I**, 137,
354, 428; **8.II**, 262; **8.III**, 56; **9**, 177,
271; **10.I**, 167, 202, 232; **10.III**, 12,
13; **11.I**, 36, 58, 172; **12.I**, 163; **12.II**,
105, 149, 154, 155; **12.III**, 77, 81,
112, 158, 159, 170; **12.IV**, 19, 20, 74;
12.V, 11; **13**, 72, 146; **14**, 213; **15.IV**,
123–30; **16.I**, 261; **17**, 85, 93, 94
Marxism,
8.I, 73, 79, 181, 209, 438; **8.III**, 50,
51, 69, 97, 103, 110, 115, 132, 136,
231, 269; **9**, 14, 23, 128, 237, 246,
247, 323, 325, 343; **10.I**, 250, 338;
10.III, 100, 114; **11.I**, 57, 116, 171;
11.II, 53, 55; **11.III**, 118, 145; **12.I**,
204; **12.IV**, 36; **12.V**, 81, 82, 147,
172; **13**, 1–3, 7, 10, 179, 305; **13**,
1–3, 7, 10, 179, 305; **14**, 43, 108,
125–8, 161–3, 210, 232
mass man,
14, 148
masses, the,
14, 154, 155
matchless discovery,
7.II, 45, 98–101, 104, 107, 109,
114–20 passim, 222–5, 303, 310

materialism,
5.I, 149; **9**, 217, 218, 246, 247; **11.I**,
57, 116, 171; **11.III**, 71, 72; **13**, 312,
316; **14**, 37, 154
matter/form,
6.III, 57
meaning, meaningfulness,
meaninglessness,
9, 66, 68, 69, 71, 75, 81, 165, 201,
248, 249, 285–7, 302; **10.I**, 344, 352,
364; **10.III**, 35; **11.I**, 95, 96, 115,
136, 151, 188–90, 201, 203, 211,
217–23 passim, 230, 275, 290, 298;
11.II, 27, 28; **11.III**, 13–18, 21, 26,
42, 52, 56 61, 62, 64, 80, 93, 101,
166, 168–70, 205, 210, 221, 222;
12.I, ix, x, 9, 79, 204–6; **12.V**, 97;
13, 10, 11, 19–25, 103, 104, 113,
145, 160, 168, 188, 227, 260, 261,
267, 277, 280, 282, 290–2, 314, 318;
14, 65, 82, 83, 96, 102, 153, 223,
239, 245, 258; **16.I**, 113–18, 215,
223–5; **17**, 14, 233, 235
meaning of existence,
12.V, 78, 80
mediation. *See also Aufhebung*
1.I, 14; **2.I**, 55–9, 61, 69; **2.II**, 3–23,
44, 66, 72, 137–41, 154–6; **4**, xii; **5.I**,
5, 39–42, 55, 56, 92, 176, 182, 185;
5.III, 48; **6.I**, 5, 9–11, 31, 80, 82, 130,
134, 172, 314–18, 336, 361–5, 370;
6.II, 104, 109; **6.III**, 82, 166; **7.I**, 44,
52, 53, 57–63 passim, 67–9, 187, 294,
303, 307; **7.II**, 5, 6, 17, 234, 243, 244,
257, 275–8; **8.I**, 80, 211; **8.II**, 223;
9, 135, 188, 246, 308, 344, 380, 384,
395, 400; **10.I**, 215, 217, 253, 254,
356, 386, 387; **10.III**, 61, 70; **11.I**, 29,
33, 73, 119, 129–32, 135, 136, 170,
268; **11.II**, 9, 64, 69, 74, 77, 86, 88,
94, 95, 123, 128, 131, 242, 246, 247;
11.III, 168, 205; **12.I**, 196; **12.IV**,
70, 71; **13**, 198, 208; **14**, 44, 46, 61,
62; **15.IV**, *131–6*; **16.I**, 54, 142, 145,
224; **16.II**, 33; **17**, 54, 253

melancholy,
1.I, 110; **3**, 139, 140; **5.I**, 24, 29,
175; **5.II**, 24; **5.III**, 32, 36–9, 50,
53, 59, 66, 152, 196, 218, 219, 245,
263–5, 267, 276, 279, 280; **6.I**, 9,
80, 86, 302, 305; **6.III**, 37, 44, 121,
122, 125, 164, 197; **7.I**, 237, 250;
7.II, 32, 189, 206, 252, 328; **7.III**,
55, 59; **8.I**, 14, 19, 24, 46, 209; **8.II**,
5, 32, 307, 320; **8.III**, 5, 6, 47, 109,
110, 112, 115, 117, 129, 131, 216,
217, 237; **9**, 110, 113, 378; **10.I**, 379,
381; **10.III**, 12, 29, 30, 62, 63, 72,
89, 146; **11.I**, 52, 56, 58–61, 110,
177, 274, 284, 285; **11.II**, 163, 227;
11.III, 205, 214; **12.I**, 70–3, 83, 123,
142, 146, 228; **12.II**, 79, 115, 137,
138, 140, 144, 154; **12.III**, 74, 80,
81, 89, 90, 94, 111, 190; **12.IV**, 47,
115, 146, 151; **12.V**, 13, 29, 70, 139,
177, 181, 184; **13**, 29, 40, 49, 56, 64,
68, 71, 88, 89, 185, 302; **14**, 109,
112, 116, 121, 198; **15.IV**, *137–42*;
16.I, 148, 149, 238, 287, 292, 293;
16.II, 15, 26, 29, 36, 40, 117, 166,
170; **17**, 7, 14, 55, 57, 70, 134, 181
memory. *See also* reminiscence
8.II, 38; **11.II**, 87; **12.III**, 19, 42,
149; **12.IV**, 125, 152, 154; **12.V**, 90,
177; **13**, 139, 188, 201, 203, 302
Menippean satire,
16.II, 49, 52
mercy,
1.II, 4, 99, 118, 140, 142
Merman. *See* Agnes and the Merman
Messiah,
1.II, 6–14 passim, 39, 44, 80, 82, 97,
161, 170, 289, 293, 304, 306
metamorphosis,
13, 127–9, 132
metaphor,
15.IV, *143–50*
metaphysics,
2.II, 20; **5.I**, 11, 35–44 passim, 62,
103, 168, 173, 179; **11.II**, 71, 88,

114, 117, 124, 129, 130, 158, 179, 180, 209, 218, 223, 225, 236, 238; **11.III**, 3, 6, 7, 73, 89, 139, 179, 181, 189; **15.IV**, *151–8*; **17**, 12, 55, 118, 122, 210, 251, 255, 264, 269, 270, 276, 277

Metropolitan School in Copenhagen, **7.II**, 213, 215, 304

Middle Ages, **5.III**, 17, 19, 132; **7.III**, 52, 58, 257, 264; **10.III**, 4, 18, 28, 37, 66, 134, 136, 158; **15.IV**, *159–62*; **16.I**, 15, 17, 26, 141, 144, 151, 193, 214, 215; **16.II**, 141, 235, 242; **17**, 234, 244, 250, 253

midlife crisis, **13**, 81, 90, 155

midwife. *See maieutics*

mimesis, **13**, 65, 144

miracle, **1.I**, 97, 197; **1.II**, 17–30, 143, 170, 239, 257, 286, 291, 304, 320; **4**, 42, 60, 113, 153, 155, 159–62; **5.I**, 25, 85, 131, 168, 177, 181, 184; **5.II**, 140; **6.II**; 61, 62, 66, 209, 237, 243, 246; **6.III**, 82; **7.I**, 282; **7.II**, 306; **9**, 370, 405; **10.I**, 72; **10.II**, 5; **12.I**, 162–5; **14**, 199, 200, 214; **15.IV**, *163–8*

mission, missionary work, **10.I**, 97; **10.II**, 17, 55, 64, 67, 69–81 passim, 173

Mithnaggedism, **10.III**, 192, 207

modal categories, **6.III**, 71

Modern Breakthrough, **7.III**, 89; **8.I**, 4, 18, 33, 34, 137, 140; **12.I**, xi, xii; **12.II**, 23, 24, 32, 45, 101, 104, 108; **12.III**, 4, 15, 16, 55, 57, 66, 109, 159, 167; **12.IV**, 114, 115

modernism, Catholic, **10.III**, 75, 94, 95

modernism, modernity, modern world **8.I**, 79, 239, 241; **10.I**, xii, 6, 66, 96, 148, 268; **10.II**, 26, 33, 45, 59, 151, 176, 178–80, 182; **10.III**, 7, 8, 19, 35, 65, 66, 94, 112, 115, 116, 118, 119, 128, 134, 135; **11.II**, 2, 11–14, 34, 226; **11.III**, 119, 208, 220–7 passim; **12.I**, 38, 63, 65, 79, 98, 99, 176, 181; **12.II**, 66, 73, 86, 87, 88, 91–4, 104, 113, 122, 133; **12.III**, 3, 38; **12.IV**, 12, 13, 34, 110, 118, 119, 158, 214, 215; **12.V**, 34, 38, 41, 49, 61–4, 67, 70, 88, 93, 94, 98, 121, 162; **13**, 56, 121–9 passim, 206, 232, 235, 245, 261, 309; **14**, 29, 30, 35, 36, 154, 199, 204, 210, 218, 232; **16.I**, 11, 50, 54–6, 59–62; **16.II**, 245

modernist crisis, **10.III**, 133

modernization, **10.II**, 29

Mohammedanism, **15.IV**, *169–72*

Molbo, the men of, **17**, 77

moment, the, **1.I**, 33–5, 63, 76, 156–8, 162; **1.II**, 175, 316; **2.I**, 40, 45, 46, 49, 50, 55, 59–68 passim, 80, 132, 133, 136; **2.II**, 16, 29, 139; **5.I**, 42; **6.I**, 366–70, 371; **7.II**, 16, 19; **8.I**, 38, 54, 88, 94, 97, 249, 311, 342, 345, 357; **8.II**, 38, 308; **8.III**, 18, 20, 69, 218, 291, 322; **9**, 101, 103, 104, 170, 407; **10.I**, 8, 9, 23, 49, 60, 74, 83, 135, 149, 151, 171, 185, 199, 207–16 passim, 325, 327, 345, 365, 366, 367, 386; **10.II**, 110; **10.III**, 61, 70, 143; **11.I**, 191, 282, 283, 285; **11.II**, 245, 246; **11.III**, 5; **12.I**, 8, 25, 26, 183; **12.III**, 10, 22, 43, 179; **12.V**, 28, 53, 83, 84; **13**, 270; **14**, 23, 33, 191; **15.IV**, *173–80*

monads, **5.I**, 70

Monasticism,
   4, xii, 24, 25, 37–43, 47, 48, 51–3,
   56, 57, 63, 95, 99, 100, 123, 124, 155,
   201, 238, 244, 246, 251, 257, 262,
   265, 276, 278, 279, 284, 290; **5.II**,
   10–12, 32, 38, 39, 77, 103, 122, 170,
   178–83, 193, 196, 201, 248, 249, 254;
   5.III, **6.III**, 95; **8.III**, 74; **10.I**, 226,
   231, 232; **10.III**, 56; **15.IV**, *181–8*;
   17, 244, 250–3
money,
   15.IV, *189–96*
monotheism,
   1.I, 90, 92
Montanism,
   4, 132
mood. *See also* emotion *and* feeling,
   15.IV, *197–204*
moralism,
   11.II, 99
morality. *See also* ethics
   7.I, 130, 131, 147, 148, 231, 233,
   238, 309; **9**, 9, 14, 82, 84, 227, 264,
   275, 325, 330, 385, 399; **10.I**, 357;
   11.I, 52; **11.II**, 56; **12.I**, 202, 205;
   13, 36; **14**, 12, 79, 100, 113, 118,
   119, 264; **16.II**, 2
Moravian Society,
   7.II, 30
Morgenposten,
   7.I, 24
Mormonism,
   7.II, 195, 204
motion. *See* movement
movement, dialectical,
   2.II, 159–60
movement (in logic) *See also* κίνησις
   2.I, 56, 133; **2.II**, 4, 11, 22, 26, 31,
   41–5 passim, 113, 123–45, 153–60
   passim; **5.I**, 186; **6.I**, 130, 255, 256,
   259, 263, 313, 314, 318–29 passim,
   336; **7.I**, 55–7, 63, 67, 79, 80, 81,
   187; **7.III**, 72, 80, 81, 161; **8.II**, 223;
   11.II, 71, 86, 88–90, 93–5, 116–18,
   126, 132, 159, 182; **15.IV**, *205–12*;
   17, 54

multiculturalism,
   11.III, 220
music, the musical,
   5.III, 8, 137–63 passim, 180, 253;
   6.III, 71, 122, 139, 148–52; **7.I**,
   278–80; **7.III**, 79, 172, 173, 177; **8.I**,
   367–9; **12.I**, 82, 174, 185–9, 222;
   12.II, 34, 170; **12.IV**, 41–9, 183, 187,
   188, 201, 202; **12.V**, 72–4, 130, 133,
   177, 178; **14**, 128, 248, 253; **15.IV**,
   213–22; **16.I**, 141–9 passim, 173, 175,
   190–2, 194, 215, 247; **16.II**, 18, 45–7,
   66, 123–6, 130, 133, 169–77, 260–5;
   17, 141–9 passim
Music Association,
   7.III, 10
Myers-Brigg test,
   13, 151
mystery,
   8.I, 7, 8
mysticism, Christian,
   5.II, 52
mysticism, neoplatonic,
   5.II, 47
mysticism/mystics,
   4, 11, 28, 237–53, 265–87, 290; **5.I**,
   104, 153, 157; **5.II**, 4, 21–5, 32, 33,
   39, 43–7, 50, 51, 149, 222, 223, 251,
   252, 255; **6.II**, 46, 87, 88, 90, 96,
   138; **6.III**, 249; **7.II**, 23, 232, 233,
   238; **8.I**, 59, 286; **8.II**, 215; **8.III**, 14,
   57, 77, 80, 113, 138; **9**, 34, 44, 75,
   229, 310; **10.I**, 70, 71, 190, 337, 347,
   356, 357, 367; **10.II**, 66, 88, 108,
   128, 176; **10.III**, 76, 82, 85–7, 89;
   11.II, 48; **12.I**, 148; **12.II**, 60; **12.III**,
   4, 31; **12.V**, 8, 9; **13**, 76, 262–4, 267,
   268; **14**, 97
myth/ mythology,
   1.II, 240, 258, 295, 296; **2.II**, 211,
   263–9, 279, 290; **4**, 317, 318; **6.II**,
   5–8, 10–12, 14–18, 26, 96, 233–53
   passim; **6.III**, 19, 175; **7.I**, 2, 5, 277,
   270, 278, 298, 306; **7.II**, 95, 96, 106,
   107, 117, 126, 251; **7.III**, 264, 265;
   8.I, 365, 366; **10.III**, 7, 105; **11.I**,

18, 19, 27, 30, 40; **12.II**, 33, 102, 105, 109, 167; **12.V**, 53, 54; **13**, 4, 5, 13, 20, 55, 56, 70, 71, 139, 140, 146, 147, 170, 220, 232; **15.IV**, *223–6*; **16.I**, xi, 1, 41, 65–8, 83, 97–100, 133–41, 145, 167, 171, 187, 209–13, 218–21, 224, 229–41, 253, 256, 293, 294; **16.II**, 40, 133–7, 155–62, 187–98, 223–33

N

Naqshbandi,
  8.III, 57
narcissism,
  13, 107, 112, 202
narrative,
  11.III, 119, 126, 129
nationalism,
  10.I, 160; **12.IV**, 120; **14**, 138, 144; **16.II**, 69
National Socialism,
  10.I, ix, 3, 15, 44, 45, 60, 105, 160, 161, 169, 170, 321, 339, 358, 366; **10.III**, 26, 47, 99, 100, 134, 136, 158, 165, 198; **11.I**, 35, 36, 40, 167; **11.II**, 55, 187; **11.III**, 100; **12.I**, 31, 95, 171, 173, 198, 200; **12.II**, 25, 80; **12.IV**, 3; **12.IV**, 3; **12.V**, 34, 42; **14**, 3, 7, 9, 11, 12, 73, 74, 76, 107, 119, 120, 122, 125, 126, 181, 182, 196, 197, 205, 209, 225
naturalism,
  5.I, 34, 35, 77; **7.I**, 292, 293 **7.III**, 105; **8.I**, 154; **10.II**, 144, 145, 180; **10.III**, 67; **11.I**, 149, 152, 156–60; **12.I**, 65; **12.II**, 68, 88; **12.III**, 17, 22, 55
natural language. *See* language, ordinary
natural law,
  4, 150; **9**, 219; **10.II**, 5; **12.IV**, 168, 169; **14**, 215–17, 219
natural man,
  2.I, 307; **5.I**, 25; **17**, 40, 42
natural sciences,
  6.I, 53, 59, 215–17, 222, 293–305; **7.I**, 215–27, 231, 238, 264, 269, 277,

298, 304, 305, 307, 310, 311; **7.III**, 258; **15.IV**, *227–30*
nature,
  6.III, 12, 74–8,118, 151, 198; **10.III**, 7, 56, 57, 61, 62, 71, 101, 102, 181; **15.IV**, *227–30*
nausea,
  12.V, 80
Nazism. *See* National Socialism
necessity,
  2.II, 12, 16–19, 27, 35, 36, 38, 44, 45, 64, 65; **4**, 128, 214, 215; **5.I**, 17, 35, 53, 55, 59–66 passim, 72, 167; **6.I**, 129, 315, 324, 327, 330; **7.I**, 41; **10.II**, 11; **10.III**, 117; **11.III**, 53, 55; **15.IV**, *231–6*
necessity and possibility,
  12.III, 40
negation, negativity,
  2.I, 90, 94, 98, 99, 102, 118, 126, 127, 135, 239, 279–83, 287, 288, 291, 292, 301, 302, 306–8; **2.II**, 4, 9, 10, 12, 18, 132, 139–40, 189, 192; **4**, 243, 250; **5.I**, 42; **5.III**, 267, 269; **6.I**, 4, 9–11, 72, 81, 102, 105, 106, 113, 114, 117, 120, 122, 126, 127, 314, 321–5, 329; **6.III**, 206, 208, 247, 252, 253, 257, 260, 262–6; **9**, 9, 84, 174, 254, 310–12, 316, 318, 332, 384; **10.I**, 87, 370; **11.I**, 14, 17, 25, 26, 28, 32, 117, 118, 191, 193–6, 202; **11.II**, 4, 49, 52, 65, 74, 77, 242; **12.I**, 21, 22, 123, 197, 202–4, 207, 210, 238–40, 244; **12.V**, 8, 85; **13**, 301, 304, 319; **15.IV**, *237–44*; **16.I**, 134, 138, 139, 263; **16.II**, 7, 159, 209
negativity, absolute infinite,
  2.I, 89, 90, 94, 101, 127, 184, 205, 206, 209, 297; **2.II**, 183, 192; **6.III**, 206, 252, 256, 257; **8.III**, 46, 136; **10.II**, 35; **11.III**, 42; **12.I**, 203, 239; **16.I**, 133; **16.II**, 5; **17**, 9, 10, 13, 15, 16, 46, 134
Nemesis,
  7.I, 104; **7.III**, 119, 120, 146

neo-evangelicalism,
  10.II, 4
Neo-Kantianism,
  10.I, xii, 2, 74, 341; **10.III**, 81, 190,
  191, 193–5, 197, 202, 206; **11.I**, 127,
  128, 133; **11.III**, 211; **12.V**, 109
neology,
  5.I, 84
Neo-Marxism,
  10.I, 346; **10.II**, 130
neo-orthodoxy,
  10.I, x, 1, 6, 99; **10.II**, 51, 144
Neoplatonism,
  4, 11, 168, 207–11, 218, 219; **5.II**,
  44, 46, 51, 52, 222, 251; **10.I**, 346;
  10.III, 84
neo-pragmatism,
  11.III, 177, 182, 190, 198
neo-rationalism,
  7.II, 61
neo-scholasticism,
  10.III, 4, 27, 99, 109, 133
New Hermeneutic,
  10.I, 146
New Testament Christianity. *See*
  Christianity, New Testament
nihilism,
  1.I, 57, 183; **2.II**, 189, 192; **6.III**, 9,
  56, 70, 164, 166, 202, 207, 208, 242,
  250, 257, 261, 264; **7.I**, 123, 130–5,
  138, 145, 151, 152, 157, 159; **8.I**,
  184, 442; **8.II**, 166, 306, 307; **8.III**,
  45; **9**, 85, 264, 266, 278–82, 286;
  10.I, 133; **10.II**, 12; **10.III**, 105, 108;
  11.I, 117, 118, 163, 167, 168, 170,
  171, 176, 188, 189, 198, 201; **11.III**,
  22, 51, 52, 60, 64, 119; **12.I**, 3, 23,
  154; **12.II**, 157; **12.III**, 35; **12.IV**,
  163; **12.V**, 18, 69; **13**, 269, 278, 298;
  14, 124, 154, 196, 214; **16.II**, 9, 29,
  30, 103, 238; **17**, 16, 17, 189, 210
nisses. *See* elves, trolles, and nisses
nominalism,
  4, 146; **11.II**, 114
Nook of the Eight Paths. *See* Grib
  Forest

noology,
  11.II, 96
Nordic Mythology,
  16.II, 65–72
Nord og Syd,
  7.I, 247, 248, 249; **7.III**, 90, 96,
  114–16, 132–8 passim, 141–6
Den Nordiske Kirketidende,
  7.II, 102, 193, 217
nothing, nothingness,
  1.I, 4, 12, 13, 16, 23, 27, 34–6, 39,
  40, 168; **9**, 7, 9, 65, 110–13, 161,
  225, 281, 323, 330–5, 345, 346, 361,
  365, 366; **10.I**, 20; **10.III**, 125; **11.I**,
  139, 190, 282; **12.I**, 36, 49, 73, 148,
  201; **12.IV**, 126; **12.V**, 18, 78, 79,
  96; **13**, 20, 24, 47, 209, 222, 225,
  227, 277, 283–5, 292, 299; **14**, 101,
  103, 126, 143, 151, 190, 214, 218,
  219, 238–40, 263
novel,
  12.I, ix, 6, 24, 38, 39, 63, 66, 83, 175,
  203; **12.II**, 3, 4, 9, 43–61 passim, 67,
  102–4, 108, 110, 113–16, 121–33
  passim, 137–45 passim, 149, 150,
  155, 156, 159, 169; **12.V**, 77–86;
  15.IV, *245–52*; **17**, 51, 57, 67–9, 119,
  162, 205, 207, 209, 210, 212
Nunc Dimittis,
  1.II, 3
Ny Samling af fædrelandske Sange,
  20, A II 313
Nyt Aftenblad,
  7.I, 247

O
obedience,
  5.II, 11; **10.II**, 71; **11.II**, 17; **12.II**,
  6, 12
objectivity,
  15.V, *1–6*
offense,
  1.I, 124; **1.II**, 6, 18, 22, 24, 26,
  29–30, 38, 47, 49, 82–4, 110, 157,
  160–2, 241, 244, 321, 323; **2.I**, 37,
  43, 67, 80, 141–4, 305; **2.II**, 92; **3**,

136, 159; **4**, 58, 107, 137; **5.I**, 27, 132, 180; **5.II**, 27, 188, 242; **6.I**, 37, 38, 41, 42; **6.II**; 4–8, 11, 17, 49, 219; **6.III**, 102, 295; **7.II**, 169, 323; **8.I**, 40, 65, 78, 79, 155, 249, 311, 340, 442; **8.II**, 325; **8.III**, 234; **9**, 78, 81, 90, 150, 265, 274, 282, 367, 407; **10.I**, 9, 10, 15, 27–9, 59, 60, 95, 123, 127, 132, 135, 366; **10.II**, 7, 11, 12, 16, 20, 55, 93, 131, 136, 161; **10.III**, 22, 34, 35, 69; **11.II**, 120, 123, 125, 145, 147; **12.I**, 53; **12.III**, 4, 5; **12.V**, 84; **13**, 74; **14**, 151, 155; **15.V**, *7–14*; **16.I**, 98; **17**, 40, 44, 45, 48

ontological argument,
  4, 168, 169, 171, 173–5, 177, 198, 202; **5.I**, 177, 178; **9**, 397, 406; **10.III**, 63

ontology,
  9, 51, 96, 102, 132, 135–7, 145, 200, 205, 244, 246, 250–2, 325, 402; **11.I**, 9, 31, 34, 35, 39, 77; **11.II**, 115, 130, 133, 176, 177, 185, 209, 219; **14**, 41, 42, 44–6, 55

opera,
  7.III, 69, 70, 171–3, 177; **14**, 128; **16.I**, 243–9; **16.II**, 169–79, 115, 116, 130, 217, 218, 257–67; **17**, 34–6

opposites,
  2.II, 7, 8, 10, 126, 132, 140, 147–60 passim, 289; **7.I**, 60, 62

opposites, unity of,
  2.II, 157–8

ordeal,
  12.IV, 188

Order of Cistercians of Strict Observance,
  10.III, 111

ordinary language,
  11.III, 2, 3, 7, 15, 16, 18, 21, 22, 157, 164, 170

orthodoxy/orthodox,
  15.V, *15–22*

orthography,
  7.III, 239, 241

Other, the/otherness. *See also* alterity
  9, 1, 11, 15, 45, 51, 206, 211, 303, 343, 404; **11.I**, 127, 136, 137, 202; **13**, 8, 22, 102, 110–12, 131, 144, 145, 208–11, 253, 254, 308–11; **14**, xiv, 79; **15.V**, *23–8*

Ottoman Empire,
  5.II, 2; **5.III**, 2, 13

outer and inner. *See* inner/outer

P

paganism,
  1.II, 70; **4**, 51, 58, 59, 90, 124, 125, 150, 230; **15.V**, *29–34*; **16.I**, 23, 27, 28, 254, 273; **16.II**, 46, 47, 194, 228; **17**, 9, 186, 189

painting,
  16.II, 69

panentheism,
  10.II, 107, 138; **15.V**, *35–42*

Pantheism,
  4, 51, 239, 241–3, 274, 277; **5.I**, 34, 87, 167, 173, 182; **5.II**, 47; **5.III**, 103, 107; **6.I**, 52, 56; **6.II**, 89, 101, 102, 109, 147, 148, 199, 208, 220, 240; **7.I**, 223, 294; **7.II**, 57; **10.I**, 87, 88, 91, 348, 387; **10.III**, 67, 86

Pantheism Controversy,
  5.I, 33; **16.II**, 196

pantomime,
  7.III, 78

parable,
  11.III, 25

paradox,
  1.I, 52, 65, 71, 75, 123, 163, 164, 170, 215, 240, 247, 259; **1.II**, 18, 22–4, 26, 29, 30, 107, 115, 197, 198, 238, 240–4, 252, 253, 262–8 passim, 275, 277, 279, 314–16, 319; **2.I**, 28, 32, 33, 40–3, 63, 66, 67–71, 80, 82, 132–7, 145, 179, 189, 305–7; **2.II**, 22, 67, 72, 93, 94, 97, 172, 230, 240, 242; **3**, 30, 61, 62; **4**, 63, 113, 136, 137, 150; **5.I**, 5, 55, 56, 135, 167; **5.II**, 246; **6.I**, 37, 38, 41, 59, 60, 351, 370; **6.II**, 4, 8, 16, 17, 138; **6.III**,

102, 194, 195, 295; **7.I**, 5; **7.II**, 58,
65, 76–83 passim, 91, 92, 130, 176,
179, 185, 242, 248, 276, 277; **8.I**,
6–8, 14–16, 20, 22, 23, 35–40, 59,
66, 72, 78, 86–8, 94, 144, 155, 178,
211, 221, 249, 255, 256, 279, 280,
311, 320, 323, 333, 342, 345, 359,
361, 377, 425, 426, 439, 440, 442,
444, 454, 456; **8.II**, 4, 8, 92, 158,
223, 225, 226, 253, 256, 290, 304,
324, 325; **8.III**, 70, 75, 85, 138, 213;
9, 79, 81, 90, 137, 170, 171, 179,
188, 223, 229, 242, 248, 250, 265,
273, 300, 302, 306, 310, 338, 379,
383, 399, 400, 404; **10.I**, 8, 9, 14, 23,
79, 88, 127, 135, 164, 167, 171, 189,
201, 253, 254, 323–8, 344, 347, 359,
360, 365, 366, 369, 370, 382, 386;
10.II, 3, 6, 10–20 passim, 32, 69, 76,
77, 88, 90–7 passim, 112, 113,
123–6, 128, 131, 133, 134, 135, 137,
139, 147, 148, 151, 161, 182, 183,
199; **10.III**, 7, 19, 107, 109, 120, 180;
11.I, 17, 30, 36, 59, 61, 78, 159, 167,
168, 171, 227, 228, 253, 259–62,
270, 272, 279, 297; **11.II**, 16, 17, 27,
31, 32, 64, 66, 69, 71, 120, 128, 131,
145, 209, 212–15, 229, 237, 241,
242, 244–6, 249, 250; **11.III**, 25, 39,
123, 148, 225; **12.I**, 53, 54, 74, 103,
106, 143–7, 152, 199, 210; **12.II**, 7,
23, 126, 138, 154, 174; **12.III**, 43, 80,
90; **12.IV**, 17, 69, 85, 167, 180, 181,
202, 207; **12.V**, 70, 83, 84, 129, 144,
153, 180; **13**, 19–21, 24, 61, 72–4,
77, 89, 107, 108, 134, 166, 209,
212, 226, 227, 234, 235, 270, 284,
289–91, 299, 304, 305, 316, 318;
14, 6, 15, 20, 34, 37, 46–9, 60–3, 70,
109, 110, 155, 165, 166, 185, 233,
238, 239, 264, 265; **15.V**, *43–8*; **16.I**,
43, 177–9, 183, 269, 271; **16.II**, 102;
17, 122, 145, 188, 275
paradox, absolute,
   4, 137; **5.I**, 57, 177, 180; **8.III**, 234,
   242, 256; **10.I**, xii; **10.II**, 30, 132;

10.III, 32, 53, 63, 65, 69, 70, 72;
   11.III, 3, 5, 8, 75, 76, 165, 168–70;
   17, 122
parody. *See also* satire
   14, 59, 60, 68–70, 97; **15.V**, *49–54*
parousia,
   10.I, 224, 225, 239
particular. *See* universal
passion. *See also* pathos
   1.I, 64, 65, 67, 187, 222; **1.II**, 80,
   129, 151–8 passim, 163, 164, 169,
   172, 178, 180; **2.I**, 34, 41, 70, 78,
   108, 113, 136, 220, 275, 286, 287,
   291, 306, 307; **2.II**, 195–208; **4**, xii,
   201, 202, 261; **5.I**, 93, 100; **7.II**, 73,
   85, 122, 132, 164, 169, 225; **7.III**,
   33, 160–3, 198–204 passim, 269,
   277, 293; **8.I**, 15, 16, 59, 72, 155,
   456; **8.III**, 85, 115, 242; **9**, 72, 80,
   82, 98, 100, 101, 263, 272, 273–5,
   286, 378, 379, 381–6, 400; **10.II**,
   11, 18, 32, 69, 92, 93, 119, 184, 212,
   213; **10.III**, 34, 72, 105, 120, 202;
   11.I, 55, 58, 59, 72, 73, 77, 117, 152,
   251, 258, 259, 275, 292; **11.II**, 71,
   150, 185, 226, 245, 249; **11.III**, 9,
   51, 67, 77, 80, 83, 171, 221, 224;
   12.I, 10, 11, 16, 84, 107, 190, 206;
   12.II, 79, 82, 89, 93, 101, 154, 155;
   12.III, 89, 158; **12.IV**, 16–20, 90;
   12.V, 47, 110, 169, 177, 179, 183;
   13, 37, 38, 45, 48, 91, 104, 110,
   181–6, 226, 230, 233, 281, 282; **14**,
   7, 14, 15, 48, 59, 61, 62, 113, 153,
   163, 164, 184, 188, 190, 191, 198,
   223, 249; **15.V**, 55–62; **16.I**, 20, 21,
   34, 38, 74, 127, 141, 149–51, 174–7,
   187, 198, 240, 271; **16.II**, 8, 91; **17**,
   123, 133, 145, 251, 253, 261, 268,
   271, 305
pastor,
   15.V, *63–6*
pastoral care,
   5.II, 40, 247
pastoral seminary,
   7.II, 268, 292, 335

pataphysics,
  13, 1, 3
pathos. *See also* passion
  2.II, 44–5, 76, 91, 92, 203, 264; **4**, 5,
  81, 172, 175, 177, 319; **15.V**, *55–62*;
  17, 123, 125, 126, 130, 132, 134–6,
  184, 253, 261–3, 268, 278
patience,
  1.I, 29, 160, 164, 215, 218, 223;
  1.II, 3–14, 181; **15.V**, *67–74*
Peasants' Revolt (1525),
  5.II, 85, 86, 89
Pelagianism,
  1.I, 6; **1.II**, 4; **4**, 11, 15; **6.I**, 9, 56;
  10.II, 148, 149
persecution. *See also* martyr/
  martyrdom
  1.II, 37, 44–50 passim, 164, 177,
  198, 201, 205; **15.IV**, *123–30*
Perseus. See Heiberg, Johan Ludvig,
  Perseus
personalism,
  10.I, 99, 194, 195, 213–15; **10.III**,
  60, 67, 71; **14**, 92, 95–7, 99, 101
personality,
  15.V, *75–82*
personhood,
  10.III, 58
perspectivism,
  14, 147, 153
pessimism,
  13, 58
Pharisees, the,
  1.II, 40, *93–103*, 108, 113, 116, 117,
  119, 125, 131, 132, 237
phenomenology,
  8.I, 205, 282, 364, 443, 450; **8.II**,
  7, 88, 95, 215, 228, 307; **8.III**, 11,
  12, 15, 48, 67, 70, 72, 74, 82, 84;
  9, 108, 114, 127–54, 150, 158, 174,
  180, 220, 234–6, 239, 240, 244,
  245, 249, 309, 323, 325, 357, 365,
  394, 395, 398, 401, 406, 408; **10.I**,
  44, 86, 341, 346, 369; **10.II**, 34,
  108; **10.III**, 46, 194; **11.I**, x, xi, 129,
  147–60 passim, 167, 182, 195, 202;
  11.II, 114, 115, 130, 173, 175, 185,
  207–10, 213, 214, 216–18, 220, 221,
  225, 227, 228, 229, 233; **11.III**, 5,
  65, 121, 138, 148; **12.I**, 148; **12.V**,
  7, 10, 14, 80, 82; **13**, 30, 33, 34, 44,
  49, 55, 71, 76, 167, 179, 197, 219;
  14, 45, 53, 117, 159, 160, 220; **17**,
  123–7, 129, 137
phenomenon,
  6.III, 71, 203
philistine,
  12.I, 35; **12.III**, 10
philistinism,
  13, 22, 23, 59, 156
philosophers,
  15.V, *83–94*
philosophy,
  8.I, 7; **15.V**, *83–94*
philosophy, analytic,
  8.I, 182, 183, 204, 209, 239, 259;
  11.I, xi, 209, 210, 214, 223, 224,
  234, 235; **11.III**, 11–18 passim, 21,
  22, 26, 72, 118, 177, 179–81, 195,
  196
philosophy, beginning of. *See*
  beginning of philosophy
philosophy, existential,
  8.I, 39, 159, 205, 246, 279, 282,
  352, 379
philosophy, Greek,
  8.I, 6, 8, 357
philosophy, moral,
  11.II, 233
philosophy, ordinary,
  11.III, 1, 11, 13, 15, 19, 21, 24
philosophy, rational,
  5.I, 34, 39, 43, 44
philosophy, speculative. *See*
  speculative philosophy
philosophy, transcendental,
  5.I, 41; **10.I**, 44
philosophy and Christianity,
  7.I, 282
philosophy of history,
  6.II, 72–4; **12.I**, 31, 34, 37; **14**, 210,
  220, 224

philosophy of identity,
  7.I, 237
philosophy of religion,
  4, 57; **6.III**, 61, 66; **10.III**, 7; **11.I**,
  xi; **11.III**, 2–4, 100, 103, 118,
  157–60
physiognomy,
  12.I, 143, 146–54
Pietism,
  1.I, 179, 232, 241, 255, 260, 261;
  1.II, 191–5, 200, 205, 211, 285; **2.I**,
  133, 139; **4**, 244, 245, 251, 268–277,
  281, 284; **5.I**, x; **5.II**, 8, 44, 56, 57,
  63–79, 149–56 passim, 247, 249,
  252, 253, 256; **5.III**, 63, 68, 125,
  246; **6.II**, 46; **7.II**, 24, 29, 30, 38,
  189, 211, 216, 267; **8.I**, 127–30, 140,
  141, 145, 165, 333, 345; **10.I**, 13,
  15, 16, 18, 19, 32, 33, 173, 369; **11.I**,
  298; **12.II**, 66, 69, 127, 131; **12.III**,
  57, 72, 73, 78, 124–8 passim
Pietism, Halle,
  5.II, 28, 64–8, 149–53
Pietism, Moravian. *See* Herrnhutism
πίστις or pistis. *See also* faith
  2.II, 84, 88, 91, 94–7; **10.II**, 193,
  198, 199, 201; **10.III**, 14
Platonism,
  4, 111, 118; **6.II**, 24, 26–8, 31–3,
  200; **11.III**, 139
pleasure,
  17, 4–6, 9, 10, 13, 15, 17
pluralism,
  11.III, 87, 89, 183
pneumatology,
  10.I, 190–2, 206, 328
poem,
  6.III, 8, 10, 14, 27, 35, 36, 41, 45,
  131, 307
poet,
  6.III, 33, 70, 125, 171–84 passim
poetic living,
  6.III, 278–83, 302–5
poetry,
  1.I, 141, 142; **2.I**, 252, 262; **3**, ix–
  xii, 4, 39–48 passim, 87–9, 93, 94,

  112, 167, 180, 197; **4**, 210–12, 219,
  223–32, 257, 259–61, 299–320;
  5.III, 5, 36, 63–75 passim, 99, 189,
  205, 206, 273–80 passim; **6.I**, 128,
  129, 295, 297, 298; **6.III**, 32, 34,
  56, 57, 66, 71, 124, 126, 127,
  145–7, 149, 162, 163, 177, 192,
  202, 217, 218, 225, 244, 245, 254,
  264, 280–5, 305, 306; **7.I**, 35, 50,
  58, 60, 123, 126–8, 132, 139, 140,
  142, 279; **7.II**, 18, 96, 97, 118, 179,
  180, 230–2, 244, 246, 251, 304, 305,
  340, 345; **7.III**, 33–48, 172, 173–7,
  210, 221, 233, 238, 241, 248, 253,
  257–73, 285–97; **12.I**, 25, 39, 65,
  150, 154, 215; **12.II**, 21, 65, 66, 70,
  72, 74, 75, 77, 78, 84–92 passim,
  103, 108, 110, 167, 169; **12.IV**, 1,
  2, 5, 7, 11, 21, 23, 27, 36, 37, 43,
  53, 54, 56, 61–8, 70, 71, 73, 75, 85,
  101, 102, 122, 139, 196, 202; **12.V**,
  22, 23, 57–76; **15.V**, *95–100*; **16.I**,
  50, 52; **16.II**, 45, 67, 79, 80, 91, 96,
  97, 144, 150, 187; **17**, 4, 6, 21, 39,
  59, 68, 69, 72–5, 93, 101, 103, 120,
  143–50, 155, 156, 160, 164–6, 168,
  186, 189, 194, 201, 207, 251–3,
  261, 281, 282, 304–6, 308
poetry, apocalyptic,
  7.II, 230, 232, 241
poetry, Romantic,
  6.III, 202, 218, 220
poetry, speculative. *See* speculative
  poetry
poetry, troubadour,
  4, 299–320
politics,
  2.II, 83, 96, 149; **5.III**, 93–107; **7.I**,
  13–33, 77–82, 85–100, 169–75,
  247–9; **8.I**, 81–6; **9**, 45, 64, 219;
  11.I, 107, 110, 113, 119, 166, 174,
  289; **11.II**, 2, 151, 152; **12.I**, 67, 96,
  172; **13**, 2, 10, 24, 56, 63, 81, 91,
  95, 98, 125, 141, 152, 153, 179, 185,
  190, 206, 261–71, 297, 301, 319;
  15.V, *101–6*

Politiken,
  8.I, 83
pornography,
  13, 10, 11
positivism,
  8.I, 154, 160, 161; **8.II**, 5; **8.III**, 136;
  9, 217, 218, 243, 376; **10.I**, 367;
  10.III, 115, 116, 195; **11.I**, x, 88, 108,
  272, 273; **11.III**, 17, 18, 71, 77; **12.I**,
  31, 37; **12.II**, 23, 45, 56, 69, 91, 92;
  13, 250, 269; **14**, 125, 147, 214, 217
positivism, logical,
  11.III, 15, 72, 137
possibility,
  1.I, 17, 20, 31–9 passim, 52, 109,
  163, 164, 200, 201, 216, 244; **1.II**,
  11, 28, 39, 48, 66–9, 139, 141, 145;
  2.II, 18, 30, 33, 34, 37, 38 75, 113;
  4, 128, 175, 212, 214; **6.I**, 315, 324,
  329; **6.III**, 71; **8.II**, 87, 88; **8.III**, 8,
  54, 240; **9**, 113, 114, 140, 141, 329,
  332–4, 363, 365, 405, 407; **10.I**,
  204, 205, 214, 217, 218; **10.III**, 35,
  117; **11.I**, 75, 77, 81, 189, 200, 233,
  271, 281, 282; **11.III**, 53, 55; **12.I**, 4,
  6, 7, 23, 26, 27, 84, 202; **12.II**, 60;
  13, 22–4, 43–5, 66, 130, 143, 163,
  220, 222–4, 284, 288, 300, 312; **14**,
  3, 4, 61, 65, 110, 184, 218, 241–4,
  247–50, 266; **17**, 12, 16, 54, 72, 123,
  161, 171–3, 185, 187, 219, 251, 267,
  271, 272, 275, 278, 305
possibility and actuality,
  2.II, 16, 17, 19, 27–31, 35–6, 92,
  154
possibility and necessity,
  11.II, 152, 153; **11.III**, 57, 58, 60;
  12.V, 144; **16.II**, 89, 90
possible worlds,
  5.I, 53, 58, 59, 66–9, 83
postmodernism, postmodernity,
  8.I, 79, 164, 238, 263; **8.III**, 110,
  111, 249; **10.I**, 1, 148; **10.II**, 45, 54;
  11.I, xi; **11.II**, 3, 31, 84, 124, 207;
  11.III, 214; **12.I**, ix; **12.IV**, 193;
  17, xiii

post-structuralism,
  8.I, 421, 450; **11.I**, xi; **11.II**, 31, 43;
  12.IV, 193; **14**, 54
poverty,
  5.II, 17, 178, 188, 252, 256
pragmatism,
  8.III, 14, 134, 136, 138, 177, 231;
  11.III, 87, 88, 92, 179–82; **14**, 232,
  233, 246
prayer,
  5.II, 12, 25, 26, 75, 139, 169, 179,
  193, 249; **6.II**, 204; **7.I**, 223, 282;
  10.I, 77, 148, 164, 166; **11.II**, 142,
  143, 153; **15.V**, *107–12*; **16.II**, 34
preaching,
  5.II, 18, 38, 67, 87–9, 98, 113, 150,
  192, 195, 199, 202, 206, 238; **10.I**,
  165
Preces Catholico-Christianæ,
  20, M 460
predestination,
  1.I, 6, 11; **4**, 114, 115, 123–8; **10.I**,
  207, 242
pre-established harmony,
  5.I, 52, 57, 59
present age, the,
  10.II, 29; **15.V**, *113–20*
press, freedom of,
  17, 29, 32
press, the,
  7.III, 163; **9**, 173; **10.I**, 268; **10.III**,
  116–18; **11.I**, 174, 295; **11.II**, 226;
  11.III, 51, 63, 64; **12.I**, 69, 159,
  160–4; **12.V**, 109; **13**, 56; **15.V**,
  121–8
presuppositionless science,
  6.I, 9
pride,
  15.V, *129–34*; **16.II**, 25, 26, 59, 60,
  62, 127, 211, 224, 227, 253
primitivity,
  15.V, *135–40*
Privatdozent,
  7.II, 73, 75, 88; **14**, 108, 117–19
privatism,
  10.I, 216

progress,
  10.I, 87; **15.V**, *141–4*
proofs of God's existence,
  10.II, 11, 20, 127, 130; **12.I**, 39
prophecy,
  1.II, 286, 291
Protestantism. *See also* Reformation
  1.II, 254, 259, 276; **2.I**, 38; **4**, 36,
  47, 193, 241; **6.I**, 32, 288; **6.III**, 16,
  22; **7.II**, 100, 169, 176, 193; **7.III**,
  56; **8.III**, 45; **11.I**, 175; **11.III**, 99,
  121; **12.I**, 32, 84, 164; **12.II**, 88, 93;
  12.III, 57; **12.V**, 34; **13**, 107, 164–7,
  298; **15.V**, *145–52*; **16.II**, 46
prototype, the,
  1.II, 43, 79, 82, 85, 87, 100, 101,
  113, 114, 118, 123, 127–9, 130–5,
  151, 162–4, 169, 178, 180; **4**, 13, 36,
  289, 291; **5.II**, 83, 97–101, 106, 107,
  169, 193–7, 207, 219, 220, 229, 239,
  241, 242; **10.III**, 85; **13**, 145, 146;
  14, 17, 195; **17**, 47
providence,
  1.I, 19, 23, 27, 29, 36–8, 44, 53, 56,
  57, 63, 159, 162; **4**, 208; **5.III**, 98,
  99; **16.II**, 158
provincialism,
  14, 152
Psalmebog (collected and ed. by
  Roskilde-Konvents Psalmekomite),
  20, A I 94
pseudonym/pseudonymity,
  5.III, 109, 121, 122; **6.II**, 206, 207;
  8.I, 68, 456, 457; **8.II**, 5, 8, 41, 44,
  45, 48, 218, 220, 249, 271, 293; **8.III**,
  6, 83, 107, 111, 206, 213, 214, 236,
  239, 256; **9**, 2, 10, 40, 77, 146, 187,
  202, 223, 226, 271, 283, 377, 398;
  10.I, 96, 217, 322–3; **10.II**, 55, 69, 73,
  138, 147; **10.III**, 85, 141; **11.I**, ix, x,
  24, 52, 56, 59, 60, 173, 175, 178, 180,
  200, 226, 231, 251, 254, 258–61, 270,
  278, 291–3; **11.II**, 39, 105, 111, 113,
  114, 116, 146, 147, 162, 163; **11.III**,
  31, 64–7, 209; **12.I**, ix, x, xiii, 24,
  107; **12.II**, 34; **12.III**, 6, 7, 28, 33, 36;
  12.V, 19, 57–76, 122, 131, 176; **13**,

21, 45, 74, 180, 182, 279, 292; **14**, 35,
  36, 192; **15.V**, *153–8*; **16.I**, 263
psychiatry,
  10.III, 62, 63; **13**, 29, 30, 32, 33, 42,
  48, 49, 143, 151, 242, 275, 277, 279
psychoanalysis,
  8.I, 73, 205, 253, 440; **9**, 128, 239,
  240; **10.III**, 8, 141, 143, 144, 146;
  11.I, 20; **11.II**, 5, 6, 8, 233; **11.III**,
  112; **12.I**, 149, 151, 184; **12.II**, 168;
  12.IV, 4; **12.V**, 36, 66; **13**, xi, 1,
  8–10, 21, 30, 32–4, 82, 83, 91, 95–7,
  103, 140, 151–4, 177–85 passim,
  190, 195–216, 218, 219, 224, 230,
  242, 275, 286, 297, 305, 319; **14**, 35;
  16.I, 152; **17**, 252, 255
psychobiography,
  13, 91
psychohistory,
  13, 91
psychological experiment,
  15.V, *159–66*
psychology,
  1.I, 29, 30, 32; **6.I**, 5, 7; **6.II**, 181–91
  passim; **7.I**, 236, 237; **8.I**, 13, 19, 20,
  46, 205, 209, 280, 285, 372, 451; **9**,
  110, 132, 134, 136, 143, 146, 157,
  169, 174, 239, 240, 241; **10.I**, 48,
  80, 85, 90, 93, 150, 159, 256–8, 263,
  266, 339, 352, 353, 364, 368, 369,
  387; **10.II**, 89, 90, 93, 97, 143, 144,
  196, 201; **10.III**, 7, 8, 62, 63, 71,
  72, 82, 87, 102, 123, 125–7, 200;
  11.I, 18, 20, 52, 68, 91, 93, 98, 99,
  115, 116, 148–51, 159, 193, 202,
  272, 273, 278, 280–2, 284; **11.II**, 9,
  102, 128, 240, 243; **11.III**, 88, 89,
  92, 93, 95, 109, 111, 119, 137–9;
  12.I, 31, 36, 66, 68, 146–9, 153, 154,
  196, 210; **12.II**, 33, 71, 76, 94, 110,
  168–70, 172, 176; **12.III**, 81, 82,
  111, 120, 134; **12.V**, 18, 36, 39; **13**,
  18, 20, 21, 24, 30–3, 35–7, 39, 41–3,
  47, 49, 76, 83–6, 91, 92, 95, 97, 115,
  116, 134, 140, 143, 144, 151–60 passim, 163, 208, 217–19, 221, 228–30,
  232–4, 239–44, 247, 248, 255, 276,

277, 280, 319; **14**, ix, xv, 32, 33, 77, 218, 222; **15.V**, *167–72*; **17**, 259–80

psychology, analytical,
13, xi, 151, 154, 158

psychology, Christian,
13, xii, 248, 255

psychology, depth,
13, 97, 152

psychology, developmental,
13, xi, 86

psychology, existential,
13, xi, xii, *217–38*, 273–80 passim

psychology, humanistic,
13, xi, 49, 218, 243, 245

psychopathology,
13, 32, 39, 41, 42, 45, 273, 283, 285, 286, 290, 292

psychotherapy,
13, 151, 158, 218–20, 229, 239, 242, 273, 274, 276, 278, 280, 284, 291–3

public, the,
2.I, 191; **5.III**, 101; **7.III**, 163; **10.I**, 268; **10.III**, 116–18; **11.III**, 51; **12.I**, 149, 163, 166; **14**, xii, 188, 190, 201; **16.I**, 264, 267, 276

public opinion,
14, xiii

punctuation,
7.III, 239–43; **15.V**, *173–8*

purgatory,
1.I, 254; **5.II**, 10; **10.III**, 88

purity of heart,
1.II, 37, 43, 47, 116, 117, 213; **10.III**, 160; **11.III**, 126

Pyrrhonism,
5.I, 133Q

Q

qualitative difference. *See* difference, qualitative

Quickborn,
10.III, 46, 47

R

race,
15.V, *185–90*

racism,
14, xiii, 235, 236, 247

rationalism, rationality,
1.II, 191, 194, 211, 258, 286, 288, 300, 304; **2.II**, 7, 9, 16; **3**, 189, 190; **5.I**, 12, 27, 33, 61, 63, 83, 84, 88, 156, 180; **5.II**, 68, 69, 163; **6.II**, 39–50 passim; **7.II**, 63, 98, 99, 101, 105, 185, 186, 191, 214, 231, 267, 268, 276–8, 289, 303, 306; **9**, 2, 64, 65, 76, 77, 380, 381; **10.I**, xii, 323, 324, 358, 366; **10.II**, 11–13, 16, 112, 125, 144, 145, 146, 151, 176, 180, 184; **10.III**, 104, 105, 108, 176; **11.I**, 12, 26, 30, 39, 40, 76, 88–90, 109, 116, 126, 128, 132, 136, 148–52, 157–9, 170, 192, 202, 203, 250, 277, 281; **11.II**, 246; **11.III**, 11, 71, 75, 77, 90–2, 117, 120, 122, 129, 158, 160, 167, 173, 180, 188, 221, 225; **12.I**, 34, 94, 131; **12.II**, 22, 23, 28, 35, 79; **12.V**, 78, 82, 84, 90–5, 98; **13**, 101, 125, 224, 229, 263, 267, 269, 270; **14**, 37, 69, 83, 98, 130, 138, 139, 143, 147, 188, 193

realism,
12.III, 3, 6, 7, 66, 75

reality,
5.I, 17, 35, 41, 42; **6.III**, 147; **11.I**, 189

reappropriation,
10.I, 151

reason,
5.III, 96, 98, 99, 126, 273; **10.I**, 1, 90, 228, 241, 245–7, 250, 255, 268, 270, 342, 348, 386; **10.II**, 17, 20, 33, 51, 112, 124, 125, 131, 137, 152, 153, 162, 174, 175, 180, 182, 183, 185; **15.V**, *191–6*; **16.II**, 127, 135

rebellion,
9, 63, 65, 71, 72, 80, 84–9; **10.II**, 150; **11.I**, 196, 197; **13**, 92, 98, 132

recognition,
9, 343, 344; **11.I**, 6, 77, 110, 111, 281; **11.II**, 184; **12.V**, 78, 80; **13**, 116, 156, 159, 198; **14**, 18, 29, 143

recollection,
  2.I, *28–44*, 47, 54–61 passim, 65,
  66, 69–73, 79, 80, 96, 119, 120, 132,
  292; **2.II**, **4**, 172, 173, 177; **5.I**, 52,
  69, 70; **5.III**, 178; **6.II**, 32, 33; **7.II**,
  278; **8.I**, 78, 155; **8.II**, 5, 308; **10.II**,
  126; **11.II**, 9; **12.I**, 86, 182; **12.III**,
  19, 20, 42, 43, 95, 98, 150, 154;
  12.IV, 51, 73, 74, 148; **12.V**, 68;
  15.V, *197–204*; **16.I**, 260, 265, 266,
  270, 274; **17**, 6, 18, 54, 98, 99, 121,
  130, 283, 288–91, 293, 296, 297
reconciliation,
  1.I, xii, 19, 60; **2.I**, 43, 51, 55, 56,
  63, 64, 69; **4**, 154, 177, 194, 211;
  7.I, 66, 198–202, 205, 208, 218–27
  passim; **8.I**, 144, 442; **9**, 72, 149,
  236, 315, 317; **10.I**, 4, 6, 21, 24, 30,
  325, 336, 344, 345; **11.I**, 16, 61, 131,
  177, 252; **12.I**, 79, 87; **12.V**, 85; **13**,
  140, 309; **14**, 63, 101, 167; **16.I**, 21,
  52–7, 220, 222, 223, 227, 255; **16.II**,
  17, 29, 30, 61, 79, 261
redemption,
  1.I, 15, 27, 36, 70; **1.II**, 8, 214; **2.I**,
  43, 53, 64, 65, 78, 84, 111, 113, 187,
  188; **4**, 11, 63, 90, 123, 168, 211;
  7.III, 77; **8.I**, 338; **9**, 66, 85, 89, 278,
  282, 300, 305–18 passim; **10.I**, 4, 29,
  71, 76, 194, 207, 330, 389; **10.II**, 151,
  181; **10.III**, 57, 71, 92, 100, 162; **11.I**,
  119, 193, 200; **11.II**, 93; **11.III**, 5;
  12.I, 7, 8, 178; **12.IV**, 46, 162, 163,
  217, 219, 220; **12.V**, 39, 129; **13**, 20,
  23, 71, 72, 267, 271; **14**, 24, 114, 248;
  16.I, 167, 269
reduplication/redoubling,
  1.II, 27; **2.I**, 138, 140, 141; **2.II**,
  137; **4**, 13; **5.I**, 119, 131–3; **5.II**,
  219; **6.I**, 32, 33, 38, 80, 81, 85; **7.I**,
  191, 192, 194; **8.I**, 439; **10.I**, 28, 29;
  12.III, 5; **15.V**, *205–12*
reflection, reflectivity,
  6.I, 5, 107; **7.II**, 8, 27, 37, 42, 115,
  164, 235, 348; **7.III**, 20, 61, 112,
  160–3, 173, 174, 177, 178, 200,
  263–7, 279–82, 294; **8.I**, 154; **10.II**,
  16; **12.II**, 58, 79, 80, 82, 84, 85, 87,
  92–4; **12.III**, 115, 117; **12.IV**, 151,
  152, 215; **12.V**, 17; **16.I**, 150; **16.II**,
  20, 21, 23, 29; **17**, 164, 172, 183,
  187
reflective sorrow, 6, 101, 102
  16.II,
Reformation. *See also* Protestantism
  1.I, 232; **1.II**, 3, 214, 254, 256, 269,
  275, 276; **4**, 40, 191, 268, 272–4; **5.I**,
  x; **5.II**, 21, 33, 81, 82, 84, 113, 118,
  119, 154, 159, 174–83 passim, 195,
  199, 200, 203–6, 226, 237; **5.III**, 106;
  7.II, 173–6, 211, 214, 291, 315; **8.I**,
  246; **10.I**, 74, 91, 163, 189, 214, 229,
  266; **10.II**, 39, 51, 144; **10.III**, 108,
  136; **15.V**, *145–52*
refugee,
  14, 9, 19–21
Regensen College in Copenhagen,
  2.I, 229; **7.II**, 304; **7.III**, 248
reincarnation,
  11.III, 73–5
relativism,
  2.II, 189; **6.II**, 69; **6.III**, 55, 56, 70,
  86; **8.II**, 290; **10.I**, 342, 383; **10.II**,
  177, 178; **11.III**, 118, 183; **13**,
  234, 269
religion,
  6.III, 12, 37, 84, 98, 220, 221, 224,
  227, 249, 256, 303–8
religious/religiousness,
  15.V, *213–20*
religiousness A and B,
  1.I, 136; **2.I**, 42, 70; **2.II**, 64, 72;
  4, 81, 89; **5.I**, 103–5; **8.I**, 245, 345,
  370; **8.III**, 117, 183, 207, 216; **9**,
  165, 187; **10.I**, 88, 132, 168, 327,
  327, 354, 368; **10.II**, 10; **10.III**, 79,
  163, 179; **11.I**, 253; **11.III**, 51, 55,
  56, 61–7; **12.V**, 151; **13**, 62, 76, 166;
  14, 1, 141; **16.II**, 30, 31; **17**, 21,
  124–7, 130, 131, 137, 151
religious spheres of existence,
  10.II, 184
remembrance,
  12.III, 154, 168

reminiscence,
  13, 197–201, 209
Renaissance,
  5.II, 222
renunciation,
  1.II, 11, 12, 14, 36, 80, 81; **9**, 45, 53,
  72, 87, 171, 266, 280; **11.I**, 105, 107,
  219, 263, 280; **11.III**, 37; **13**, 71, 73,
  168, 211, 313
repentance,
  1.I, 71, 72, 106, 136, 169, 185, 186,
  187, 201, 220; **1.II**, 27, 47, 86, 88,
  89, 118, 127, 156, 159, 213; **4**, 50,
  63; **5.II**, 24, 27–9, 87, 150; **6.I**, 73,
  74, 87; **10.I**, 357; **10.II**, 49, 76, 198,
  202; **10.III**, 68; **13**, 121; **15.V**, *221–
  4*; **16.I**, 67, 68, 191, 192; **16.II**, 25–7,
  60, 124, 158; **17**, 273, 277, 278
repetition,
  1.I, 109, 122–7 passim, 137, 138;
  1.II, 26–8, 130; **2.I**, 56, 58, 59, 61,
  71, 116, 141; **2.II**, 44, 136, 138, 141,
  154; **3**, 98; **5.I**, 52, 69, 70, 71, 175,
  185; **5.III**, 72, 106, 176, 182; **6.II**,
  180; **6.III**, 75–8, 101; **7.I**, 63, 67–9;
  7.II, 111, 156; **7.III**, 72, 80; **8.I**, 69,
  97, 148, 183, 212, 246, 358, 382,
  451, 452, 453; **8.II**, 2, 27, 38, 51,
  227, 291, 304, 308, 324, 325; **8.III**,
  70, 111, 219, 286, 322; **9**, 83, 96,
  101, 270, 271, 366, 399, 405, 407;
  10.I, xii; **10.II**, 126, 127; **10.III**, 79,
  83, 196, 197, 200, 202; **11.I**, 37, 130,
  167, 169, 176; **11.II**, 13, 14, 47, 71,
  85, 86, 87, 88, 98, 100, 101, 114,
  116, 245, 251, 252; **11.III**, 21, 22,
  39–41, 44, 152, 207, 215; **12.I**, 26,
  82–5, 105, 130, 179, 182; **12.II**, 49;
  12.III, 41–4, 82, 83, 91, 94–9, 105,
  190; **12.IV**, 51, 59, 69–74, 75, 93,
  110, 118, 124–6, 148, 149, 153, 154,
  179, 185; **12.V**, 6, 7, 9, 85, 179; **13**,
  xi, 6, 38, 45–8, 69, 196–204, 208–
  13, 301–3, 317; **14**, 23, 191, 198;
  15.V, *225–30*; **16.I**, 113, 116–18,
  241, 266; **16.II**, 26, 82; **17**, 53–5, 58,
  99, 234, 286, 292, 293, 305–8

repression,
  13, 22, 103, 154, 284, 286
resignation,
  1.I, 53, 66–9, 117, 213, 214, 246; **9**,
  71, 81, 86, 264, 266, 274, 360, 368;
  11.I, 115, 155, 269, 274, 284, 285,
  295, 297; **11.III**, 37, 149, 209, 210,
  214; **12.I**, 73, 239; **12.II**, 155; **13**,
  253, 314; **14**, 66, 223; **15.V**, *231–8*;
  16.I, 9, 113, 117; **17**, 78, 126, 130,
  133, 151, 186, 255
resignation, knight of,
  17, 150, 151
resoluteness,
  9, 113; **11.I**, 31; **12.I**, 96
responsibility,
  9, 11–14, 44, 45, 83, 171, 245, 263,
  264, 266, 267, 284–7, 317, 323, 325,
  341, 405; **10.I**, 80, 363; **10.II**, 122;
  11.I, 80, 109, 119, 155, 228, 299;
  11.II, 112, 114, 117–22, 130–2, 170,
  191, 215; **11.III**, 101, 102, 113; **12.I**,
  3, 6, 10, 11, 76, 81, 144, 159; **12.V**,
  111, 112, 135; **13**, 109, 129, 153,
  154, 179, 225–7, 248, 259–61, 268,
  270, 271, 277; **14**, 76, 77, 116, 194,
  201, 239, 241, 244, 245; **17**, 21, 82,
  91, 95, 102, 109, 110, 113, 123, 124,
  129, 136, 137, 144, 246, 264, 266,
  271, 272, 275–8, 281
Restoration,
  6.II, 2
Resurrection,
  1.I, 67, 221, 238; **1.II**, 22, 80, 85, 87,
  169–85, 257, 291, 308, 322; **2.I**, 48,
  50; **4**, 6, 54, 57, 104, 107, 117, 132;
  6.I, 51; **7.II**, 111, 197; **10.I**, 135, 189,
  190, 199, 200, 201, 243, 244, 247,
  248, 284, 344; **10.II**, 86; **11.II**, 250,
  251; **12.I**, 24; **12.III**, 171; **13**, 63,
  260, 261
*Den Rette uforandrede augsburgske
  Troesbekjendelse*,
  20, M 386
revelation,
  1.I, 21, 126, 136, 169, 176, 177, 224,
  241; **1.II**, 205, 259, 260, 286, 288,

290, 300, 312, 314, 315, 320, 323;
2.I, 39, 80–3 passim, 145, 275; **2.II**,
7, 8; **4**, 111, 153, 157, 189, 197, 199,
242, 243; **5.I**, 13, 39, 55, 56, 168,
181; **6.I**, 353, 366; **6.II**, 42, 43, 49,
108, 125, 129, 131–8 passim, 175;
6.III, 75, 145, 250; **7.I**, 298, 310;
7.III, 1, 5, 10–19 passim, 26, 42, 44,
45, 59, 60, 83, 99, 163–8, 235, 256,
269, 278, 329; **8.I**, 6, 37, 39, 78, 155,
240, 249, 336, 340, 374; **8.II**, 215;
8.III, 202, 245, 255; **9**, 129, 149,
179, 182, 183, 189, 273, 300, 305,
307, 308, 310–12, 316, 362; **10.I**,
1, 2, 6, 22–4, 27, 29, 30, 32, 33, 43,
44, 47, 48, 50, 59, 67, 70, 72, 74, 75,
80, 84, 85, 88, 90, 94, 127, 128, 131,
132, 135, 136, 171, 192, 199, 242–50
passim, 252, 266, 325, 327–9, 342,
347, 348, 358, 365, 366; **10.II**, 86,
88, 97, 125, 134, 136, 152, 161, 175,
178, 180, 183, 185; **10.III**, 14, 15,
19, 57, 69, 71, 79, 149, 162; **11.I**, 28,
30, 98, 297; **11.II**, 52, 53, 58, 118,
141, 145, 184, 208, 214, 216, 218,
227, 229; **11.III**, 5, 6, 129, 160, 210;
12.I, 24–7, 94, 107; **12.III**, 8; **13**,
247, 305–7, 314; **14**, 80, 83, 97, 129,
130, 210, 220, 224; **15.V**, *239–44*;
16.II, 33, 230; **17**, 18, 122, 215–20

revocation,
    12.I, 22, 205
revolt. *See* rebellion
revolution,
    15.V, *245–54*
Revolution of 1848,
    10.III, 120; **12.I**, 61, 64, 67; **14**, xi,
    24, 193–5
Der Rheingraf,
    20, A II 263
rhetoric,
    7.III, 242; **8.I**, 89, 381; **10.I**, 21; **14**,
    53, 56–60, 68, 69, 92, 94, 104; **15.V**,
    255–62
rigorism,
    15.V, *263–8*

Der Ritter von Santjago,
    20, A II 255
Romantic/Romanticism,
    1.I, xii, 236, 237; **1.II**, 57, 193; **2.I**,
    126, 217, 220, 251, 263, 284, 298,
    308; **2.II**, 62, 73; **4**, 265, 301, 305,
    308, 312–19 passim; **5.I**, 33, 147,
    154–6; **5.II**, 50, 51; **5.III**, 1, 5, 6,
    9, 15–25 passim, 32, 35, 36, 52,
    53, 56, 84, 94, 98, 102, 107, 110,
    112, 137–41 passim, 145, 147, 157,
    175–80, 185–213 passim, 247, 267,
    273; **6.III**, 8, 19, 22, 25–49 passim,
    77, 118, 121, 123, 125, 128, 131,
    145, 156, 157, 162, 240, 252, 253,
    264, 271, 275–82 passim, 298, 302;
    7.I, 115, 129, 134, 224, 261–84, 278;
    7.II, 28, 96, 304; **7.III**, 36, 37, 39,
    52, 55, 60, 70, 71, 105, 110, 119,
    120, 169, 173, 176, 195, 209–12,
    216, 218–22, 238, 241, 247, 257,
    258, 263, 264, 287, 290; **8.I**, 67, 68,
    210, 278, 370, 430; **8.II**, 156, 286,
    290; **8.III**, 6, 112, 237, 254; **9**, 396,
    397, 399; **10.I**, 367, 382, 387; **10.II**,
    144; **10.III**, 9, 55, 61, 62, 70, 71,
    108; **11.I**, 127, 198, 284; **11.III**, 23,
    32, 44, 139, 143, 144, 151; **12.I**, 153;
    12.II, 22, 60, 105, 108; **12.III**, 21, 29,
    35, 118, 119, 147, 150; **12.V**, 80, 81,
    93; **13**, 184, 267; **14**, 35, 124, 151,
    184, 193–7; **15.V**, *269–72*; **16.I**, 15,
    17, 66, 100, 131–2, 138, 145, 151,
    160–4, 181, 190; **16.II**, 14, 65–7, 69,
    72, 75, 79, 176; **17**, 162, 307
Romanticism, Danish,
    16.I, 17, 32, 229
Romanticism, German,
    6.III, 28, 99, 115, 185, 188, 191,
    192, 198, 209, 212, 213, 216, 236,
    243; **7.I**, 140; **8.III**, 15; **10.I**, 173,
    342, 346; **10.III**, 19; **12.IV**, 195;
    12.V, 93; **16.I**, 123, 128, 160, 187;
    17, xi
Romantic literature,
    10.II, 212, 213

Royal Ballet School,
  7.III, 275
Royal Danish Academy of Sciences
  and Letters,
  7.I, 216
Royal Danish Ballet,
  7.III, 69, 70, 71
Royal Danish Library,
  7.III, 233, 236; **8.I**, 9, 27
Royal Military College,
  7.I, 38, 41, 47; **7.III**, 87
Royal Theater in Copenhagen,
  5.III, 65, 68, 77, 84, 121, 122,
  129–31, 141–5, 150, 163, 173–5,
  236–9, 250, 253, 259; **6.III**, 53,
  173, 174; **7.I**, ix, xii, 37–9; **7.III**, 9,
  10, 12, 40, 68, 71, 76, 87, 153, 173,
  189–94, 211, 235, 258, 276, 277;
  8.I, 147; **12.I**, x; **16.I**, 18, 32, 72, 89,
  106, 145, 244; **17**, 107

S

sacraments,
  10.I, 149
sacrifice,
  1.II, 5, 30, 83, 118, 151, 153–5,
  160–4, 192, 202, 300; **9**, 9, 14, 49,
  279, 338, 359, 368, 399; **11.I**, 12,
  16, 17, 23, 30, 40, 118, 297; **11.II**, 4,
  15, 16, 18, 26, 27, 36, 38, 47, 48, 54,
  72, 73, 78, 98, 99, 100, 116–21, 126,
  132, 168, 186, 187, 213, 216; **12.I**,
  24, 27, 124, 127, 184; **12.III**, 39, 60,
  159; **12.V**, 133; **13**, 56, 73, 76, 107,
  111, 131, 139–41, 146–8, 157, 170,
  187, 210, 213, 263, 269, 270, 287,
  299, 302, 305–14 passim, 317; **14**,
  63, 66, 112, 113, 118, 119, 129, 130;
  15.V, *273–80*
*Salomo der Weise und sein Narr
  Markolph*,
  20, A II 227
salvation. *See also* happiness, eternal
  1.I, 9, 10, 27, 46, 66, 80, 92, 153,
  173, 192, 232, 253, 260; **1.II**, 4,
  37, 49, 76, 81, 126, 158, 178, 181,

203, 204, 214, 269, 303; **4**, 14, 29,
  50, 62, 80, 82, 83, 90, 91, 123, 150,
  151, 176; **5.II**, 12, 22, 27, 82, 85,
  88, 93, 96, 105, 106, 115, 152, 179,
  181, 190, 197, 198, 201, 237, 239;
  7.II, 120, 121, 124; **7.III**, 77; **8.I**,
  90, 177, 345; **9**, 46, 48, 49, 65, 89,
  147–51, 317, 363; **10.I**, 16, 19, 22,
  25, 28, 33, 34, 127, 127, 200, 244,
  265, 328, 336, 349; **10.II**, 77, 183,
  208, 216; **10.III**, 19, 37, 71, 100,
  146, 168; **11.I**, 79, 80, 200, 203;
  11.II, 48, 52, 58, 67, 73, 100, 184,
  186, 192, 216, 224, 227; **11.III**, 6,
  143; **12.III**, 34, 171; **13**, 71, 98,
  265–8; **14**, 25, 34, 37, 139, 154,
  210, 225, 268; **15.VI**, *1–8*; **16.I**,
  239; **17**, 125
Sange for det smukke Kjøn,
  20, U 93
satire. *See also* parody
  15.V, *49–54*; **16.II**, 1, 3, 7, 9, 49
Saxo Grammaticus,
  20, M 2008–2010
scandal. *See* offense
Scandinavian Society,
  8.I, 154
scapegoat,
  13, 139–41, 146, 171; **14**, xii, xiii
Die Schildgenossen,
  10.III, 46–8, 50, 63
schizophrenia,
  13, 23, 31, 36, 42, 43, 47
Schleswig Wars (1848–51,1864),
  7.I, xi, 80, 86–90, 171, 247, 248;
  7.II, 109, 155; **7.III**, 88, 115, 193;
  12.I, 62, 65, 67
Scholasticism,
  4, 27, 135–47, 151, 161, 167, 168,
  191, 199, 219, 274, 275, 290, 316,
  318, 319; **5.II**, 4, 117, 119, 150, 155,
  178; **10.III**, 25; **12.V**, 38, 41
School of Civic Virtue in Copenhagen.
  See Borgerdydskolen in Copenhagen
Schwärmerei,
  16.I, 216

science. *See also* speculation
  10.III, 62, 70, 71, 75, 76, 85, 115,
  116, 190, 191, 194–7, 199, 201, 208;
  12.IV, 14, 96, 176, 179, 180, 182,
  185–8; **15.VI**, *65–74*
Scripture. *See* Bible
Second Adam,
  1.I, 4, 7, 9, 14–16, 28, 33, 37, 39
secret,
  11.II, 7, 9–19 passim, 67, 70, 115,
  117–20, 122, 123, 128, 130–2, 182,
  192; **13**, 2, 4, 9, 12, 13, 64, 68, 145
secret note, the,
  8.I, 47, 77
secularism, secularization. *See also*
  worldliness
  10.I, xii, xiii, 115, 116, 119, 228,
  229, 387; **10.II**, 25, 27, 28, 31, 32,
  39, 42; **11.I**, 117, 158, 166; **12.I**,
  37; **14**, 34, 38, 80, 81, 112, 118;
  15.VI, *267–70*; **16.I**, 162–5, 261,
  268, 284
seducer,
  5.III, 7, 9; **12.I**, 74, 75, 82
seduction,
  2.I, 128; **5.III**, 5, 56; **7.III**, 83; **8.I**,
  80; **9**, 5, 6, 12, 76, 84; **11.I**, 179;
  12.II, 55; **12.III**, 46; **12.IV**, 59,
  149, 153; **12.V**, 178; **13**, xii, 1–5,
  9–13, 58, 60–2; **15.VI**, *17–22*; **16.I**,
  46, 84, 86, 173, 210, 224–7, 238;
  16.II, 95–109, 116, 124–30 passim,
  175, 176, 211, 212, 257–67; **17**,
  2, 3, 5, 21, 22, 32, 77, 147, 162,
  164–72
self,
  11.II, 9, 25, 35, 114, 115, 123, 125–7,
  130, 132, 133, 148, 216, 234; **15.VI**,
  23–8
self-consciousness,
  1.I, ix, x, 11, 122, 146; **8.I**, 348
self-deception,
  1.II, 116, 118; **10.II**, 120; **11.III**,
  101, 103, 105, 106, 109, 111–13;
  12.III, 137; **12.V**, 153; **13**, 23, 101,
  154, 158; **15.VI**, *29–34*

self-examination,
  1.I, 111, 147, 148, 151, 154, 177,
  214, 217, 223, 226; **12.II**, 147, 161
selfhood,
  1.I, 24, 37, 38, 122; **10.I**, xii;
  10.II, 110; **11.II**, 209, 216, 218,
  228; **12.IV**, 82, 122
selfishness,
  13, 106–11, 252, 289
semiology,
  13, 1, 3, 7, 179, 181–3, 190
semiotics,
  11.I, xi; **12.IV**, 193
sensuality/sensuousness,
  16.I, *141–53*, 182, 191, 192, 210,
  214–18, 223–7; **16.II**, 81, 102, 103,
  125, 165, 242
sentimentality,
  7.I, 131, 143
seriousness,
  9, 12–14, 105, 285, 340, 341, 342,
  399; **10.I**, 60; **11.I**, 25, 189, 214,
  263, 274; **12.I**, 22, 27, 39, 205; **12.V**,
  28; **14**, 69, 82, 184
Sermon on the Mount,
  1.II, 33–50
Seven Years' War (1756–63),
  5.II, 249
sexes,
  11.II, 2
shame,
  12.I, 184, 213
The Shepherd of Hermas,
  1.I, 8
sickness,
  1.I, 127; **1.II**, 19, 27, 28, 146, 147,
  175; **8.III**, 65; **11.III**, 35, 55, 88;
  12.II, 155; **12.III**, 46; **12.IV**, 81, 91,
  218; **12.V**, 162; **15.VI**, *35–40*; **17**, 43
sickness unto death,
  9, 90, 114, 210; **10.I**, 94, 206, 304,
  357, 364; **11.I**, 113, 118, 171; **11.II**,
  127, 128; **12.I**, 15–18, 72, 74, 178;
  12.III, 47; **12.V**, 19; **13**, 31, 36, 43,
  92, 230, 254; **14**, 4, 187, 265; **17**,
  42, 48

sign,
2.II, 92; **10.III**, 14, 21, 35; **11.II**,
5–7, 28, 30, 31, 39, 88, 92, 113, 128,
129, 131; **11.III**, 38, 42; **13**, 3, 11,
12, 181–3, 200

signified and signifier,
11.II, 113

sign of contradiction,
1.II, 7, 24, 159, 162, 180

silence,
1.I, 163, 188–90, 200, 215, 248;
1.II, 60; **2.II**, 66; **7.II**, 158, 202, 273;
8.III, 56; **10.I**, 47; **10.II**, 163, 165;
11.I, 227, 229, 234; **11.II**, 26, 33, 35,
36, 38, 118–20; **11.III**, 39; **12.II**, 6,
8, 10–12; **12.III**, 101–3, 105, 179;
12.V, 130, 135, 180; **15.VI**, *41–4*;
16.I, 22, 43, 45, 46; **16.II**, 23, 58, 61,
63, 76, 82; **17**, 68, 71, 72, 267, 291

simplicity,
10.I, 60

simultaneity,
8.I, 159, 160; **10.I**, 167, 171, 172,
265

sin,
1.I, 4–18 passim, 21, 22, 25–40
passim, 70, 71, 116, 121, 123, 126,
135–7, 151–3, 160, 163, 167, 172,
185, 201, 219, 223, 226, 241; **1.II**,
4, 6, 27, 28, 36, 37, 43, 45, 47, 67,
69, 73, 75, 81, 99–101, 108, 115,
116, 123, 130–2, 135, 144, 146, 151,
152–8, 175, 177, 195, 196, 249; **2.I**,
39, 40, 43, 48, 50, 64, 69–72, 73,
77–84 passim, 136, 142, 145, 303;
2.II, 44, 51, 53, 70–4, 78, 140, 215,
216, 319; **3**, 17, 62, 65, 84, 139, 174,
178; **4**, 3, 12, 15, 28–31, 38, 50, 62,
63, 73–6, 84, 89, 90, 104, 107, 108,
123–7, 148, 170, 171, 176, 197,
223–36; **5.I**, 5, 7, 27, 58, 59, 65, 95,
99, 150, 159, 180; **5.II**, 15, 17, 26,
28, 43, 49, 53–7, 66, 91–3, 98–100,
104, 106, 162, 167, 180, 181, 183,
189; **5.III**, 191, 218, 220, 221, 223;
6.I, 3–12 passim, 133, 135, 185,

189, 191, 193, 194, 225, 226, 259,
293, 294, 298, 300–5; **6.II**, 6–9, 13,
32, 33, 35, 42, 44, 45, 48, 50, 69,
106–10, 143, 145–57 passim, 174,
183–6, 190, 191, 202, 210, 214–16,
219, 245, 247, 252; **6.III**, 221, 224,
227, 262, 310; **7.I**, 272, 282; **7.II**,
3, 5, 10, 27, 69, 257, 278, 280, 281;
8.I, 22, 23, 35–7, 62, 66, 183, 246,
257, 338, 345, 375, 427, 440, 443,
450, 451; **8.II**, 21, 217, 227, 263,
291, 294, 308, 324, 325; **8.III**, 15,
16, 58, 60, 65, 69, 74, 256, 322; **9**,
9, 25, 29, 73, 84, 102, 107, 108, 111,
112, 114, 133, 147–51; **10.I**, x, 6, 22,
25, 26, 29, 30, 32, 47, 48, 69, 70, 85,
89, 91, 94, 135, 205, 214, 248, 252,
253, 256–61, 266, 267, 269, 270,
304, 326, 336, 348, 357, 364; **10.II**,
10, 36, 39, 50, 51, 53, 73, 76, 77, 88,
90–3, 97, 98, 121, 122, 129, 131,
137, 143, 144, 148, 149, 150, 153,
166, 183, 185; **10.III**, 8, 9, 64, 85,
101, 125–7, 161, 196, 208; **11.I**, 54,
154, 155, 171, 198, 199, 272, 275,
281, 282; **11.II**, 48, 50, 54–8, 92,
123, 182, 184, 216, 218, 224, 229,
230, 241–3, 248–51; **11.III**, 5, 7, 8,
128, 148, 188, 192, 205, 225; **12.I**,
26, 50, 53, 76, 148, 178, 183; **12.II**,
26, 85, 153; **12.III**, 4, 34, 181, 185;
12.IV, 15, 33, 56, 83, 151; **12.V**, 13,
15, 28, 39, 85, 93, 96, 113, 134, 135,
160, 165, 171, 193; **13**, 47, 71, 98,
111, 196, 205, 208–10, 251–5, 304,
315, 318, 319; **14**, 63, 100, 114–16,
118, 119, 165, 223, 243, 244, 246;
15.VI, *45–52*; **16.I**, 22, 271, 272;
16.II, 52, 59, 60, 63, 91, 200, 219,
220, 227–31; **17**, 17, 40–2, 44, 45,
48, 121, 259, 262, 263, 267, 271,
272, 274–8

sin, original,
2.I, 37; **4**, 11, 12, 15, 123, 125–8,
133, 170, 193, 197; **9**, 146–8, 149,
150, 151, 228, 272, 273, 279, 281–3,

300, 305, 315, 317, 318, 334, 336,
340, 357, 361–8 passim, 378, 400,
405, 407; **10.I**, 86, 265; **10.II**, 122,
150, 151; **11.I**, 281; **11.II**, 3, 10,
11, 93, 132; **12.I**, 147; **12.II**, 170;
12.III, 183; **13**, 205, 208, 316; **14**,
100, 264, 267; **16.I**, 239, 269; **16.II**,
29; **17**, 41, 42, 264, 265, 269, 270,
275, 276
sincerity,
    12.I, 108, 209
sin-consciousness,
    2.I, 71, 72, 290, 306, 307
single individual, the,
    1.II, 120, 129, 130, 252, 265, 318; **2.I**,
    128, 130; **2.II**, 259; **3**, 131, 178; **4**, 14;
    5.III, 101–5, 193; **7.II**, 176, 318, 329;
    8.I, 178–81, 208, 272, 322, 323, 326,
    350, 440, 456; **8.III**, 56, 57, 65, 68,
    120, 130, 131, 133, 138, 142; **9**, 39,
    42–4, 48–53, 64, 147, 210, 225, 323,
    338, 377, 396, 403, 407; **10.I**, xii, 9,
    30, 55; **10.II**, 8, 10, 12, 17, 27, 29, 32,
    36, 37, 39, 40, 114; **10.III**, 7, 15, 70,
    71; **11.I**, 28–30, 39, 40, 73, 81, 118,
    155, 169, 172, 173, 178, 180, 254,
    272, 295, 298, 300; **11.II**, 16, 75, 119,
    121, 144, 170, 216; **11.III**, 39; **12.I**,
    143–7, 150, 151, 210; **12.II**, 5, 89,
    91, 93, 94, 150; **12.III**, 34, 45, 56, 58,
    131, 158, 169; **12.IV**, 121; **12.V**, 40,
    109, 126, 146, 153, 191–6; **13**, 114,
    146, 147, 182, 219; **14**, x, 24, 32, 33,
    48, 97, 140, 164, 195, 196, 198, 264;
    16.I, 5, 22, 43, 214, 264, 266, 275;
    16.II, 239; **17**, 45, 144, 264
Sittlichkeit. See ethical life
skepticism. *See also* doubt
    2.II, 113, 114, 138, *165–82*; **5.I**, 2,
    11, 13, 14, 17, 23, 24, 28, 29, 35,
    115; **6.III**, 73; **7.I**, 120; **9**, 66, 226,
    253, 380, 396; **10.II**, 12; **11.I**, 109;
    11.III, 11; **12.I**, 50; **12.V**, 84; **13**,
    314; **14**, 34, 81; **15.VI**, *53–8*
skepticism, Greek,
    5.I, 15, 62, 63

Skeptics, the,
    2.I, x
*En Skiøn Historie om de Syv viise
    Mestere*, **M** 1470
Smalcald Articles,
    6.I, 5, 225; **17**, 270
socialism,
    14, 140, 142, 196
socialism, Christian,
    10.I, 2, 7
socialism, religious,
    10.I, 156
social philosophy,
    6.I, 17–24
Sociedad Iberoamericana de Estudios
    Kierkegaardianos (SIEK),
    8.III, 278–80, 287
society,
    15.VI, *59–64*
Society for the Promotion of the
    Natural Sciences in Copenhagen,
    7.I, 216
Society of Jesus,
    10.III, 4, 98, 133
sociology,
    10.III, 102; **11.III**, 119, 203; **13**, 2,
    3, 8, 76, 84, 95, 121, 264, 297
Socratic method. *See* Socrates, method
sola gratia,
    5.II, 197, 199, 202
solidarity,
    9, 63, 71, 87, 88; **14**, xiii, 82, 83, 119
solipsism,
    1.II, 76; **9**, 4, 170, 343; **12.V**, 9
solitude,
    8.III, 10, 52, 62, 85, 115, 129; **9**,
    47, 48, 82, 91; **11.I**, 56, 77, 78, 216;
    11.II, 63, 64, 66–8, 70, 71, 78, 79,
    118, 170; **12.I**, 7, 10, 11, 54, 121,
    130; **12.IV**, 130, 146; **12.V**, 93, 94,
    184, 195; **13**, 58, 66; **17**, 254, 255
Sophists, the,
    1.II, 94; **2.I**, 8, 10–15 passim, 20, 49,
    51, 52, 167, 169, 174, 188, 194, 207,
    229, 232, 236, 250, 253, 257, 280,
    302, 303, 306; **2.II**, 112, 128, 165,

172, 183–94, 307, 314; **3**, 42; **6.I**,
105, 110–14, 117, 283; **6.III**, 69, 76;
7.I, 82; **16.I**, 264, 267, 269, 270, 276
Søren Kierkegaard Library at the
University of Copenhagen,
8.II, 41, 45; **8.III**, 141
Søren Kierkegaard Research Centre at
the University of Copenhagen,
8.II, 48, 96, 97, 173, 174, 218; **8.III**,
98, 106, 238
*Søren Kierkegaard Selskabets
Populære Skrifter*,
8.I, 70, 71
Søren Kierkegaard Society/*Søren
Kierkegaard Selskab* (Denmark),
8.I, 54–6, 58
sorites,
2.II, 22, 23, 173, 201
Sorø Academy,
5.III, 82; **7.III**, 20, 209, 210, 215
sorrow,
16.I, 6, 51, 52, 59, 72–6, 103, 107,
108, 148, 176–9, 253; **16.II**, 7,
59–61, 63, 90, 101, 102, 219, 240,
242, 254; **17**, 7
soteriology,
1.II, 62, 75, 76; **4**, 5, 11, 50, 54, 57,
61–3, 177; **8.III**, 88, 246; **10.I**, 25,
30, 264; **10.II**, 97, 166, 167; **10.III**,
46; **12.V**, 19; **13**, 58, 71–4,
303, 317
soul,
2.I, 18, 21, 27, 30, 32, 38, 46–50, 54,
63, 65, 68, 75, 98, 106, 119–22, 131,
222; **2.II**, 273, 279, 293
Spanish Civil War,
12.IV, 2, 3
The Spectator,
20, A II 269–276
speculation. *See also* science
2.I, 28–30, 33–8, 41, 44, 46–8, 51,
60, 69–72, 79, 83–6, 104, 127, 203,
207, 209; **2.II**, 254, 259, 261, 291,
292, 295, 305–7; **5.II**, 43, 45; **5.III**,
22, 205; **8.I**, 39; **10.II**, 15; **11.II**,
122, 126, 174, 183, 226, 237, 238,

247; **15.VI**, *65–74*; **16.I**, 134, 137,
138, 269; **17**, 29, 33, 39, 54, 95,
118–20, 122, 123, 129, 134, 137,
179, 181, 188, 262, 264, 267, 276,
277
speculative dogmatics,
5.II, 53
speculative idea,
7.I, 238
speculative idealism,
4, 172, 175; **10.I**, 81; **11.I**, 131, 132,
139; **11.II**, 122, 244
speculative logic,
2.II, 4, 11, 14, 123, 132, 137; **7.I**, 59,
69, 181, 188, 291, 292; **7.II**, 341
speculative method,
2.II, 4, 137
speculative philosophy,
2.II, 3, 5, 13, 14, 141, 190; **4**, 137,
151; **5.I**, 28, 43, 182; **5.II**, 52,
54, 56; **6.I**, 2, 3, 312, 336, 362–5,
369–71; **7.I**, 1–10, 53, 59, 185, 232,
239, 253, 255, 264; **7.II**, 8, 63, 75,
339; **8.III**, 117–20; **9**, 201, 202, 273,
362, 364, 365, 399, 406, 407; **10.I**,
166, 388; **10.II**, 15, 95; **11.I**, ix, 35,
87, 129, 176, 259, 262, 263; **11.II**,
145, 182, 243, 244, 250; **12.I**, 34,
54; **12.V**, 109; **14**, 79, 98
speculative poet,
6.III, 70
speculative poetry,
4, 225–7
speculative system,
7.I, 147
speculative theology,
6.I, 2, 3, 26, 52; **6.II**, 57, 58, 64, 65,
127, 134, 136, 143, 147, 164; **7.I**, 59,
234, 290, 294, 297, 298, 300, 307;
7.II, 2, 3, 5, 7, 10, 50, 51, 56, 57, 62,
71, 89, 92, 187; **11.II**, 128
spidsborger. *See* bourgeois
Spießbürgertum. *See* bourgeois
spirit,
6.III, 61, 74, 78, 210, 243; **7.II**, 3,
5, 10; **9**, 142–4, 244, 250, 305, 306,

309, 310, 365, 400; **10.I**, 22, 49, 70,
87, 149, 192, 196, 206, 215, 216,
238, 260, 261, 263, 328, 344, 345,
350, 370, 383; **10.II**, 10; **10.III**, 59,
60, 67, 71, 82, 105; **11.I**, 12–17, 21,
27, 36, 72, 94, 114, 130, 152, 157,
194, 251, 252, 258, 263, 281, 282;
12.I, 37, 63, 70, 99, 100, 126, 150–3,
174, 178; **12.V**, 53, 95, 99; **13**, 7,
23, 32, 34, 37–9, 41, 60, 76, 88, 128,
197, 222, 228, 229, 269, 287, 292,
318; **14**, 4, 59, 102, 196, 198, 216,
217, 219, 244; **15.VI**, *75–82*
spiritlessness,
  15.VI, *83–8*; **17**, 273, 277
spiritualism,
  5.II, 23, 46
spiritual trial,
  1.II, 26; **5.III**, 23; **16.I**, 7, 10, 45, 46,
  75, 165
spurious infinity. *See* bad infinity
stagecoach horn,
  17, 52
stages,
  5.III, 59; **6.III**, 46, 78, 122, 124,
  151; **7.II**, 177, 178; **7.III**, 218, 222;
  8.I, 15, 19, 20, 80, 201, 210, 249,
  285, 287, 336, 371, 425, 430, 433;
  8.II, 2, 6, 38, 50, 157, 217, 220, 223,
  287, 289, 296, 303, 304; **8.III**, 61,
  70, 89, 106, 112, 136, 141, 237–41,
  257; **9**, 47, 56, 165, 186, 187, 399,
  404; **10.I**, 86, 171, 322, 365, 369;
  10.II, 27, 92, 97, 110, 198–200, 211;
  10.III, 7, 14, 61, 70; **11.I**, 190, 258,
  278; **11.II**, 32, 103, 162; **11.III**, 17,
  43, 51, 110, 141, 146, 147, 149, 167;
  12.I, 1, 2, 71, 85, 105, 177, 187;
  12.II, 32, 59, 61, 71, 115, 132, 170,
  175; **12.III**, 5, 6, 21, 29, 32, 33, 34,
  36, 40–2, 44, 46, 83, 158, 159, 166,
  167; **12.IV**, 11, 13, 14–19, 30, 37,
  126, 179, 186, 187, 225; **12.V**, 40,
  70, 151; **13**, xi, 67, 81, 82, 85–92,
  128, 129, 302, 315–18; **14**, 46, 111,
  124, 267; **15.VI**, *89–96*; **16.I**, 36–8,

43, 47, 103, 127, 153, 166, 190, 191,
238, 239; **16.II**, 95, 174–6, 240;
17, 1–3, 9–11, 15, 19, 22, 69, 72–5,
107, 114, 126, 127, 131, 136, 146,
147, 159, 166, 172, 180, 181, 185,
187–91, 226, 244, 250, 251, 254,
259, 265
stages, aesthetic,
  10.I, 365; **10.III**, 7, 11; **11.II**, 103,
  152, 162, 185; **11.III**, 148, 165, 223;
  12.II, 59, 61, 71, 132, 170, 175;
  12.III, 21, 145, 153, 157, 159, 166,
  167; **12.IV**, 14, 16–19, 30, 37, 126,
  179, 186, 187, 225; **12.V**, 70, 151;
  16.I, 36, 37, 47, 103, 143, 153, 166,
  191, 238, 239; **16.II**, 95, 174, 176,
  240; **17**, 1, 107, 114, 131, 159, 166,
  180, 181, 187, 189, 191, 226, 244,
  250, 251, 254
stages, ethical,
  10.II, 198; **10.III**, 13; **11.II**, 103,
  122, 162, 185; **11.III**, 110, 138, 148,
  149, 165, 223; **12.II**, 59, 61, 71, 115,
  132, 170, 175; **12.III**, 21, 153, 157,
  159, 166, 167; **12.IV**, 14–19, 30, 37,
  126, 186, 225; **12.V**, 70, 151; **16.I**,
  36, 38, 43, 127, 153, 166, 238; **17**,
  2, 3, 9–11, 15, 17, 19–22, 131, 180,
  181, 187, 226, 244, 250, 254, 265
stages, religious,
  10.III, 11, 13; **11.II**, 103, 122, 162,
  185; **11.III**, 110, 138, 148, 149, 165;
  12.II, 71, 115, 132, 175; **12.III**, 166,
  167; **12.IV**, 14, 17–19, 30, 37, 126,
  186, 225; **12.V**, 70, 151; **16.I**, 127,
  166, 190; **17**, 22, 69, 72–5, 107, 131,
  147, 185, 188, 190, 244, 250, 251,
  254, 265
Stalinism,
  12.V, 50, 161, 171
state,
  15.VI, *97–100*
Statsvennen,
  7.I, 94, 114
Die Stimme im Rosenthal,
  20, A II 256–257

Stimmen der Zeit,
   10.III, 134
Stoicism/Stoics,
   2.I, x; **2.II**, 119, 152, 166, 195–208;
   3, 12, 18, 25–32 passim, 44, 62,
   69–73, 111–19 passim, 166, 173; **6.I**,
   20, 21, 23, 255, 287; **6.II**, 24, 207;
   10.III, 7; **11.II**, 167; **12.V**, 70
story-telling,
   15.VI, *101–8*
Strandveien,
   5.III, 41
striving,
   15.VI, *109–14*
strong Jutlanders,
   7.II, 28, 30
structuralism,
   11.I, xi; **11.II**, 31; **12.V**, 143
Student Association,
   7.I, 26, 92, 97, 98, 103, 121, 147;
   7.III, 10, 20
stumbling block,
   1.II, 6, 80, 162
Stunden der Andacht,
   20, A I 45–52
Sturm und Drang,
   16.I, 105, 123; **16.II**, 14, 96, 97
subjective freedom,
   16.I, 53
subjective thinking, subjective thinker,
   9, 171, 175, 206, 208, 384, 400, 407;
   11.I, 73; **12.I**, 54, 165; **17**, 134, 135
subjective truth,
   12.I, 7; **13**, 8, 38–41; **17**, 144, 185,
   250, 254
subjectivism,
   6.II, 69; **8.II**, 169, 207, 214, 216;
   8.III, 5, 6, 16, 68, 85, 113, 127; **9**,
   28, 90; **10.I**, xii, 15, 166, 214–16,
   250; **10.II**, 92, 114, 199, 200; **10.III**,
   107, 202; **11.I**, 31, 32, 36, 39, 87,
   149, 159, 171; **11.II**, 112; **11.III**,
   172, 224; **12.I**, 107; **12.V**, 82; **14**, 97
subjectivity. *See also* objectivity
   1.I, 23, 29, 31, 34, 40, 119, 122,
   144, 155, 164, 176, 216; **2.I**, 184,

186, 187, 206, 207, 232, 251, 281,
282, 294, 304, 308; **2.II**, 191, 192,
204; **4**, 47, 63, 115, 125, 157, 161,
310, 312; **5.I**, 15, 16, 88, 101, 167;
5.III, 186; **6.I**, 121; **6.III**, *185–233*,
240, 251, 253, 254; **7.I**, 130, 138,
159, 160, 235, 236, 239, 240, 254,
293, 304; **7.II**, 3, 4, 6, 10, 115, 225;
8.I, 80, 81, 90, 91, 144, 181, 255,
261, 282, 345, 372, 433, 452, 454,
457; **8.II**, 6, 8, 37; **8.III**, 47, 68, 108,
111, 133, 151, 180, 242, 292; **9**, 9,
26, 27, 28, 87, 132, 134–8, 145, 147,
149, 164, 187, 207, 224–8, 239, 243,
247, 248, 254, 274, 277, 319, 341,
378–80, 383, 386, 399, 402–4, 407;
10.I, 14, 18, 25, 172, 196, 206, 213,
242, 249, 263, 265, 268, 323, 324,
328, 329, 348, 356, 361, 369; **10.
II**, 3, 10, 12, 16–20, 30–2, 36, 40,
42, 55, 65, 89, 92, 97, 117–19, 144,
146–8, 151, 153, 159, 182–5, 193,
200; **11.I**, 14, 16, 27–9, 32, 35, 54,
55, 71, 73, 75, 77, 78, 87, 116, 119,
136, 137, 147–60 passim, 253, 258,
260, 261, 267, 268, 271, 272, 275,
276, 279; **11.II**, 11, 12, 51, 53, 54,
57, 67–70, 74, 77, 111–16, 121–3,
125, 128, 130, 132, 174, 180, 182–4,
186, 187, 192, 196, 208, 209, 214,
216, 217, 219, 226, 235; **11.III**, 2, 6,
7, 9, 76, 78, 93, 94, 166, 171–3, 193,
227; **12.I**, 38, 44, 53–5, 94, 106,
107; **12.III**, 17, 30, 31, 36, 38, 170;
12.IV, 3, 20, 166, 177; **12.V**, 11, 42,
80, 81, 84, 99, 113–17, 153; **13**, 8,
45, 66, 70, 310; **14**, 13, 33, 34, 41–9,
124, 128, 139, 163, 166; **15.V**, *1–6*;
16.I, 54, 198, 238, 264; **16.II**, 7, 9,
26, 135, 148; **17**, 45, 118, 123–6,
132, 136, 180, 182, 183, 250, 254,
255, 271
subjectivity, isolated,
   12.III, 9
subjectivity and objectivity,
   10.I, 31

subjectivity is truth. *See* also truth as
  subjectivity
  12.II, 62
sublation. *See Aufhebung*
sublime, sublimity,
  11.II, 14–16, 18, 66, 183; **11.III**, 19,
  23, 26, 210, 211, 215
sub specie aeternitatis,
  2.I, 84; **5.I**, 182, 183; **12.IV**, 84,
  179, 180
suffering,
  1.I, 4, 7–10, 23, 25, 27, 28, 35, 36,
  39, 44, 53, 56, 57, 63–6, 70–80 passim, 115–40, 148, 149, 152, 155–60,
  163, 165, 177, 186, 222, 231, 261;
  1.II, 6–8, 11, 30, 38–40, 44–9, 61,
  63, 66, 82–8 passim, 110, 135, 139,
  140, 145, 146, 151–64, 176–80, 184,
  197, 198, 201, 202, 205, 230, 231;
  2.I, 137, 138, 143; **2.II**, 62, 113, 211–
  19 passim, 229–30, 289, 304; **3**, 6, 7,
  29, 62, 64, 65, 94, 95, 114, 116, 118,
  132, 133, 154, 159, 174, 198, 206;
  5.I, 58, 156, 160; **5.II**, 26, 45, 49,
  50, 55, 72, 116, 162, 170, 229, 238,
  239; **5.III**, 5, 22, 38, 40; **7.II**, 111,
  112, 127, 132, 202, 328; **7.III**, 114;
  8.I, 78, 179, 180; **9**, 69, 75, 78, 91,
  135, 136, 145, 151, 225, 266, 282,
  304, 310–19 passim, 361, 363, 367,
  368–70; **10.I**, 27–9, 57, 58, 76, 98,
  190, 198, 202, 213, 239; **10.II**, 19,
  31, 73, 76, 77, 128, 164, 198; **10.III**,
  33, 36, 77, 83, 85, 86, 88, 91, 102,
  104, 106, 143, 147, 166; **11.I**, 36, 55,
  56, 58, 59, 199–201, 263, 279, 280,
  285, 290, 293, 299; **11.II**, 143, 144,
  147, 184, 195, 196, 230; **11.III**, 143;
  12.I, 130, 179, 209, 238; **12.II**, 7,
  32, 54, 58, 62, 71, 88–93, 116, 123,
  125, 127, 128, 130, 133, 148, 153–5,
  162; **12.III**, 46, 60, 80, 112, 113, 137,
  161, 170; **12.IV**, 16, 21, 46, 74, 147,
  163, 165, 206, 220; **12.V**, 12, 18, 19,
  129, 130, 144, 164–6; **13**, 45, 58, 63,
  65, 68, 71, 72, 104, 147, 303, 307;

14, 10, 58, 65, 236, 239, 249; **15.VI**,
  115–20; **16.I**, 3, 7, 35, 53, 54, 57–62,
  108, 109, 148, 151, 164–6, 190, 254,
  255; **16.II**, 58, 59, 63, 210, 243; **17**,
  15, 18, 47, 48, 57, 69, 72, 74, 125,
  126, 130, 131, 133, 151, 208, 226 n,
  227–9, 234, 251
sufficient reason, the principle of,
  5.I, 59–63, 65
Sufism,
  8.III, 3, 4, 6, 9, 18–21, 54, 56–62,
  69, 74
suicide,
  2.II, 201, 303; **3**, 72, 98, 135, 137,
  140, 192; **9**, 69, 76, 80, 87, 88, 147,
  217, 279, 301, 381; **11.I**, 50, 291;
  11.II, 27, 75, 76; **12.I**, 15, 66, 74;
  12.IV, 187, 217; **12.V**, 85; **13**, 36,
  87, 143, 277; **14**, 103, 241; **15.VI**,
  121–6; **16.II**, 33, 34, 78, 98, 123,
  164, 170, 193, 240
supernaturalism,
  1.I, x; **1.II**, 170; **2.II**, 7–9, 16; **7.II**,
  4, 276–8; **10.I**, 249, 338, 361, 370;
  11.I, 159
surrealism,
  12.V, 10, 80
suspension. *See* teleological suspension
  of the ethical
Svenska Psalmboken,
  20, A I 99
syllogism,
  16.I, 202, 206
symbol,
  10.I, 342, 343, 345, 359, 368; **11.II**,
  30–2, 92, 100; **11.III**, 38, 42; **13**, 4,
  9–11, 13, 19, 20, 22, 23, 25, 71, 116,
  125, 140, 160, 161, 164, 177, 181–3,
  188, 190, 200–2, 206–11, 251, 310, 311
symbolism,
  11.II, 30, 76; **12.III**, 55
sympathy/empathy,
  15.VI, *127–34*
synthesis,
  2.I, 58, 60, 64, 65, 139; **10.I**, 261,
  350, 357; **10.II**, 10, 13, 121, 123,

127, 145, 152, 153, 175; **10.III**, 55, 70, 79, 87, 125, 179; **11.I**, 278; **11.II**, 64, 105, 126, 152, 153, 184, 234, 235, 241; **11.III**, 43, 52, 54, 57, 66, 90; **13**, 22, 36, 100, 139, 155, 228, 288; **14**, 4, 59–61, 89, 92, 93, 102, 217, 219, 265; **17**, 10, 42, 43, 186, 188, 255
system, the,
  7.I, 120, 185–7, 197, 232, 292–4, 308; **7.II**, 3, 8, 161, 166, 231, 243, 247, 343, 349, 352; **7.III**, 171, 172; **8.I**, 440; **9**, 3, 38, 47, 75, 171, 175, 177, 182, 185, 187, 200, 201, 209, 225, 236, 240, 244, 252, 302, 310, 342–4, 394–7, 399, 405, 407; **10.I**, 18, 50, 88, 323, 335, 347, 348, 380; **10.II**, 48, 111, 145; **10.III**, 106; **11.I**, 9, 17, 67, 70–2, 74, 80, 87, 94–6, 98, 110, 116, 124, 130, 133, 135, 138, 147, 156, 159, 211, 227, 250, 258, 272, 278; **11.II**, 45, 47, 50–2, 58, 68, 88, 93, 100, 111, 113, 128, 129, 131, 141, 142, 145, 146, 150, 158, 174, 180, 182, 183, 185, 236, 237, 239, 240, 244, 246–8, 251; **11.III**, 7, 13, 14, 17, 30, 42, 43, 51, 81, 90, 93, 105, 139, 142, 143, 171, 173, 185, 186, 188, 205, 206, 208, 210, 219; **12.I**, 19, 153; **12.III**, 35; **13**, 33, 35, 37, 48, 123, 124; **14**, 32, 34, 59, 61, 64, 96, 150, 163, 164, 216; **16.II**, 147; **17**, 8, 54, 119, 120, 123, 127, 137, 200–2, 264
systematic philosophy. *See* speculative philosophy

T
Talmud,
  10.III, 157, 158, 165, 203, 204
Taming of the Shrew,
  16.II, 43
Taoism,
  8.III, 115; **13**, 167
tax collector,
  1.II, 94, 98, 101–3, 107–20, 130, 237; **11.III**, 143, 144, 149, 150, 152, 171; **12.V**, 196

teacher,
  15.VI, *135–40*
technology,
  11.II, 2, 142, 152, 153, 210; **12.V**, 80, 82
teleological suspension of the ethical,
  1.I, 52; **2.II**, 239; **5.I**, 93; **8.III**, 15, 31, 181; **9**, 49, 50, 176, 227, 228, 274, 300, 338, 360, 364; **10.I**, 82; **10.II**, 48, 49, 119, 122, 162–4, 166, 167; **10.III**, 178, 183–6; **11.I**, 253; **11.II**, 59, 86, 132, 174, 213; **11.III**, 107, 129, 172; **12.I**, 180, 210; **12.II**, 115, 148, 175; **12.IV**, 66, 169; **12.V**, 69; **13**, 301, 303, 306, 307; **14**, 63, 130, 199, 202, 264; **15.VI**, *141–6*; **17**, 151
teleology,
  5.I, 183, 186
τέλος,
  2.II, 39–44 passim, 62, 67
temporal and eternal. *See* eternal and temporal
temporality. *See also* time
  1.I, 156–8, 165, 187, 192; **9**, 104, 113, 134, 142, 305, 306, 310, 311, 316; **10.I**, 124 **11.I**, 131, 134, 140, 167, 189–91; **11.III**, 53; **12.V**, 19; **13**, 39–41, 73, 204, 277; **14**, 164; **15.VI**, *163–8*
temptation. *See also* Anfechtung
  1.II, 48; **5.II**, 36, 38; **14**, 115, 246; **15.VI**, *147–50*
Ten Commandments,
  1.II, 37, 43
terror. *See also* fear
  9, 25, 26, 359, 364; **11.I**, 169, 280; **13**, 24, 164, 177, 185, 187, 268, 282, 285, 286, 292; **14**, 65, 127, 236–8, 241, 245, 247
test. *See* trial
theater. *See* drama/theater
theater criticism,
  17, 34, 35, 109
theodicy,
  1.I, 4, 40; **5.I**, ix, 1, 2, 3, 51, 52, 58, 61, 67, 149; **6.I**, 7, 10, 50; **9**, 304, 314–19; **14**, 236, 239

Theologisk Maanedsskrift,
   7.II, 101, 102, 104, 118, 216,
   306, 312
theology, dialectical,
   8.I, 33, 35, 159, 239, 246, 279, 334,
   352, 373, 376; **8.III**, 139, 149, 205;
   10.I, ix, 3, 44, 59, 60, 71, 98, 107,
   156, 169, 187, 207, 352, 359, 383;
   10.II, 86, 88, 90; **10.III**, 10, 19, 22,
   202; **11.I**, 10, 28, 61, 168, 182
theology, dogmatic,
   10.III, 25
theology, ethical,
   8.I, 276–80, 289
theology, evangelical,
   10.II, 51
theology, existential,
   8.I, 80; **10.I**, x, 16, 60, 131, 197, 361
theology, feminist,
   10.II, 151
theology, liberal,
   8.I, 21, 22, 32, 33, 35, 334; **10.I**, 1,
   44, 99, 107, 191, 384
theology, liberation,
   10.II, 26, 27, 39
theology, Lundensian,
   10.II, 207
theology, natural,
   10.I, 3, 70–2, 193; **10.II**, 106
theology, negative,
   8.I, 184, 262; **12.III**, 35
theology, neo-orthodox,
   10.I, 98, 346
theology, political,
   10.I, 193, 202, 157, 158, 189–91,
   193, 202
theology, postmodern,
   10.II, 39
theology, Princeton,
   10.II, 173, 177, 185
theology, radical,
   10.II, 27
theology, Shekinah,
   10.I, 194
theology, systematic,
   10.I, 148, 161, 166, 167, 170, 175,
   191–3, 207, 243, 250, 252, 264, 267,

   321, 335, 340, 341, 355, 358, 360,
   362, 370, 377
theology of crisis,
   8.I, 33, 238; **10.III**, 19; **14**, 98
theology of the cross,
   10.I, 91, 95, 187–90, 194, 198,
   200–2, 207, 213, 326
theonomy,
   2.I, 85
theory,
   8.II, 50
the they. *See das Man*
Thirty Years' War (1618–48),
   5.II, 46, 50, 54
Thomism,
   9, 218, 224, 226; **10.II**, 130; **10.III**,
   101
thorn in the flesh,
   1.II, 140, 198, 205; **12.III**, 8, 80
thought and being,
   7.I, 291, 310; **7.II**, 3, 8; **12.I**, 19
thoughtlessness,
   15.VI, *157–62*
Thousand and One Nights,
   16.II, 43
Tidehverv,
   8.I, 32–4, 38, 40, 41, 44, 64, 82,
   85, 96
Tidsskrift for Litteratur og Kritik,
   7.II, 6
*Tidsskrift for udenlandsk theologisk
   Litteratur*,
   7.I, 156
Till Uglspil,
   20, M 1469
time,
   2.I, 45–72; **5.I**, 38, 41, 42; **6.I**, 10;
   8.I, 357; **8.II**, 38, 48, 296, 308; **8.III**,
   3, 5, 13, 20, 21, 32, 41, 50, 51, 53,
   54, 57, 61, 66, 135, 239, 240, 280,
   288, 290; **9**, 101, 103, 104, 240, 245,
   246, 272, 302, 303, 305, 307, 310–
   12, 316; **10.I**, 186, 194, 207, 212;
   11.I, 149, 152, 167, 168, 188–93,
   200, 250, 251, 270, 279, 281; **12.I**,
   25, 178, 179, 183; **12.III**, 42, 44;
   12.V, 53, 108; **13**, 39, 69, 123, 184,

185, 204, 219, 220; **14**, 23, 45, 46,
48, 99, 100, 239, 243; **15.VI**, *163–8*
time, fullness of,
10.I, 328
time and eternity,
10.I, 14, 74, 185, 198, 199, 207–13
passim, 261, 325–8, 360; **10.II**, 10,
11, 15–17, 20, 31, 90, 92, 95, 96,
107, 127; **10.III**, 107, 179; **12.IV**,
205; **12.V**, 83; **15.VI**, *163–8*
Tivoli,
13, 181
totalitarianism,
11.I, 40; **11.II**, 183; **12.V**, 94, 95,
158, 160, 162, 163; **14**, 29, 36, 38,
127, 207, 225
tragedy/tragic,
2.II, 59–79, 211–34, *303–25*; **4**,
210–12; **6.I**, 131, 132; **6.II**, 29;
6.III, 4, 69, 243, 249; **7.III**, 177,
195; **8.III**, 119; **10.III**, 16, 103, 104;
11.II, 12; **12.I**, 20–2, 49, 50; **12.IV**,
6; **12.V**, 94; **14**, 55, 129, 130, 153,
232, 245; **15.VI**, *169–76*; **16.I**, 1–6,
9–11, 49–61, 71, 104, 105, 109, 125,
128, 161, 176, 180, 183, 204, 207,
252–6; **16.II**, 13, 57–64, 85–94,
199–213, 219, 220
tragedy, Greek,
16.II, 190
tragic hero,
16.I, *2–11*, 43, 58, 60, 82, 109, 126
transcendence,
1.II, 58, 60, 62, 65, 71, 73, 75, 76,
147, 197; **2.I**, 56; **2.II**, 42–5, 75; **4**,
42, 63, 99; **6.III**, 18, 26, 56, 242;
8.II, 227; **8.III**, 85, 86; **9**, 2, 7, 25,
85, 130, 131, 137, 147, 149, 151,
173, 179, 190, 209, 210, 211, 228,
236, 304, 312, 316, 404, 407; **10.I**,
6, 243, 246; **10.III**, 75–95 passim,
98, 102, 107, 109, 144–6, 149; **11.I**,
15–17, 21, 27, 30, 32, 96, 252; **12.V**,
111, 184; **13**, 9–11, 13, 25, 121, 128,
290, 304, 311, 315; **14**, 61, 65, 210,
220, 222, 224, 225; **15.III**, *209–14*;
16.II, 59, 63

transcendence and immanence
9, 52, 130, 131, 132, 136, 137, 147,
149, 150, 253–5, 308–10; **10.II**, 11,
51, 53, 90, 91, 96, 107, 127, 130,
139, 146; **10.III**, 136, 138, 139;
11.II, 77, 106, 107, 166, 177, 187,
188, 192, 194, 195, 209, 212, 216,
217, 221, 223, 225, 227–9, 247;
12.IV, 179, 182, 185, 187; **12.V**,
153; **13**, 135, 311; **15.III**, *209–14*;
17, 91, 94, 124, 132, 180, 188
transfiguration,
1.I, 94; **15.VI**, *177–84*
transition,
2.I, 50, 55, 58, 59–63, 66, 118, 127,
131, 132, 139, 220, 233, 241, 260,
287; **2.II**, 11, 17; **4**, 29, 36, 92, 139;
10.III, 61, 70; **15.VI**, *185–92*
*Tre Hundrede udvalgte og lystige Ny
Historier*,
20, M 1468
trial,
12.IV, 74, 123 177, 178, 188, 208;
15.VI, *193–202*
tribulation. *See* trial
trinitology,
10.III, 57, 71
Trinity,
1.I, 43; **4**, 3, 4, 51, 132, 169, 223;
5.II, 46–9; **6.II**, 44, 59, 102, 113,
130, 130–2, 209; **7.I**, 63, 297; **7.II**,
27, 57, 63, 64, 70, 79; **8.I**, 23;
8.III, 246; **9**, 137–9, 144, 150, 305,
307; **10.I**, 4, 31, 186, 190, 192,
199, 214–17, 250, 263; **10.II**, 58,
96; **14**, 251
Trojan War,
16.I, 1
troll. *See* elves, trolles, and nisses
Tröst Einsamkeit,
20, M 912
troubadours,
3, 93; **4**, 299–320
trust,
9, 302, 311–19 passim; **11.I**, 192,
200, 201; **13**, 81, 85, 87–92, 122–35
passim, 186

truth,
  8.III, 108; **9**, 26, 29, 100, 101, 164,
  378–80, 383, 386, 399, 405; **10.I**,
  86, 97, 165, 196, 206, 210, 213, 214,
  269, 330, 352, 354; **10.II**, 3–20 passim, 31, 32, 35, 39, 42, 52, 55, 64, 69,
  70, 73–7, 80, 81, 89, 117–19, 122–4,
  127, 129, 131, 133, 145, 147, 151–3,
  175–9, 181, 183–5, 200, 214; **15.VI**,
  203–8
truth as subjectivity,
  11.III, 77, 82, 104, 110, 160, 161,
  165, 166, 172, 173
truth-witness,
  16.I, 162–8
*T & T Clark Foreign Theological
  Library*,
  8.I, 240
Tübingen School,
  1.II, 179, 184, 191, 240, 307, 308,
  310, 311; **6.II**, 23–36
Turks. *See* Ottoman Empire

U
Übermensch,
  10.III, 7
Uebungen des lateinischen Stils,
  20, M 1008
ultimate concern,
  13, 20, 280–6, 291, 292
ultraism,
  12.V, 21
ultramontanism,
  10.III, 75
uncanny,
  12.IV, 55
uncertainty,
  9, 379, 380, 384, 385, 400; **11.I**, 21,
  213, 259, 275, 298; **12.I**, 4, 239, 240,
  244; **13**, 91, 304, 313–16; **14**, 48, 218,
  222, 245
unconscious,
  6.I, 293, 294, 297, 298, 302–5
*Underlige Spørgsmaal, lystige at høre
  og læse*,
  20, M 1464

*Underlig og selsom Historie am Tiile
  Ugelspegel*,
  20, M 1469
understanding,
  15.VI, *209–14*
unhappy consciousness,
  6.I, 132, 133; **7.II**, 4; **8.I**, 439; **9**,
  337, 396, 397; **11.I**, 29; **11.II**, 247;
  12.I, 244; **12.V**, 84; **13**, 162; **14**, 64
Unheimlichkeit,
  13, 184, 185
Unitarianism,
  7.II, 70, 71
unity, higher,
  7.I, 60
unity of opposites,
  6.III, 58
unity of thought and being, the,
  2.I, 29, 30, 43, 51; **5.II**, 54
universal and particular,
  2.I, 292; **6.I**, 134; **6.III**, 252; **7.II**, 34
universals,
  4, 146, 147, 169
University of Berlin,
  7.II, 191; **9**, 34, 38; **11.I**, 85, 88
University of Copenhagen,
  1.II, 221, 223, 258, 310; **2.I**, 54, 137,
  255; **2.II**, 6, 26, 151; **3**, 151; **5.III**,
  84; **7.I**, ix, 2, 3, 14, 15, 26, 37, 59,
  86, 180–2, 184, 215, 216, 230, 233,
  241, 245, 290, 306; **7.II**, 2, 7, 24, 29,
  41, 50, 154, 193, 232, 239, 268, 308,
  337; **7.III**, 51, 93, 110, 210, 214,
  225, 230, 234, 248, 258, 259, 287
University of Erlangen,
  7.II, 308
University of Kiel,
  7.II, 154, 308; **7.III**, 210
University of Leipzig,
  9, 34–8
University of Vienna,
  9, 34, 36, 38; **11.I**, 223
University of Zurich,
  9, 34
unmoved mover,
  2.II, 27, 39–42

upbuilding discourses,
  8.III, 87
Urania. See Heiberg, Johan, Ludvig,
  Urania
urbanization,
  10.II, 25, 27–9, 33, 39
Utilitarism,
  8.III, 136; **11.I**, 108; **11.III**, 138

V
Valkendorfs Collegium,
  5.III, 64, 71
value,
  9, 12, 13, 83, 89, 206, 266, 285, 336,
  337, 339, 341, 342, 360; **11.I**, 94,
  151, 158, 224, 279, 285, 298; **12.I**,
  31–7, 94, 102; **13**, 10, 21, 61, 76, 114,
  115, 226, 260, 261, 266–9, 314; **14**,
  20, 57, 80, 81, 90, 97, 140, 143, 154,
  213, 264, 267
vanity,
  1.I, *179–92*
Vatican Council, First (1869–70),
  10.III, 33
Vatican Council, Second (1962–65),
  10.III, 54, 102, 119, 121, 135, 149,
  158
vaudeville,
  7.I, 39; **7.III**, 169, 171–4, 179, 181,
  190–2, 195, 199, 276; **9**, 380; **12.IV**,
  122; **15.VI**, *215–20*; **16.II**, 115
*Das Verstandesthum und das
  Individuum*,
  20, M 868
vertigo,
  9, 141, 327, 329, 335, 336, 366;
  10.I, 257, 263; **10.II**, 39, 121;
  10.III, 9, 125; **11.I**, 282, 283; **11.II**,
  243; **12.I**, 75, 76, 148, 208; **12.III**,
  39; **13**, 227, 233; **14**, 102, 218, 238,
  240, 243, 244, 266, 267; **14**, 238,
  240, 247
Vienna Circle,
  11.III, 15, 71, 72, 78
Vienna school,
  12.III, 36

virgin birth,
  10.I, 72, 98, 246, 284
virtue,
  2.I, 11, 15, 16, 31, 32, 54, 98–100,
  118–22 passim, 185, 228, 234, 250,
  253, 271, 279–81; **2.II**, 47, 50, 308;
  5.II, 10, 11, 18, 85, 98, 163, 179, 194,
  251, 255; **11.III**, 117, 119, 120, 121,
  125–7, 129
virtue by the absurd,
  16.I, 9
vitalism,
  9, 139, 406
Die Volksharfe,
  20, M 1472–1473
voluntarism,
  10.I, 359, 370
vortex,
  15.VI, *221–8*
voting,
  15.VI, *229–34*
Vulgate,
  1.II, 3, 226, 228, 229, 231

W
Weimar Classicism,
  6.III, 53, 156, 157
Weimar Court Theater,
  6.III, 53
Weimar Republic,
  10.I, xi, 156, 160, 377; **10.III**, 48,
  50; **14**, 180, 181, 187, 191, 198
Weltanschauung,
  9, 159; **11.I**, 94, 95; **13**, 62; **14**, 108,
  114, 115, 120, 125, 127
*Wilhelmine, eine Geschichte
  in Briefen*,
  20, A II 238
will,
  15.VI, *235–42*
without authority,
  1.I, 181, 223, 224
witness,
  1.I, x, 24, 51, 74, 76, 79, 92, 97, 109,
  111, 119, 129, 138–40, 176, 213;
  1.II, 86, 198, 259, 260, 266; **10.I**,

xii, 84, 95; **10.II**, 37, 81; **11.II**, 123;
15.VI, *243–50*
witness to the truth,
10.III, 17; **12.II**, 163; **16.I**, 159, 163,
164, 168
women,
5.III, 218; **6.III**, 10, 18, 80, 84,
174; **8.I**, 80, 91, 125, 263, 447–9;
9, 15–19, 82; **12.I**, 86; **13**, 10, 132;
14, xii, xiii, 54; **15.VI**, *251–8*; **17**,
29, 63, 99, 159, 169–71, 252–4,
292
woman in sin,
1.II, 94, 98–100, 103, *123–35*
women's equality. *See* emancipation of
women
wonder,
15.VI, *259–67*
word, the,
10.I, 3, 69–74 passim, 78, 80, 81, 83,
86, 93, 146, 147, 202, 244, 246, 247,
277, 321, 327
works, good works,
10.I, 16, 18, 24, 33, 55, 147
worldliness. *See also* secularism,
secularisation
15.VI, *267–70*

World War I,
12.I, xi, 2, 31, 32, 95, 98, 146, 160,
195, 198, 215, 229; **12.II**, 25; **12.IV**,
113; **12.V**, 140
World War II,
12.I, 5, 6, 172, 173; **12.II**, 67; **12.IV**,
3, 12, 42, 113, 134, 214, 216; **12.V**,
140, 171
writing,
15.VI, *271–7*

Y
yoga,
13, 55, 167
Young Germany,
6.III, 157; **7.I**, 135, 137, 139

Z
Zaubereien und Wunder,
20, A II 230
*Zeitschrift für Philosophie und
speculative Theologie*,
20, M 877–911
Zionism,
9, 35; **10.III**, 172; **14**, 30
*Zollverordnung für Schleswig und
Holstein*,
20, A II 200

Overview of the Articles in the Series

Section I: Sources

1.I: Barrett, Lee C. and Jon Stewart (eds.), *Kierkegaard and the Bible*, Tome I, *The Old Testament*, Farnham and Burlington: Ashgate 2010 (*Kierkegaard Research: Sources, Reception and Resources*, vol. 1).

    (Timothy Dalrymple, "Adam and Eve: Human Being and Nothingness," pp. 3–42; Timothy Dalrymple, "Abraham: Framing *Fear and Trembling*," pp. 43–88; Paul Martens, "Moses: The Positive and Negative Importance of Moses in Kierkegaard's Thought," pp. 89–99; Matthias Engelke, "David and Solomon: Models of Repentance and Evasion of Guilt," pp. 101–13; Timothy H. Polk, "Job: Edification against Theodicy," pp. 115–42; Matthias Engelke, "Psalms: Source of Images and Contrasts," pp. 143–78; Will Williams, "Ecclesiastes: Vanity, Grief, and the Distinctions of Wisdom," pp. 179–94; Matthias Engelke, "Nebuchadnezzar: The King as Image of Transformation," pp. 195–204; Iben Damgaard, "Kierkegaard's Rewriting of Biblical Narratives: The Mirror of the Text," pp. 207–30; Lori Unger Brandt, "Kierkegaard's Use of the Old Testament: From Literary Resource to the Word of God," pp. 231–51; W. Glenn Kirkconnell, "Kierkegaard's Use of the Apocrypha: Is It 'Scripture' or 'Good for Reading'?" pp. 253–64.)

1.II: Barrett, Lee C. and Jon Stewart (eds.), *Kierkegaard and the Bible*, Tome II, *The New Testament*, Farnham and Burlington: Ashgate 2010 (*Kierkegaard Research: Sources, Reception and Resources*, vol. 1).

    (Lee C. Barrett, "Simeon and Anna: Exemplars of Patience and Expectancy," pp. 3–16; Jolita Pons, "Jesus' Miracles: Kierkegaard on the Miracle of Faith," pp. 17–32; Lee C. Barrett, "The Sermon on the Mount: The Dialectic of Exhortation and Consolation," pp. 33–53; Leo Stan, "The Lily in the Field and the Bird of the Air: An Endless Liturgy in Kierkegaard's Authorship," pp. 55–78; Kyle A. Roberts, "Peter: The 'Pitiable Prototype,'" pp. 79–91; Paul Martens, "The Pharisee: Kierkegaard's Polyphonic Personification of a Univocal Idea," pp. 93–105; Timothy H. Polk, "The Tax Collector: Model of Inwardness," pp. 107–22; Paul Martens, "The Woman in Sin: Kierkegaard's Late Female Prototype," pp. 123–37; Kyle A. Roberts, "Lazarus: Kierkegaard's Use of a Destitute Beggar and a Resurrected Friend," pp. 139–49; Lee C. Barrett, "The Crucifixion: Kierkegaard's Use of the New Testament Narratives," pp. 151–67; Lee C. Barrett, "The Resurrection: Kierkegaard's Use of the Resurrection as Symbol and as Reality," pp. 169–87; Lori Unger Brandt, "Paul: Herald of Grace and Paradigm of Christian Living," pp. 189–208; Kyle A. Roberts, "James: Putting Faith to Action," pp. 209–17; Niels W. Bruun and Finn Gredal Jensen,

"Kierkegaard's Latin Translations of the New Testament: A Constant Dialogue with the Vulgate," pp. 221–36; Timothy H. Polk, "Kierkegaard's Use of the New Testament: Intratextuality, Indirect Communication, and Appropriation," pp. 237–48; Joel D.S. Rasmussen, "Kierkegaard's Biblical Hermeneutics: Imitation, Imaginative Freedom, and Paradoxical Fixation," pp. 249–84; Mogens Müller, "Kierkegaard and Eighteenth- and Nineteenth-Century Biblical Scholarship: A Case of Incongruity," pp. 285–327.)

2.I: Nun, Katalin and Jon Stewart (eds.), *Kierkegaard and the Greek World*, Tome I, *Socrates and Plato*, Farnham and Burlington: Ashgate 2010 (*Kierkegaard Research: Sources, Reception and Resources*, vol. 2).

(Paul Muench, "*Apology*: Kierkegaard's Socratic Point of View," pp. 3–25; David D. Possen, "*Meno*: Kierkegaard and the Doctrine of Recollection," pp. 27–44; Janne Kylliäinen, "*Phaedo* and *Parmenides*: Eternity, Time, and the Moment, or From the Abstract Philosophical to the Concrete Christian," pp. 45–71; David D. Possen, "*Phaedrus*: Kierkegaard on Socrates' Self-Knowledge – and Sin," pp. 73–86; David D. Possen, "*Protagoras* and *Republic*: Kierkegaard on Socratic Irony," pp. 87–104; Rick Anthony Furtak, "*Symposium*: Kierkegaard and Platonic Eros," pp. 105–14; Marius Timmann Mjaaland, "*Theaetetus*: Giving Birth, or Kierkegaard's Socratic Maieutics," pp. 115–46; Katalin Nun, "Cumulative Plato Bibliography," pp. 147–64; Eric Ziolkowski, "Aristophanes: Kierkegaard's Understanding of the Socrates of the 'Clouds,'" pp. 167–98; William McDonald, "Xenophon: Kierkegaard's Use of Socrates of the 'Memorabilia,'" pp. 199–211; Tonny Aagaard Olesen, "Kierkegaard's Socrates Sources: Eighteenth- and Nineteenth-Century Danish Scholarship," pp. 215–66; Harald Steffes, "Kierkegaard's Socrates Sources: Eighteenth- and Nineteenth-Century Germanophone Scholarship," pp. 267–311.)

2.II: Nun, Katalin and Jon Stewart (eds.), *Kierkegaard and the Greek World*, Tome II, *Aristotle and Other Greek Authors*, Farnham and Burlington: Ashgate 2010 (*Kierkegaard Research: Sources, Reception and Resources*, vol. 2).

(Håvard Løkke and Arild Waaler, "*Organon* and *Metaphysics* IV: The First Principles of Logic and the Debate about Mediation," pp. 3–23; Håvard Løkke and Arild Waaler, "*Organon* and *Metaphysics*: Change, Modal Categories, and Agency," pp. 25–45; Håvard Løkke, "*Nicomachean Ethics*: Ignorance and Relationships," pp. 47–58; Daniel Greenspan, "*Poetics*: The Rebirth of Tragedy and the End of Modernity," pp. 59–79; Heiko Schulz, "*Rhetoric*: Eloquence, Faith and Probability," pp. 81–98; Katalin Nun, "Cumulative Aristotle Bibliography," pp. 99–108; Nicolae Irina, "Diogenes Laertius: Kierkegaard's Source and Inspiration," pp. 111–21; Jon Stewart, "The Eleatics: Kierkegaard's Metaphysical Considerations of Being and Motion," pp. 123–45; Finn Gredal Jensen, "Heraclitus: Presocratic Ideas of Motion, Change and Opposites in Kierkegaard's Thought," pp. 147–63; Anthony Rudd, "The Skeptics: Kierkegaard and Classical Skepticism," pp. 165–82; K. Brian Söderquist, "The Sophists: Kierkegaard's Interpretation of Socrates and the Sophists," pp. 183–94; Rick Anthony Furtak, "The Stoics: Kierkegaard on the Passion for Apathy," pp. 195–208; Finn Gredal Jensen, "Aeschylus:

Kierkegaard and Early Greek Tragedy," pp. 211–34; Nicolae Irina, "Euripides: Kierkegaard and the Ancient Tragic Heroes," pp. 235–46; Finn Gredal Jensen, "Herodotus: Traces of 'The Histories' in Kierkegaard's Writings," pp. 247–62; Nicolae Irina, "Hesiod: Kierkegaard and the Greek Gods," pp. 263–9; Finn Gredal Jensen, "Homer: Kierkegaard's Use of the Homeric Poems," pp. 271–99; Nicolae Irina, "Plutarch: A Constant Cultural Reference," pp. 301–11; Nicolae Irina, "Sophocles: The Tragic of Kierkegaard's Modern 'Antigone,'" pp. 313–25.)

3: Stewart, Jon (ed.), *Kierkegaard and the Roman World*, Farnham and Burlington: Ashgate 2009 (*Kierkegaard Research: Sources, Reception and Resources*, vol. 3).

(Stacey E. Ake, "Apuleius: Direct and Possible Indirect Influences on the Thought of Kierkegaard," pp. 1–9; Thomas Eske Rasmussen, "Cicero: A Handy Roman Companion. Marcus Tullius Cicero's Appearance in Kierkegaard's Works," pp. 11–37; Thomas Miles, "Horace: The Art of Poetry and the Search for the Good Life," pp. 39–51; Nataliya Vorobyova, "Livy: 'The History of Rome' in Kierkegaard's Works," pp. 53–67; Rick Anthony Furtak, "Marcus Aurelius: Kierkegaard's Use and Abuse of the Stoic Emperor," pp. 69–74; Jon Stewart, "Nepos: Traces of Kierkegaard's Use of an Edifying Roman Biographer," pp. 75–85; Steven P. Sondrup, "Ovid: Of Love and Exile. Kierkegaard's Appropriation of Ovid," pp. 87–103; Niels W. Bruun, "Sallust: Kierkegaard's Scarce Use of a Great Roman Historian," pp. 105–9; Niels W. Bruun, "Seneca: *Disjecta Membra* in Kierkegaard's Writings," pp. 111–24; Sebastian Hőeg Gulmann, "Suetonius: Exemplars of Truth and Madness. Kierkegaard's Proverbial Uses of Suetonius' 'Lives,'" pp. 125–45; Jon Stewart, "Tacitus: Christianity as *odium generis humani*," pp. 147–61; Mikkel Larsen, "Terence: Traces of Roman Comedy in Kierkegaard's Writings," pp. 163–83; Nataliya Vorobyova, "Valerius Maximus: Moral 'Exempla' in Kierkegaard's Writings," pp. 185–95; Steven P. Sondrup, "Virgil: From Farms to Empire: Kierkegaard's Understanding of a Roman Poet," pp. 197–212.)

4: Stewart, Jon (ed.), *Kierkegaard and the Patristic and Medieval Traditions*, Aldershot and Burlington: Ashgate 2008 (*Kierkegaard Research: Sources, Reception and Resources*, vol. 4).

(Robert Puchniak, "Athanasius: Kierkegaard's Curious Comment," pp. 3–9; Robert Puchniak, "Augustine: Kierkegaard's Tempered Admiration of Augustine," pp. 11–22; Jack Mulder, Jr., "Bernard of Clairvaux: Kierkegaard's Reception of the Last of the Fathers," pp. 23–45; Leo Stan, "Chrysostom: Between the Hermitage and the City," pp. 47–65; Jack Mulder, Jr., "Cyprian of Carthage: Kierkegaard, Cyprian, and the 'Urgent Needs of the Times,'" pp. 67–94; Joseph Ballan, "Gregory of Nyssa: Locating the Cappadocian Fathers in Kierkegaard's Church-Historical Narrative," pp. 95–102; Paul Martens, "Irenaeus: On Law, Gospel and the Grace of Death," pp. 103–10; Paul Martens, "Origen: Kierkegaard's Equivocal Appropriation of Origen of Alexandria," pp. 111–21; Robert Puchniak, "Pelagius: Kierkegaard's Use of Pelagius and Pelagianism," pp. 123–30; Pierre Bühler, "Tertullian: The Teacher of the credo quia absurdum," pp. 131–42; István Czakó, "Abelard: Kierkegaard's Reflections on the Unhappy Love of a Scholastic Dialectician," pp. 145–65; Lee C. Barrett, "Anselm of

Canterbury: The Ambivalent Legacy of Faith Seeking Understanding," pp. 167–81; Benjamín Olivares Bøgeskov, "Thomas Aquinas: Kierkegaard's View Based on Scattered and Uncertain Sources," pp. 183–206; Joseph Westfall, "Boethius: Kierkegaard and 'The Consolation,'" pp. 207–21, Thomas Miles, "Dante: Tours of Hell. Mapping the Landscape of Sin and Despair," pp. 223–35; Peter Šajda, "Meister Eckhart: The Patriarch of German Speculation Who Was a 'Lebemeister': Meister Eckhart's Silent Way into Kierkegaard's Corpus," pp. 237–53; Karl Verstrynge, "Petrarch: Kierkegaard's Few and One-Sided References to a Like-Minded Thinker," pp. 255–64; Peter Šajda, "Tauler: A Teacher in Spiritual Dietethics. Kierkegaard's Reception of Johannes Tauler," pp. 265–87; Joel D.S. Rasmussen, "Thomas à Kempis: 'Devotio Moderna' and Kierkegaard's Critique of 'Bourgeois-Philistinism,'" pp. 289–98; Tonny Aagaard Olesen, "Troubadour Poetry: The Young Kierkegaard's Study of Troubadours – 'with Respect to the Concept of the Romantic,'" pp. 299–321.)

5.I: Stewart, Jon (ed.), *Kierkegaard and the Renaissance and Modern Traditions*, Tome I, *Philosophy*, Farnham and Burlington: Ashgate 2009 (*Kierkegaard Research: Sources, Reception and Resources*, vol. 5).

(Karl Verstrynge, "Pierre Bayle: Kierkegaard's Use of the 'Historical and Critical Dictionary,'" pp. 1–10; Anders Moe Rasmussen, "René Descartes: Kierkegaard's Understanding of Doubt and Certainty," pp. 11–21; Thomas Miles, "David Hume: Kierkegaard and Hume on Reason, Faith, and the Ethics of Philosophy," pp. 23–32; Anders Moe Rasmussen, "Friedrich Heinrich Jacobi: Two Theories of the Leap," pp. 33–49; Håvard Løkke and Arild Waaler, "Gottfried Wilhelm Leibniz: Traces of Kierkegaard's Reading of the 'Theodicy,'" pp. 51–76; Curtis L. Thompson, "Gotthold Ephraim Lessing: Appropriating the Testimony of a Theological Naturalist," pp. 77–112; Søren Landkildehus, "Michel de Montaigne: The Vulnerability of Sources in Estimating Kierkegaard's Study of 'Essais,'" pp. 113–28; Søren Landkildehus, "Blaise Pascal: Kierkegaard and Pascal as Kindred Spirits in the Fight against Christendom," pp. 129–46; Vincent A. McCarthy, "Jean-Jacques Rousseau: Presence and Absence," pp. 147–65; Clare Carlisle, "Baruch de Spinoza: Questioning Transcendence, Teleology and Truth," pp. 167–94.)

5.II: Stewart, Jon (ed.), *Kierkegaard and the Renaissance and Modern Traditions*, Tome II, *Theology*, Farnham and Burlington: Ashgate 2009 (*Kierkegaard Research: Sources, Reception and Resources*, vol. 5).

(Peter Šajda, "Abraham a Sancta Clara: An Aphoristic Encyclopedia of Christian Wisdom," pp. 1–20; Joseph Ballan, "Johann Arndt: The Pietist Impulse in Kierkegaard and Seventeenth-Century Lutheran Devotional Literature," pp. 21–30; Peter Šajda, "Ludovicus Blosius: A Frightful Satire on Christendom," pp. 31–41; Lee C. Barrett, "Jacob Böhme: The Ambiguous Legacy of Speculative Passion," pp. 43–61; Christopher B. Barnett, "Hans Adolph Brorson: Danish Pietism's Greatest Hymn Writer and His Relation to Kierkegaard," pp. 63–79; David Yoon-Jung Kim, "John Calvin: Kierkegaard and the Question of the Law's Third Use," pp. 81–110; Finn Gredal Jensen, "Erasmus of Rotterdam: Kierkegaard's Hints at a Christian Humanist," pp. 111–27; Peter Šajda, "François de Salignac de la Mothe-Fénelon: Clearing the Way

for *The Sickness unto Death*," pp. 129–47; Joseph Ballan, "August Hermann Francke: Kierkegaard on the Kernel and the Husk of Pietist Theology," pp. 149–56; Christopher B. Barnett, "Thomas Kingo: An Investigation of the Poet's and Hymnist's Impact on Kierkegaard," pp. 157–71; David Yoon-Jung Kim and Joel D.S. Rasmussen, "Martin Luther: Reform, Secularization, and the Question of His 'True Successor,'" pp. 173–217; Ivan Ž. Sørensen, "Hieronimus Savonarola: Kierkegaard's Model for the Blood-Witness," pp. 219–43; Christopher B. Barnett, "Gerhard Tersteegen: Kierkegaard's Reception of a Man of 'Noble Piety and Simple Wisdom,'" pp. 245–58.)

5.III: Stewart, Jon (ed.), *Kierkegaard and the Renaissance and Modern Traditions*, Tome III, *Literature, Drama and Music*, Farnham and Burlington: Ashgate 2009 (*Kierkegaard Research: Sources, Reception and Resources*, vol. 5).

(Bartholomew Ryan, "Lord George Gordon Byron: Seduction, Defiance, and Despair in the Works of Kierkegaard," pp. 1–11; Óscar Parcero Oubiña, "Miguel de Cervantes: The Valuable Contribution of a Minor Influence," pp. 13–29; Ingrid Basso, "François-René de Chateaubriand: The Eloquent Society of Symparanekromenoi," pp. 31–62; Kim Ravn, "Johannes Ewald: Poetic Fire," pp. 63–76; Julie K. Allen, "Ludvig Holberg: Kierkegaard's Unacknowledged Mentor," pp. 77–92; Ingrid Basso, "Alphonse de Lamartine: The Movement 'en masse' versus the Individual Choice," pp. 93–108; Nataliya Vorobyova, "Prosper Merimée: A New Don Juan," pp. 109–24; Jeanette Bresson Ladegaard Knox, "Molière: An Existential Vision of Authenticity in Man across Time," pp. 125–35; Elisabete M. de Sousa, "Wolfgang Amadeus Mozart: The Love for Music and the Music of Love," pp. 137–67; Elisabete M. de Sousa, "Eugène Scribe: The Unfortunate Authorship of a Successful Author," pp. 169–83; Joel D.S. Rasmussen, "William Shakespeare: Kierkegaard's Post-Romantic Reception of 'the Poet's Poet,'" pp. 185–213; Bartholomew Ryan, "Percy Bysshe Shelley: Anxious Journeys, the Demonic, and 'Breaking the Silence,'" pp. 215–24; Nataliya Vorobyova, "Richard Brinsley Sheridan: A Story of One Review – Kierkegaard on 'The School for Scandal,'" pp. 225–43; Tonny Aagaard Olesen, "Johan Herman Wessel: Kierkegaard's Use of Wessel, or: The Crazier the Better," pp. 245–71; Joseph Ballan, "Edward Young: Kierkegaard's Encounter with a Proto-Romantic Religious Poet," pp. 273–81.)

6.I: Stewart, Jon (ed.), *Kierkegaard and His German Contemporaries*, Tome I, *Philosophy*, Aldershot and Burlington: Ashgate 2007 (*Kierkegaard Research: Sources, Reception and Resources*, vol. 6).

(Peter Koslowski, "Baader: The Centrality of Original Sin and the Difference of Immediacy and Innocence," pp. 1–16; J. Michael Tilley, "Bayer: Kierkegaard's Attempt at Social Philosophy," pp. 17–24; István Czakó, "Feuerbach: A Malicious Demon in the Service of Christianity," pp. 25–47; Hartmut Rosenau, "I.H. Fichte: Philosophy as the Most Cheerful Form of Service to God," pp. 49–66; David J. Kangas, "J.G. Fichte: From Transcendental Ego to Existence," pp. 67–95; Jon Stewart, "Hegel: Kierkegaard's Reading and Use of Hegel's Primary Texts," pp. 97–165; Johannes Adamsen, "Herder: A Silent Background and Reservoir," pp. 167–77; Ronald M. Green,

"Kant: A Debt Both Obscure and Enormous," pp. 179–210; Smail Rapic, "Lichtenberg: Lichtenberg's Aphoristic Thought and Kierkegaard's Concept of the 'Subjective Existing Thinker,'" pp. 211–28; Tonny Aagaard Olesen, "Schelling: A Historical Introduction to Kierkegaard's Schelling," pp. 229–75; Simonella Davini, "Schopenhauer: Kierkegaard's Late Encounter with His Opposite," pp. 277–91; Stefan Egenberger, "Schubert: Kierkegaard's Reading of Gotthilf Heinrich Schubert's Philosophy of Nature," pp. 293–307; Darío González, "Trendelenburg: An Ally against Speculation," pp. 309–34; Jon Stewart, "Werder: The Influence of Werder's Lectures and 'Logik' on Kierkegaard's Thought," pp. 335–72.)

6.II: Stewart, Jon (ed.), *Kierkegaard and His German Contemporaries*, Tome II, *Theology*, Aldershot and Burlington: Ashgate 2007 (*Kierkegaard Research: Sources, Reception and Resources*, vol. 6).

(David James and Douglas Moggach, "Bruno Bauer: Biblical Narrative, Freedom and Anxiety," pp. 1–21; David D. Possen, "F.C. Baur: On the Similarity and Dissimilarity between Jesus and Socrates," pp. 23–38; Lee C. Barrett, "Bretschneider: The Tangled Legacy of Rational Supernaturalism," pp. 39–52; Jon Stewart, "Daub: Kierkgaard's Paradoxical Appropriation of a Hegelian Sentry," pp. 53–78; Stephan Bitter, "Erdmann: Appropriation and Criticism, Error and Understanding," pp. 79–100; Christoph Kronabel and Jon Stewart, "Günther: Kierkegaard's Use of an Austrian Catholic Theologian," pp. 101–15; Heiko Schulz, "Marheineke: The Volatilization of Christian Doctrine," pp. 117–42; Christine Axt-Piscalar, "Julius Müller: Parallels in the Doctrines of Sin and Freedom in Kierkegaard and Müller," pp. 143–59; Heiko Schulz, "Rosenkranz: Traces of Hegelian Psychology and Theology in Kierkegaard," pp. 161–96; Richard E. Crouter, "Schleiermacher: Revisiting Kierkegaard's Relationship to Him," pp. 197–231; George Pattison, "D.F. Strauss: Kierkegaard and Radical Demythologization," pp. 233–57.)

6.III: Stewart, Jon (ed.), *Kierkegaard and His German Contemporaries*, Tome III, *Literature and Aesthetics*, Aldershot and Burlington: Ashgate 2008 (*Kierkegaard Research: Sources, Reception and Resources*, vol. 6).

(Judith Purver, "Achim von Arnim: Kierkegaard's Encounters with a Heidelberg Hermit," pp. 1–24; Judith Purver, "Eichendorff: Kierkegaard's Reception of a German Romantic," pp. 25–49; Jon Stewart and Katalin Nun, "Goethe: A German Classic through the Filter of the Danish Golden Age," pp. 51–96; Sergia Karen Hay, "Hamann: Sharing Style and Thesis: Kierkegaard's Appropriation of Hamann's Work," pp. 97–113; Judit Bartha, "E.T.A. Hoffmann: A Source for Kierkegaard's Conceptions of Authorship, Poetic-Artistic Existence, Irony and Humor," pp. 115–37; Joachim Grage, "Hotho: A Dialogue on Romantic Irony and the Fascination with Mozart's 'Don Giovanni,'" pp. 139–53; Markus Kleinert, "Jean Paul: Apparent and Hidden Relations between Kierkegaard and Jean Paul," pp. 155–70; András Nagy, "Schiller: Kierkegaard's Use of a Paradoxical Poet," pp. 171–84; K. Brian Söderquist, "Friedrich Schlegel: On Ironic Communication, Subjectivity and Selfhood," pp. 185–233; Jon Stewart, "Solger: An Apostle of Irony Sacrificed to Hegel's System," pp. 235–69; Marcia

C. Robinson, "Tieck: Kierkegaard's 'Guadalquivir' of Open Critique and Hidden Appreciation," pp. 271–314.)

7.I: Stewart, Jon (ed.), *Kierkegaard and His Danish Contemporaries*, Tome I, *Philosophy, Politics and Social Theory*, Farnham and Burlington: Ashgate 2009 (*Kierkegaard Research: Sources, Reception and Resources*, vol. 7).

(K. Brian Söderquist, "Andreas Frederik Beck: A Good Dialectician and a Bad Reader," pp. 1–12; Andrea Scaramuccia, "Jens Finsteen Giødwad: An Amiable Friend and a Despicable Journalist," pp. 13–34; Jon Stewart, "Johan Ludvig Heiberg: Kierkegaard's Criticism of Hegel's Danish Apologist," pp. 35–76; J. Michael Tilley, "J.L.A. Kolderup-Rosenvinge: Kierkegaard on Walking Away from Politics," pp. 77–83; Julie K. Allen, "Orla Lehmann: Kierkegaard's Political Alter-Ego?" pp. 85–100; Finn Gredal Jensen, "Poul Martin Møller: Kierkegaard and the Confidant of Socrates," pp. 101–67; J. Michael Tilley, "Ditlev Gothard Monrad: Kierkegaard on Politics, the Liberal Movement, and the Danish Constitution," pp. 169–77; Jon Stewart, "Rasmus Nielsen: From the Object of 'Prodigious Concern' to a 'Windbag,'" pp. 179–213; Bjarne Troelsen, "Hans Christian Ørsted: Søren Kierkegaard and 'The Spirit in Nature,'" pp. 215–27; Carl Henrik Koch, "Frederik Christian Sibbern: 'The Lovable, Remarkable Thinker, Councilor Sibbern' and 'the Political Simple-Peter Sibbern,'" pp. 229–60; Andrew J. Burgess, "Henrich Steffens: Combining Danish Romanticism with Christian Orthodoxy," pp. 261–87; Carl Henrik Koch, "Peter Michael Stilling: As Successor? 'Undeniably a Possibility,'" pp. 289–301; Carl Henrik Koch, "Frederik Ludvig Zeuthen: 'I Struck a Light, Lit a Fire – Now It Is Burning and This 'Fire' Dr. Zeuthen Wants to Extinguish – with an 'Enema Syringe,'" pp. 303–17.)

7.II: Stewart, Jon (ed.), *Kierkegaard and His Danish Contemporaries*, Tome II, *Theology*, Farnham and Burlington: Ashgate 2009 (*Kierkegaard Research: Sources, Reception and Resources*, vol. 7).

(Carl Henrik Koch, "Adolph Peter Adler: A Stumbling-Block and an Inspiration for Kierkegaard," pp. 1–22; Christopher B. Barnett, "Nicolai Edinger Balle: The Reception of His 'Lærebog' in Denmark and in Kierkegaard's Authorship," pp. 23–39; Hugh S. Pyper, "Henrik Nicolai Clausen: The Voice of Urbane Rationalism," pp. 41–8; Gerhard Schreiber, "Magnús Eiríksson: An Opponent of Martensen and an Unwelcome Ally of Kierkegaard," pp. 49–94; Anders Holm, "Nicolai Frederik Severin Grundtvig: The Matchless Giant," pp. 95–151; Søren Jensen, "Hans Frederik Helveg: A Receptive Grundtvigian," pp. 153–88; Thorkild C. Lyby, "Peter Christian Kierkegaard: A Man with a Difficult Family Heritage," pp. 189–209; Søren Jensen, "Jacob Christian Lindberg: An Acceptable Grundtvigian," pp. 211–28; Curtis L. Thompson, "Hans Lassen Martensen: A Speculative Theologian Determining the Agenda of the Day," pp. 229–66; Christian Fink Tolstrup, "Jakob Peter Mynster: A Guiding Thread in Kierkegaard's Authorship?" pp. 267–87; Søren Jensen, "Just H.V. Paulli: Mynster's Son-in-Law," pp. 289–302; Søren Jensen, "Andreas Gottlob Rudelbach: Kierkegaard's Idea of an 'Orthodox' Theologian," pp. 303–33; Jon Stewart, "Eggert Christopher Tryde:

A Mediator of Christianity and a Representative of the Official Christendom,"
pp. 335–54.)

7,III: Stewart, Jon (ed.), *Kierkegaard and His Danish Contemporaries*, Tome III,
Literature, Drama and Aesthetics, Farnham and Burlington. Ashgate 2009
(*Kierkegaard Research: Sources, Reception and Resources*, vol. 7).

(Lone Koldtoft, "Hans Christian Andersen: Andersen Was Just an Excuse,"
pp. 1–31; Henrik Blicher, "Jens Baggesen: Kierkegaard and His Master's Voice,"
pp. 33–48; Sven Hakon Rossel, "Steen Steensen Blicher: The Melancholy Poet
of the Jutland Heath," pp. 49–65; Nathaniel Kramer, "August Bournonville:
Kierkegaard's Leap of Faith and the 'Noble Art of Terpsichore,'" pp. 67–82;
Katalin Nun, "Mathilde Fibiger: Kierkegaard and the Emancipation of Women,"
pp. 83–103; Johnny Kondrup, "Meïr Goldschmidt: The Cross-Eyed Hunchback,"
pp. 105–49; Katalin Nun, "Thomasine Gyllembourg: Kierkegaard's Appreciation
of the Everyday Stories and 'Two Ages,'" pp. 151–67; George Pattison, "Johan
Ludvig Heiberg: Kierkegaard's Use of Heiberg as a Literary Critic," pp. 169–87;
Katalin Nun, "Johanne Luise Heiberg. An Existential Actress," pp. 189–208;
Poul Houe, "Carsten Hauch: A Map of Mutual Misreadings," pp. 209–23; Jesper
Eckhardt Larsen, "Johan Nicolai Madvig: The Master of Latin in Kierkegaard's
Parnassus," pp. 225–32; Kim Ravn, "Christian Molbech: Proverbs and Punctuation:
The Inspiration of a Danish Philologist," pp. 233–45; K. Brian Söderquist, "Peder
Ludvig Møller: 'If He Had Been a Somewhat More Significant Person . . .,'"
pp. 247–55; Bjarne Troelsen, "Adam Oehlenschläger: Kierkegaard and the Treasure
Hunter of Immediacy," pp. 257–73; William Banks, "Joachim Ludvig Phister: The
Great Comic Actor of Reflection and Thoughtfulness," pp. 275–83; Nathaniel
Kramer, "Christian Winther. Kierkegaard as Lover and Reader," pp. 285–97.)

Section II: Reception

8.I: Stewart, Jon (ed.), *Kierkegaard's International Reception*, Tome I, *Northern and
Western Europe*, Farnham and Burlington: Ashgate 2009 (*Kierkegaard Research:
Sources, Reception and Resources*, vol. 8).

(Steen Tullberg, "Denmark: The Permanent Reception – 150 Years of
Reading Kierkegaard," pp. 3–120; Thor Arvid Dyrerud, "Norway: 'You Have
No Truth Onboard!' Kierkegaard's Influences on Norway," pp. 121–72; Jonna
and Lars-Erik Hjertström Lappalainen, "Sweden: Kierkegaard's Reception in
Swedish Philosophy, Theology, and Contemporary Literary Theory," pp. 173–
96; Janne Kylliäinen, "Finland: The Reception of Kierkegaard in Finland,"
pp. 197–217; Vilhjálmur Árnason, "Iceland: 'Neglect and Misunderstanding.'
The Reception of Kierkegaard in Iceland," pp. 219–34; George Pattison, "Great
Britain: From 'Prophet of the Now' to Postmodern Ironist (and after)," pp. 237–
69; Karl Verstrynge, "The Netherlands and Flanders: Kierkegaard's Reception
in the Dutch-Speaking World," pp. 271–306; Heiko Schulz, "Germany and
Austria: A Modest Head Start: The German Reception of Kierkegaard," pp. 307–
419; Jon Stewart, "France: Kierkegaard as a Forerunner of Existentialism and
Poststructuralism," pp. 421–74.)

8.II: Stewart, Jon (ed.), *Kierkegaard's International Reception*, Tome II, *Southern, Central and Eastern Europe*, Farnham and Burlington: Ashgate 2009 (*Kierkegaard Research: Sources, Reception and Resources*, vol. 8).

(Elisabete M. de Sousa, "Portugal: Discontinuity and Repetition," pp. 1–15; Dolors Perarnau Vidal and Óscar Parcero Oubiña, "Spain: The Old and New Kierkegaard Reception in Spain," pp. 17–80; Ingrid Basso, "Italy: From a Literary Curiosity to a Philosophical Comprehension," pp. 81–151; András Nagy, "Hungary: The Hungarian Patient," pp. 155–88; Roman Králik, "Slovakia: A Joint Project of Two Generations," pp. 189–204; Helena Brezinova, "The Chech Republic: Kierkegaard as a Model for the Irrationalist Movements," pp. 205–12; Antoni Szwed, "Poland: A Short Story of the Reception of Kierkegaard's Thought," pp. 213–43; Darya Loungina, "Russia: Kierkegaard's Reception through Tsarism, Communism, and Liberation," pp. 247–83; Desislava Töpfer-Stoyanova, "Bulgaria: The Long Way from Indirect Acquaintance to Original Translation," pp. 285–99; Nicolae Irina, "Romania: A Survey of Kierkegaard's Reception, Translation, and Research," pp. 301–15; Ferid Muhic, "Macedonia: The Sunny Side of Kierkegaard," pp. 317–22; Safet Bektovic, "Serbia and Montenegro: Kierkegaard as a Post-Metaphysical Philosopher," pp. 323–8.)

8.III: Stewart, Jon (ed.), *Kierkegaard's International Reception*, Tome III, *The Near East, Asia, Australia and the Americas*, Aldershot and Burlington: Ashgate 2009 (*Kierkegaard Research: Sources, Reception and Resources*, vol. 8).

(Türker Armaner, "Turkey: The Reception of Kierkegaard in Turkey," pp. 3–24; Jacob Golomb, "Israel: Kierkegaard's Reception in *Fear and Trembling* in Jerusalem," pp. 25–38; Habib C. Malik, "The Arab World: The Reception of Kierkegaard in the Arab World," pp. 39–95; Ramin Jahanbegloo, "Iran: Kierkegaard's Reception in Iran," pp. 97–9; Wang Qi, "China: The Chinese Reception of Kierkegaard," pp. 103–23; Pyo Jae-myeong, "Korea: The Korean Response to Kierkegaard," pp. 125–48; Satoshi Nakazato, "Japan: Varied Images through Western Waves," pp. 149–73; William McDonald, "Australia: An Archaeology of Silence of Kierkegaard's Philosophical Reception," pp. 175–93; Abrahim H. Khan, "Canada: Kierkegaard on the Canadian Academic Landscape," pp. 197–227; Lee C. Barrett, "The USA: From Neo-Orthodoxy to Plurality," pp. 229–68; Leticia Valadez, "Mexico: Three Generations of Kierkegaard Studies," pp. 269–84; Patricia Carina Dip, "Hispanophone South America: Kierkegaard's Latin American Reception. An Oxymoron," pp. 285–317; Alvaro Luiz Montenegro Valls, "Brazil: Forty Years Later," pp. 319–28.)

9: Stewart, Jon (ed.), *Kierkegaard and Existentialism*, Farnham and Burlington: Ashgate 2011 (*Kierkegaard Research: Sources, Reception and Resources*, vol. 9).

(Ronald M. Green and Mary Jean Green, "Simone de Beauvoir: A Founding Feminist's Appreciation of Kierkegaard," pp. 1–21; George Pattison, "Nicholas Berdyaev: Kierkegaard amongst the Artists, Mystics, and Solitary Thinkers," pp. 23–32; Peter Šajda, "Martin Buber: 'No-One Can so Refute Kierkegaard as Kierkegaard Himself,'" pp. 33–61; Leo Stan, "Albert Camus: Walled within God," pp. 63–94; Vincent McCarthy, "Martin Heidegger: Kierkegaard's

Influence Hidden and in Full View," pp. 95–125; Leo Stan, "Michel Henry: The Goodness of Living Affectivity," pp. 127–54; István Czakó, "Karl Jaspers: A Great Awakener's Way to Philosophy of Existence," pp. 155–97; Jeanette Bresson Ladegaard Knox, "Gabriel Marcel: The Silence of Truth," pp. 199–215; Nathaniel Kramer, "Jacques Maritain: Kierkegaard as 'Champion of the Singular,'" pp. 217–32; Elisabetta Basso, "Maurice Merleau-Ponty: Kierkegaard's Influence on His Work," pp. 233–61; Thomas Miles, "Friedrich Nietzsche: Rival Visions of the Best Way of Life," pp. 263–98; Claudia Welz, "Franz Rosenzweig: A Kindred Spirit in Alignment with Kierkegaard," pp. 299–321; Manuela Hackel, "Jean-Paul Sartre: Kierkegaard's Influence on His Theory of Nothingness," pp. 323–54; George Pattison, "Lev Shestov: Kierkegaard in the Ox of Phalaris," pp. 355–73; Jan E. Evans, "Miguel de Unamuvol: Kierkegaard's Spanish 'Brother,'" pp. 375–91; Alejandro Cavallazzi Sánchez and Azucena Palavicini Sánchez, "Jean Wahl: Philosophies of Existence and the Introduction of Kierkegaard in the Non-Germanic World," pp. 393–414.)

10.I: Stewart, Jon (ed.), *Kierkegaard's Influence on Theology*, Tome I, *German Protestant Theology*, Farnham and Burlington: Ashgate 2012 (*Kierkegaard Research: Sources, Reception and Resources*, vol. 10).

(Lee C. Barrett, "Karl Barth: The Dialectic of Attraction and Repulsion," pp. 1–41; Christiane Tietz, "Dietrich Bonhoeffer: Standing 'in the Tradition of Paul, Luther, Kierkegaard, in the Tradition of Genuine Christian Thinking,'" pp. 43–64; Curtis L. Thompson, "Emil Brunner: Polemically Promoting Kierkegaard's Christian Philosophy of Encounter," pp. 65–103; Heiko Schulz, "Rudolf Bultmann: Faith, Love, and Self-Understanding," pp. 105–44; Derek R. Nelson, "Gerhard Ebeling: Appreciation and Critical Appropriation of Kierkegaard," pp. 145–53; Matthias Wilke, "Emanuel Hirsch: A German Dialogue with 'Saint Søren,'" pp. 155–84; Curtis L. Thompson, "Jürgen Moltmann: Taking a Moment for Trinitarian Eschatology," pp. 185–221; David R. Law, "Franz Overbeck: Kierkegaard and the Decay of Christianity," pp. 223–40; Curtis L. Thompson, "Wolfhart Pannenberg: Kierkegaard's Anthropology Tantalizing Public Theology's Reasoning Hope," pp. 241–74; Gerhard Schreiber, "Christoph Schrempf: The 'Swabian Socrates' as Translator of Kierkegaard," pp. 275–319; Kyle A. Roberts, "Helmut Thielicke: Kierkegaard's Subjectivity for a Theology of Being," pp. 321–34; Lee C. Barrett, "Paul Tillich: An Ambivalent Appropriation," pp. 335–76; Mark Chapman, "Ernst Troeltsch: Kierkegaard, Compromise, and Dialectical Theology," pp. 377–92.)

10.II: Stewart, Jon (ed.), *Kierkegaard's Influence on Theology*, Tome II, *Anglophone and Scandinavian Protestant Theology*, Farnham and Burlington: Ashgate 2012 (*Kierkegaard Research: Sources, Reception and Resources*, vol. 10).

(Silas Morgan, "Edward John Carnell: A Skeptical Neo-Evangelical Reading," pp. 3–23; Silas Morgan, "Harvey Gallagher Cox, Jr.: An Uncomfortable Theologian Wary of Kierkegaard," pp. 25–44; Paul Martens, "Stanley J. Grenz: An Unfinished Engagement with Kierkegaard," pp. 45–62; Mariana Alessandri, "John Alexander Mackay: The *Road* Approach to Truth," pp. 63–84; David J. Gouwens, "Hugh Ross Mackintosh: Kierkegaard as 'A Precursor of Karl Barth,'" pp. 85–103; David R. Law, "John Macquarrie: Kierkegaard as a Resource for

Anthropocentric Theology," pp. 105–41; Kyle A. Roberts, "Reinhold Niebuhr: The Logic of Paradox for a Theology of Human Nature," pp. 143–55; Sarah Pike Cabral, "Gene Outka: Kierkegaard's Influence on Outka's Writing on Neighbor Love, Equality, Individuality, and the Ethical," pp. 157–71; Kyle A. Roberts, "Francis Schaeffer: How Not to Read Kierkegaard," pp. 174–87; Svein Aage Christoffersen, "Gisle Christian Johnson: The First Kierkegaardian in Theology?" pp. 191–203; Carl S. Hughes, "Anders Nygren: Influence in Reverse?" pp. 205–18.)

10.III: Stewart, Jon (ed.), *Kierkegaard's Influence on Theology*, Tome III, *Catholic and Jewish Theology*, Farnham and Burlington: Ashgate 2012 (*Kierkegaard Research: Sources, Reception and Resources*, vol. 10).

(Joseph Ballan, "Hans Urs von Balthasar: Persuasive Forms or Offensive Signs? Kierkegaard and the Problems of Theological Aesthetics," pp. 3–24; Ulli Roth, "Eugen Biser: Rediscovering 'Christology from Inside,'" pp. 25–43; Peter Šajda, "Romano Guardini: Between Actualistic Personalism, Qualitative Dialectic, and Kinetic Logic," pp. 45–74; David R. Law, "Friedrich von Hügel: Kierkegaard as Non-Mystical Ascetic and One-Sided Defender of Transcendence," pp. 75–96; Christopher B. Barnett, "Henri de Lubac: Locating Kierkegaard Amid the 'Drama' of Nietzschean Humanism," pp. 97–110; Erik M. Hansen, "Thomas Merton: Kierkegaard, Merton, and Authenticity," pp. 111–30; Christopher B. Barnett, "Erich Przywara: Catholicism's Great Expositor of the 'Mystery' of Kierkegaard," pp. 131–51; Jack Mulder, Jr., "Abraham Joshua Heschel: Heschel's Use of Kierkegaard as Cohort in Depth Theology," pp. 155–70; Tamar Aylat-Yaguri, "Abraham Isaac Kook: Faith of Awe and Love," pp. 171–88; David D. Possen, "J.B. Soloveitchik: Between Neo-Kantianism and Kierkegaardian Existentialism," pp. 189–210.)

11.I: Stewart, Jon (ed.), *Kierkegaard's Influence on Philosophy*, Tome I, *German and Scandinavian Philosophy*, Farnham and Burlington: Ashgate 2012 (*Kierkegaard Research: Sources, Reception and Resources*, vol. 11).

(Peter Šajda, "Theodor W. Adorno: Tracing the Trajectory of Kierkegaard's Unintended Triumphs and Defeats," pp. 3–48; Joseph Westfall, "Walter Benjamin: Appropriating the Kierkegaardian Aesthetic," pp. 49–65; Alina Vaisfeld, "Ernst Bloch: The Thinker of Utopia's Reading of Kierkegaard," pp. 67–83; Elisabetta Basso, "Wilhelm Dilthey: Kierkegaard's Influence on Dilthey's Work," pp. 85–104; Dustin Feddon and Patricia Stanley, "Ferdinand Ebner: Ebner's *Neuer Mann*," pp. 105–21; Luiz Rohden, "Hans-Georg Gadamer: Kierkegaardian Traits in Gadamer's Philosophical Hermeneutics," pp. 123–45; Jamie Turnbull, "Edmund Husserl: Naturalism, Subjectivity, Eternity," pp. 147–62; Noreen Khawaja, "Karl Löwith: In Search of a Singular Man," pp. 163–86; Stefan Egenberger, "Michael Theunissen: Fortune and Misfortune of Temporality," pp. 187–207; Thomas Miles, "Ludwig Wittgenstein: Kierkegaard's Influence on the Origin of Analytic Philosophy," pp. 209–41; Carl Henrik Koch, "Hans Brøchner: Professor of Philosophy, Antagonist – and a Loving and Admiring Relative," pp. 245–65; Carl Henrik Koch, "Harald Høffding: The Respectful Critic," pp. 267–88; Roe Fremstedal, "Peter Wessel Zapffe: Kierkegaard as a Forerunner of Pessimistic Existentialism," pp. 289–302.)

11.II: Stewart, Jon (ed.), *Kierkegaard's Influence on Philosophy*, Tome II, *Francophone Philosophy*, Farnham and Burlington: Ashgate 2012 (*Kierkegaard Research: Sources, Reception and Resources*, vol. 11).

(Kevin Newmark, "Sylviane Agacinski: Reading Kierkegaard to Keep Intact the Secret," pp. 1–21; Joseph Westfall, "Roland Barthes: Style, Language, Silence," pp. 23–42; Laura Llevadot Pascual, "Georges Bataille: Kierkegaard and the Claim for the Sacred," pp. 43–61; Daniel Greenspan, "Maurice Blanchot: Spaces of Literature/Spaces of Religion," pp. 63–81; José Miranda Justo, "Gilles Deleuze: Kierkegaard's Presence in His Writings," pp. 83–110; Marius Timmann Mjaaland, "Jacques Derrida: Faithful Heretics," pp. 111–38; Sarah Pike Cabral, "Jacques Ellul: Kierkegaard's Profound and Seldom Acknowledged Influence on Ellul's Writing," pp. 139–56; Nicolae Irina, "Pierre Hadot: Philosophy as a Way of Life: Hadot and Kierkegaard's Socrates," pp. 157–72; Jeffrey Hanson, "Emmanuel Levinas: An Ambivalent but Decisive Reception," pp. 173–205; Leo Stan, "Jean-Luc Marion: The Paradoxical Givenness of Love," pp. 207–31; Joel D.S. Rasmussen, "Paul Ricoeur: On Kierkegaard, the Limits of Philosophy, and the Consolation of Hope," pp. 233–55.)

11.III: Stewart, Jon (ed.), *Kierkegaard's Influence on Philosophy*, Tome III, *Anglophone Philosophy*, Farnham and Burlington: Ashgate 2012 (*Kierkegaard Research: Sources, Reception and Resources*, vol. 11).

(Ronald E. Hustwit, Sr., "O.K. Bouwsma: Kierkegaard, Wittgenstein, and Conceptual Clarity," pp. 1–10; Joseph Westfall, "Stanley Cavell: The Sublimity of the Pedestrian," pp. 11–28; J.D. Mininger, "Paul de Man: The Unwritten Chapter," pp. 29–47; Joseph Westfall, "Hubert Dreyfus: Seeking the Self in a Nihilistic Age," pp. 49–69; Timothy J. Madigan, "Paul Edwards: A Rationalist Critic of Kierkegaard's Theory of Truth," pp. 71–85; J. Michael Tilley, "William James: Living Forward and the Development of Radical Empiricism," pp. 87–97; Andrew D. Spear, "Walter Kaufmann: 'That Authoritarian,' 'That Individual,'" pp. 99–116; Anthony Rudd, "Alasdair MacIntyre: A Continuing Conversation," pp. 117–34; Paul Martens, "Iris Murdoch: Kierkegaard as Existentialist, Romantic, Hegelian, and Problematically Religious," pp. 135–56; Jamie Turnbull, "D.Z. Phillips: Grammar and the Reality of God," pp. 157–76; J. Aaron Simmons, "Richard Rorty: Kierkegaard in the Context of Neo-Pragmatism," pp. 177–201; Vincent Lloyd, "Gillian Rose: Making Kierkegaard Difficult Again," pp. 203–17; Abrahim H. Khan, "Charles Taylor: Taylor's Affinity to Kierkegaard," pp. 219–29.)

12.I: Stewart, Jon (ed.), *Kierkegaard's Influence on Literature, Criticism and Art*, Tome I, *The Germanophone World*, Farnham and Burlington: Ashgate 2013 (*Kierkegaard Research: Sources, Reception and Resources*, vol. 12).

(Alina Vaisfeld, "Alfred Andersch: Reading Søren Kierkegaard as Flight to Freedom," pp. 1–13; Stefan Egenberger, "Thomas Bernhard: A Grotesque Sickness unto Death," pp. 15–29; Steen Tullberg, "Hermann Broch: 'Nennen's mir an Bessern,'" pp. 31–41; Pierre Bühler, "Friedrich Dürrenmatt: A Swiss Author Reading and Using Kierkegaard," pp. 43–59; Julie K. Allen, "Theodor Fontane: A Probable Pioneer in German Kierkegaard Reception," pp. 61–77; Sophie Wennerscheid, "Max Frisch: Literary Transformations of Identity,"

pp. 79–90; Markus Kleinert, "Theodor Haecker: The Mobilization of a Total Author," pp. 91–114; Nicolae Irina, "Franz Kafka: Reading Kierkegaard," pp. 115–40; Steen Tullberg, "Rudolf Kassner: A Physiognomical Appropriation," pp. 141–56; Joachim Grage, "Karl Kraus: 'The Miracle of Unison' – Criticism of the Press and Experiences of Isolation," pp. 157–69; Elisabete M. de Sousa and Ingrid Basso, "Thomas Mann: Demons and Daemons," pp. 171–93; David D. Possen, "Robert Musil: Kierkegaardian Themes in *The Man Without Qualities*," pp. 195–212; Leonardo F. Lisi, "Rainer Maria Rilke: Unsatisfied Love and the Poetry of Living," pp. 213–35; Sophie Wennerscheid, "Martin Walser: The (Un-) Certainty of Reading," pp. 237–47.)

12.II: Stewart, Jon (ed.), *Kierkegaard's Influence on Literature, Criticism and Art*, Tome II, *Denmark*, Farnham and Burlington: Ashgate 2013 (*Kierkegaard Research: Sources, Reception and Resources*, vol. 12).

(Søren Landkildehus, "Karen Blixen: Kierkegaard, Isak Dinesen, and the Twisted Images of Divinity and Humanity," pp. 1–16; Julie K. Allen, "Georg Brandes: Kierkegaard's Most Influential Mis-Representative," pp. 17–41; Esben Lindemann, "Ernesto Dalgas: Kierkegaard on *The Path of Suffering*," pp. 43–64; Esben Lindemann, "Martin A. Hansen: Kierkegaard in Hansen's Thinking and Poetical Work," pp. 65–99; William Banks, "Jens Peter Jacobsen: Denmark's Greatest Atheist," pp. 101–19; Poul Houe, "Harald Kidde: 'A Widely Traveled Stay-at-Home,'" pp. 121–35; Peter Tudvad, "Henrik Pontoppidan: Inspiration and Hesitation," pp. 137–65; Steen Tullberg, "Villy Sørensen: A Critical Initiation," pp. 167–81.)

12.III: Stewart, Jon (ed.), *Kierkegaard's Influence on Literature, Criticism and Art*, Tome III, *Sweden and Norway*, Farnham and Burlington: Ashgate 2013 (*Kierkegaard Research: Sources, Reception and Resources*, vol. 12).

(Hans-Erik Johannesson, "Lars Ahlin: Kierkegaard's Influence – an Ambiguous Matter," pp. 3–13; Camilla Brudin Borg, "Victoria Benedictsson: A Female Perspective on Ethics," pp. 15–25; Camilla Brudin Borg, "Lars Gyllensten: Inventor of Modern Stages of Life," pp. 27–51; Elise Iuul, "Selma Lagerlöf: 'More Clever than Wise,'" pp. 53–64; Ingrid Basso, "August Strindberg: 'Along with Kierkegaard in a Dance of Death,'" pp. 65–87; Jan Holmgaard, "Carl-Henning Wijkmark: Paradoxical Forms and an Interpretation of Kierkegaard and *Dacapo*," pp. 89–106; Esben Lindemann, "Bjørnstjerne Bjørnson: Kierkegaard's Positive Influence on Bjørnson in His Youth and Adulthood," pp. 109–44; Eivind Tjønneland, "Henrik Ibsen: The Conflict between the Aesthetic and the Ethical," pp. 145–76; Hans Herlof Grelland, "Edvard Munch: The Painter of *The Scream* and His Relation to Kierkegaard," pp. 177–93.)

12.IV: Stewart, Jon (ed.), *Kierkegaard's Influence on Literature, Criticism and Art*, Tome IV, *The Anglophone World*, Farnham and Burlington: Ashgate 2013 (*Kierkegaard Research: Sources, Reception and Resources*, vol. 12).

(Leonardo F. Lisi, "W.H. Auden: Art and Christianity in an Age of Anxiety," pp. 1–25; Nigel Hatton, "James Baldwin: 'Poetic Experimentators' in a Chaotic World," pp. 27–39; Diego Giordano, "Samuel Barber: Kierkegaard, from a Musical Point of View," pp. 41–9; Elisabete M. de Sousa, "Harold Bloom: Critics, Bards, and Prophets," pp. 51–79; Daniel Greenspan, "Don DeLillo: Kierkegaard

and the Grave in the Air," pp. 81–99; Nigel Hatton, "Louise Erdrich: Existence with an 'Edge of Irony,'" pp. 101–7; Bartholomew Ryan, "James Joyce: Negation, Kierkeyaard, Wake, and Repetition," pp. 109–31; Natalja Vorobyova Jørgensen, "David Lodge: A Therapy for the Self," pp. 133–56; Christopher B. Barnett, "Flannery O'Connor: Reading Kierkegaard in the Light of Thomas Aquinas," pp. 157–74; Joseph Ballan, "Walker Percy: Literary Extrapolations from Kierkegaard," pp. 175–91; Paul Martens, "George Steiner: Playing Kierkegaard's Theological-Philosophic-Psychological Sports," pp. 193–212; Nigel Hatton, "William Styron: Styron and the Assault of Kierkegaardian Dread," pp. 213–27.)

12.V: Stewart, Jon (ed.), *Kierkegaard's Influence on Literature, Criticism and Art*, Tome V, *The Romance Languages, Central and Eastern Europe*, Farnham and Burlington: Ashgate 2013 (*Kierkegaard Research: Sources, Reception and Resources*, vol. 12).

(Leo Stan, "Max Blecher: The Bizarre Adventure of Suffering," pp. 3–20; Eduardo Fernández Villar, "Jorge Luis Borges: The Fear without Trembling," pp. 21–32; María J. Binetti, "Leonardo L. Castellani: Between Suero Kirkegord and Thomas Aquinas," pp. 33–43; Patricia C. Dip, "Carlos Fuentes: 'Poor Mexico, So Far Away from God and So Close to the United States,'" pp. 45–55; Elisabete M. de Sousa and António M. Feijó, "Fernando Pessoa: Poets and Philosophers," pp. 57–76; María J. Binetti, "Ernesto Sábato: The Darker Side of Kierkegaardian Existence," pp. 77–86; Carmen Revilla and Laura Llevadot, "María Zambrano: Kierkegaard and the Criticism of Modern Rationalism," pp. 87–101; Tatiana Shchyttsova, "Mikhail Bakhtin: Direct and Indirect Reception of Kierkegaard in Works of the Russian Thinker," pp. 105–19; András Nagy, "Péter Esterházy: Semi-Serious," pp. 121–38; Wojciech Kaftanski, "Witold Gombrowicz: The Struggle for the Authentic Self," pp. 139–56; Nigel Hatton, "Ivan Klíma: 'To Save My Inner World,'" pp. 157–68; András Nagy, "Péter Nádas: Books and Memories," pp. 169–87; Sharon Krishek, "Pinhas Sadeh: The Poet as 'the Single Individual,'" pp. 189–97.)

13: Stewart, Jon (ed.), *Kierkegaard's Influence on the Social Sciences*, Farnham and Burlington: Ashgate 2011 (*Kierkegaard Research: Sources, Reception and Resources*, vol. 13).

(Stuart Kendall, "Jean Baudrillard: The Seduction of Jean Baudrillard," pp. 1–16; Anthony Furtak, "Ernest Becker: A Kirkegaardian Theorist of Death and Human Nature," pp. 17–28; Elisabetta Basso, "Ludwig Binswanger: Kierkegaard's Influence on Binswanger's Work," pp. 29–54; Leo Stan, "Mircea Eliade: On Religion, Cosmos, and Agony," pp. 55–80; Edward F. Mooney, "Erik Erikson: Artist of Moral Development," pp. 81–94; John Lippitt, "Erich Fromm: The Integrity of the Self and the Practice of Love," pp. 95–120; Søren Landkildehus, "Anthony Giddens: Kierkegaard and the Risk of Existence," pp. 121–36; Diego Giordano, "René Girard: From Mimetic Desire to Anonymous Masses," pp. 137–50; Anthony Rudd, "Carl Jung: A Missed Connection," pp. 151–77; Edward F. Mooney, "Julia Kristeva: Tales of Horror and Love," pp. 177–94; J.D. Miniger, "Jacques Lacan: Kierkegaard as a Freudian Questioner of the Soul avant la lettre," pp. 195–216; Poul Houe, "Rollo May: Existential Psychology," pp. 217–38; Simon D. Podmore, "Carl R. Rogers: 'To Be that Self Which One Truly Is,'" pp. 239–58; Dustin Feddon, "Max Weber: Weber's

Existential Choice," pp. 259–72; Almut Furchert, "Irvin D. Yalom: The 'Throw-ins' of Psychotherapy," pp. 273–96; Leo Stan, "Slavoj Zizek: Mirroring the Absent God," pp. 297–321.)

14: Stewart, Jon (ed.), *Kierkegaard's Influence on Social-Political Thought*, Farnham and Burlington: Ashgate 2011 (*Kierkegaard Research: Sources, Reception and Resources*, vol. 14).

(Leif Bork Hansen, "Giorgio Agamben: State of Exception," pp. 1–28; Marcio Gimenes de Paula: "Hannah Arendt: Religion, Politics, and the Influence of Kierkegaard," pp. 29–40; Michael Burns, "Alain Badiou: Thinking the Subject after the Death of God," pp. 41–51; Gerhard Tonhauser, "Judith Butler: Kierkegaard as Her Early Teacher in Rhetoric and Parody," pp. 53–72; J. Michael Tilley, "Jürgen Habermas: Social Selfhood, Religion, and Kierkegaard," pp. 73–87; Nigel Hatton, "Martin Luther King: Kierkegaard's *Works of Love*, King's *Strength to Love*," pp. 89–106; András Nagy, "Georg Lukács: From a Tragic Love Story to a Tragic Life Story," pp. 107–35; J. Michael Tilley, "Herbert Marcuse: Social Critique, Haecker, and Kierkegaardian Individualism," pp. 137–46; Robert Puchniak, "José Ortega y Gasset: Meditations on 'Provincial Romanticism,'" pp. 147–57; Michael Burns, "Jean-Paul Sartre: Between Kierkegaard and Marx," pp. 159–75; Bartholomew Ryan, "Carl Schmitt: Zones of Exception and Appropriation," pp. 177–207; Peter Brickey LeQuire, "Eric Voegelin: Politics, History, and the Anxiety of Existence," pp. 209–30; Marcia Robinson, "Cornel West: Kierkegaard and the Construction of a 'Blues Philosophy,'" pp. 231–56; Jennifer Veninga, "Richard Wright: Kierkegaard's Influence as Existentialist Outsider," pp. 257–73.)

Section III: Resources

15.I: Emmanuel, Steven M., Jon Stewart, and William McDonald (eds.), *Kierkegaard's Concepts*, Tome I, *Absolute to Church*, Farnham and Burlington: Ashgate 2013 (*Kierkegaard Research: Sources, Reception and Resources*, vol. 15).

(Steven M. Emmanuel, "Absolute," pp. 1–4; Sean Turchin, "Absurd," pp. 5–9; Steven M. Emmanuel, "Actuality/Ideality," pp. 11–16; Guadalupe Pardi, "Admiration," pp. 17–21; William McDonald, "Aesthetic/Aesthetics," pp. 23–9; J.D. Mininger, "Allegory," pp. 31–5; Jacobo Zabalo, "Ambiguity," pp. 37–43; Joseph Westfall, "Anonymity," pp. 45–51; Sean Anthony Turchin, "Anthropology," pp. 53–8; William McDonald, "Anxiety," pp. 59–64; Henrike Fürstenberg, "Aphorisms," pp. 65–70; Curtis L. Thompson, "Apologetics," pp. 71–5; Steven M. Emmanuel, "Apostle," pp. 77–82; Sean Anthony Turchin, "Appropriation," pp. 83–7; Sean Anthony Turchin, "Approximation," pp. 89–93; Diego Giordano, "Archimedean Point," pp. 95–7; Nathaniel Kramer, "Art," pp. 99–104; David Coe, "Asceticism," pp. 105–8; Lee C. Barrett, "Atonement/ Reconciliation," pp. 109–15; Sean Anthony Turchin, "Authority," pp. 117–22; Joseph Westfall, "Authorship," pp. 123–8; David Coe, "Baptism," pp. 129–32; Sean Anthony Turchin, "Beginning," pp. 133–6; Claudine Davidshofer, "Being/ Becoming," pp. 137–43; Robert B. Puchniak, "Calling," pp. 145–48; Gerhard

Thonhauser, "Care/Concern," pp. 149–55; Claudine Davidshofer, "Category," pp. 157–60; Christopher B. Barnett, "Catholicism," pp. 161–5; Shannon M. Nason, "Cause/Effect," pp. 167–73; Sara Carvalhais, "Certainty," pp. 175–80; Peter Fenves, "Chatter," pp. 181–3; Esben Lindemann, "Childhood," pp. 185–91; Gerhard Thonhauser, "Choice," pp. 193–9; Leo Stan, "Christ," pp. 201–6; Michael Tilley, "Christendom," pp. 207–10; Michael Tilley, "Church," pp. 211–14.)

15.II: Emmanuel, Steven M., Jon Stewart, and William McDonald (eds.), *Kierkegaard's Concepts*, Tome II, *Classicism to Enthusiasm*, Farnham and Burlington: Ashgate 2014 (*Kierkegaard Research: Sources, Reception and Resources*, vol. 15).

(Nassim Bravo, "Classicism," pp. 1–3; Oscar Parcero Oubinha, "Comic/ Comedy," pp. 5–10; Hjördis Becker-Lindenthal, "Common Man," pp. 11–16; Jamie Turnbull, "Communication/Indirect Communication," pp. 17–23; David Coe, "Communion," pp. 25–8; Stine Zink Kaasgaard, "Concept," pp. 29–34; Steven M. Emmanuel, "Concrete/Abstract," pp. 35–42; David Coe, "Confession," pp. 43–6; Curtis L. Thompson, "Conscience," pp. 47–53; Patrick Stokes, "Consciousness," pp. 55–9; Leo Stan, "Contemporaneity," pp. 61–5; Gabriel Ferreira da Silva, "Contingency/Possibility," pp. 67–71; Jakub Marek, "Contradiction," pp. 73–80; J. Michael Tilley, "Corrective," pp. 81–6; Lauren Greenspan, "Courage," pp. 87–92; Curtis L. Thompson, "Creation," pp. 93–9; Charlie Cahill, "Crisis," pp. 101–5; Leo Stan, "Crowd/ Public," pp. 107–14; Gabriel Guedes Rossatti, "Culture/Education," pp. 115– 20; Curtis L. Thompson, "Dance," pp. 121–8; Adam Buben, "Death," pp. 129– 34; Narve Strand, "Decision/Resolve," pp. 135–7; David Lappano, "Defiance," pp. 139–46; William McDonald, "Demonic," pp. 147–52; Nathaniel Kramer, "Desire," pp. 153–8; William McDonald, "Despair," pp. 159–64; Alejandro Cavallazzi Sánchez, "Dialectic," pp. 165–9; Irina Kruchinina, "Dialogue," pp. 171–7; Lee C. Barrett, "Dogma/Doctrine," pp. 179–85; Roe Fremstedal, "Double Movement," pp. 187–93; Wojciech Kaftański, "Double-Reflection," pp. 195–8; Anne Louise Nielsen, "Dreams," pp. 199–205; Azucena Palavicini Sánchez, "Duty," pp. 207–11; Adam Buben, "Dying to/Renunciation," pp. 213–18; John Davenport, "Earnestness," pp. 219–27; Kyle A. Roberts, "Edifying Discourse/Deliberation/Sermon," pp. 229–34; Carson Webb, "Enthusiasm," pp. 235–41.)

15.III: Emmanuel, Steven M., Jon Stewart, and William McDonald (eds.), *Kierkegaard's Concepts*, Tome III, *Envy to Incognito*, Farnham and Burlington: Ashgate 2014 (*Kierkegaard Research: Sources, Reception and Resources*, vol. 15).

(Janne Kylliäinen, "Envy," pp. 1–8; Nassim Bravo Jordán, "Epic," pp. 9–12; David R. Law, "Epigram," pp. 13–19; Azucena Palavicini Sánchez, "Ethics," pp. 21–7; Azucena Palavicini Sánchez and William McDonald, "Evil," pp. 29–35; Geoffrey Dargan, "Exception/Universal," pp. 37–43; Min-Ho Lee, "Existence/ Existential," pp. 45–51; Jakub Marek, "Experience," pp. 53–9; Nathaniel Kramer, "Fairytale," pp. 61–5; William McDonald, "Faith," pp. 67–72; Erik M. Hanson, "Finitude/Infinity," pp. 73–9; John Lippitt, "Forgiveness," pp. 81–7; Diego Giordano, "Freedom," pp. 89–92; Steven M. Emmanuel, "Genius," pp. 93–8; Paul Martens and Daniel Marrs, "God," pp. 99–105; Azucena Palavicini Sánchez,

"Good," pp. 107–11; Jack Mulder, Jr., "Governance/Providence," pp. 113–18; Derek R. Nelson, "Grace," pp. 119–23; Corey Benjamin Tutewiler, "Gratitude," pp. 125–30; Erik M. Hanson, "Guilt," pp. 131–5; Benjamin Miguel Olivares Bøgeskov, "Happiness," pp. 137–43; Sean Anthony Turchin, "Hero," pp. 145–9; Sean Anthony Turchin, "History," pp. 151–6; Leo Stan, "Holy Spirit," pp. 157–61; William McDonald, "Hope," pp. 163–8; Robert B. Puchniak, "Humility," pp. 169–74; Alejandro González, "Humor," pp. 175–81; Thomas Martin Fauth Hansen, "Hypocrisy," pp. 183–7; Claudine Davidshofer, "Identity/Difference," pp. 189–93; Frances Maughan-Brown, "Imagination," pp. 195–202; Leo Stan, "Imitation," pp. 203–7; Leo Stan, "Immanence/Transcendence," pp. 209–14; Zizhen Liu, "Immediacy/Reflection," pp. 215–22; Lee C. Barrett, "Immortality," pp. 223–9; Martijn Boven, "Incognito," pp. 231–6.)

15.IV: Emmanuel, Steven M., Jon Stewart, and William McDonald (eds.), *Kierkegaard's Concepts*, Tome IV, *Individual to Novel*, Farnham and Burlington: Ashgate 2014 (*Kierkegaard Research: Sources, Reception and Resources*, vol. 15).

(Lydia B. Amir, "Individual," pp. 1–7; Philipp Schwab, "Inner/Outer," pp. 9–15; Noreen Khawaja, "Intensity/Extensity," pp. 17–24; K. Brian Soderquist, "The Interesting," pp. 25–31; Christian Fink Tolstrup, "Inwardness/ Inward Deepening," pp. 33–8; Nassim Bravo Jordán, "Irony," pp. 39–44; Sean Anthony Turchin, "Irrational," pp. 45–8; Benjamin Miguel Olivares Bøgeskov, "Joy," pp. 49–54; Tamar Aylat-Yaguri, "Judaism," pp. 55–8; Steven Shakespeare, "Language," pp. 59–65; David Coe, "Law," pp. 67–70; Gerhard Schreiber, "Leap," pp. 71–8; Matthew Brake, "Legends," pp. 79–83; Leo Stan, "Leveling," pp. 85–8; Lee C. Barrett, "Life-View," pp. 89–95; Gabriel Ferreira da Silva, "Logic," pp. 97–103; William McDonald, "Love," pp. 105–10; Nassim Bravo Jordán, "Lyric," pp. 111–13; Deidre Nicole Green, "Marriage," pp. 115–22; Jack Mulder, Jr., "Martyrdom/Persecution," pp. 123–9; Jamie Turnbull, "Mediation/ Sublation," pp. 131–6; Steven M. Emmanuel, "Melancholy," pp. 137–41; Frances Maughan-Brown, "Metaphor," pp. 143–9; Corey Benjamin Tutewiler, "Metaphysics," pp. 151–7; Diego Giordano, "Middle Ages," pp. 159–61; Heiko Schulz, "Miracles," pp. 163–8; Diego Giordano, "Mohammedanism," pp. 169–71; William McDonald, "Moment," pp. 173–9; Curtis L. Thompson, "Monasticism," pp. 181–7; Gabriel Guedes Rossatti, "Money," pp. 189–95; Sara Carvalhais de Oliveira, "Mood/Emotion/Feeling," pp. 197–203; Shannon M. Nason, "Movement, Motion," pp. 205–12; William McDonald, "Music," pp. 213–21; Diego Giordano and William McDonald, "Myth," pp. 223–6; Thomas Posch, "Nature/Natural Science," pp. 227–30; Gabriel Ferreira da Silva, "Necessity," pp. 231–5; Archie Graham, "Negation," pp. 237–43; Gabriel Guedes Rossatti, "Novel," pp. 245–52.)

15.V: Emmanuel, Steven M., Jon Stewart, and William McDonald (eds.), *Kierkegaard's Concepts*, Tome V, *Objectivity to Sacrifice*, Farnham and Burlington: Ashgate 2015 (*Kierkegaard Research: Sources, Reception and Resources*, vol. 15).

(Jamie Turnbull, "Objectivity/Subjectivity," pp. 1–6; Sean Anthony Turchin, "Offense," pp. 7–13; Lee C. Barrett, "Orthodoxy/Orthodox," pp. 15–22; Marcia Morgan, "Otherness/Alterity/the Other," pp. 23–7; Avron Kulak, "Paganism," pp. 29–34; Curtis L. Thompson, "Pantheism," pp. 35–42; Sean Anthony Turchin,

"Paradox," pp. 43–8; Mads Sohl Jessen, "Parody/Satire," pp. 49–54; Jacobo Zabalo, "Passion/Pathos," pp. 55–62; J. Michael Tilley, "Pastor," pp. 63–6; Corey Benjamin Tutewiler, "Patience," pp. 67–73; Wolter Hartog, "Personality," pp. 75–82; William McDonald, "Philosophy/Philosophers," pp. 83–93; Laura Liva and K. Brian Söderquist, "Poetry," pp. 95–100; Leo Stan, "Politics," pp. 101–5; Derek R. Nelson, "Prayer," pp. 107–11; Gabriel Guedes Rossatti, "Present Age," pp. 113–20; David Lappano, "Press/Journalism," pp. 121–8; Daniel Dion, "Pride," pp. 129–34; Maxime Valcourt Blouin, "Primitivity," pp. 135–40; Matthew Brake, "Progress," pp. 141–4; Curtis L. Thompson, "Protestantism/Reformation," pp. 145–51; Joseph Westfall, "Pseudonymity," pp. 153–8; Martijn Boven, "Psychological Experiment," pp. 159–65; Nathaniel Kramer, "Psychology," pp. 167–71; Steven M. Emmanuel, "Punctuation," pp. 173–7; Leo Stan, "Qualitative Difference," pp. 179–83; Joseph Ballan, "Race," pp. 185–90; Jamie Turnbull, "Reason," pp. 191–6; Nathaniel Kramer, "Recollection," pp. 197–203; Wojciech Kaftański, "Redoubling/Reduplication," pp. 205–11; Lee C. Barrett, "Religious/Religiousness," pp. 213–20; Sean Anthony Turchin, "Repentance," pp. 221–4; Ryan Kemp, "Repetition," pp. 225–30; Geoffrey Dargan, "Resignation," pp. 231–7; Sean Anthony Turchin, "Revelation," pp. 239–44; Gabriel Guedes Rossatti, "Revolution," pp. 245–53; Gerhard Thonhauser, "Rhetoric," pp. 255–62; Roe Fremstedal, "Rigorism," pp. 263–8; Nassim Bravo Jordán, "Romanticism," pp. 269–72; Deidre Nicole Green, "Sacrifice," pp. 273–80.)

15.VI: Emmanuel, Steven M., Jon Stewart, and William McDonald (eds.), *Kierkegaard's Concepts*, Tome VI, *Salvation to Writing*, Farnham and Burlington: Ashgate 2015 (*Kierkegaard Research: Sources, Reception and Resources*, vol. 15).

(Roe Fremstedal and Timothy P. Jackson, "Salvation/ Eternal Happiness," pp. 1–7; Kyle A. Roberts, "Scriptures," pp. 9–15; Camilla Sløk, "Seduction," pp. 17–22; Pieter Vos, "Self," pp. 23–8; Claudia Welz, "Self-Deception," pp. 29–34; Jakub Marek, "Sickness," pp. 35–40; Alejandro González Contreras, "Silence," pp. 41–4; Leo Stan, "Sin," pp. 45–52; Matthew Brake, "Skepticism/Doubt," pp. 53–7; Jamie Aroosi, "Society," pp. 59–63; Curtis L. Thompson, "Speculation/ Science/Scholarship," pp. 65–73; Marcia Morgan, "Spirit," pp. 75–81; Gabriel Guedes Rossatti, "Spiritlessness," pp. 83–8; Lydia Amir, "Stages," pp. 89–96; Leo Stan, "State," pp. 97–100; Will Williams, "Story-Telling," pp. 101–7; Christian Fink Tolstrup, "Striving," pp. 109–14; Sean Anthony Turchin, "Suffering," pp. 115–19; Robert B. Puchniak, "Suicide," pp. 121–6; Victoria Davies, "Sympathy/Empathy," pp. 127–33; Matthew Brake, "Teacher," pp. 135–40; Thomas P. Miles, "Teleological Suspension of the Ethical," pp. 141–6; Sean Anthony Turchin, "Temptation," pp. 147–50; Mads Sohl Jessen, "Theater/Drama," pp. 151–6; Gabriel Guedes Rossatti, "Thoughtlessness," pp. 157–62; William McDonald, "Time/Temporality/ Eternity," pp. 163–8; Leonardo F. Lisi, "Tragic/Tragedy," pp. 169–75; Daniel Marrs, "Transfiguration," pp. 177–84; Gerhard Schreiber, "Transition," pp. 185–91; Geoffrey Dargan, "Trial, Test, Tribulation," pp. 193–201; Jamie Turnbull, "Truth," pp. 203–7; Matthew Brake and William McDonald, "Understanding/ Comprehension," pp. 209–14; Mads Sohl Jessen, "Vaudeville/Farce," pp. 215–19;

Gabriel Guedes Rossatti, "Vortex," pp. 221–7; Narve Strand, "Voting," pp. 229–33; Narve Strand, "Will," pp. 235–41; Ulrich Lincoln, "Witness," pp. 243–9; Céline Léon, "Women," pp. 251–8; Robert Wyllie, "Wonder," pp. 259–65; David Coe, "Worldliness/Secularism," pp. 267–70; Thomas J. Millay, "Writing," pp. 271–7.)

16.I: Nun, Katalin and Jon Stewart (eds.), *Kierkegaard's Literary Figures and Motifs*, Tome I, *Agamemnon to Guadalquivir*, Farnham and Burlington: Ashgate 2014 (*Kierkegaard Research: Sources, Reception and Resources*, vol. 16).

(Laura Liva, "Agamemnon: From Ancient Tragic Hero to Modern Ethical Archetype," pp. 1–13; Nathaniel Kramer, "Agnes and the Merman: Abraham as Monster," pp. 15–28; Jennifer Veninga, "Aladdin: The Audacity of Wildest Wishes," pp. 31–40; Frances Maughan-Brown, "Amor: God of Love – Psyche's Seducer," pp. 41–8; Shoni Rancher, "Antigone: The Tragic Art of *Either/Or*," pp. 49–64; Filipa Afonso, "Ariadne: Kierkegaard's View on Women, Life, and Remorse," pp. 65–9; Susana Janic, "Marie Beaumarchais: Kierkegaard's Account of Feminine Sorrow," pp. 71–8; Ian W. Panth, "Bluebeard: Demoniac or Tragic Hero?" pp. 79–87; Timothy Stock, "Captain Scipio: The Recollection of Phister's Portrayal as the Comic *par Excellence*," pp. 89–95; Filipa Afonso, "Cerberus: Deceiving a Watchdog and Relying on God," pp. 97–101; Antonella Fimiani, "Clavigo: A Little Tale about the Sense of Guilt," pp. 103–11; Wolter Hartog, "Coach Horn: Kierkegaard's Ambivalent Valedictory to a Disappearing Instrument," pp. 113–19; Ana Pinto Leite, "Desdemona: The Ill-Starred Heroine of Indirect Communication," pp. 121–30; Harald Steffes, "Diotima: Teacher of Socrates and Kierkegaard's Advocate for the Mythical," pp. 131–40; Jacobo Zabalo, "Don Juan (Don Giovanni): Seduction and Its Absolute Medium in Music," pp. 141–57; Christopher B. Barnett, "Don Quixote: Kierkegaard and the Relation between Knight-Errant and Truth-Witness," pp. 159–69; Sara Ellen Eckerson, "Donna Elvira: The Colossal Feminine Character, from *donna abbandonata* to the Embodiment of Modern Sorrow," pp. 171–86; Will Williams, "Elves, Trolls, and Nisses: The Relevance of Supernatural Creatures to Aestheticism, Philosophical Rationalism, and the Christian Faith," pp. 187–99; Julie K. Allen, "Erasmus Montanus: The Tragi-Comic Victim of the Crowd," pp. 201–8; Leonardo F. Lisi, "Faust: The Seduction of Doubt," pp. 209–28; Henrike Fürstenberg, "The Fenris Wolf: Unreal Fetters and Real Forces in Søren Kierkegaard's Authorship," pp. 229–42; Sara Ellen Eckerson, "Figaro: The Character and the Opera He Represents," pp. 243–9; Laura Liva, "Furies: The Phenomenal Representation of Guilt," pp. 251–8; Hjördis Becker-Lindenthal, "Gadfly: Kierkegaard's Relation to Socrates," pp. 259–77; Eric Ziolkowski, "Guadalquivir: Kierkegaard's Subterranean Fluvial Pseudonymity," pp. 279–96.)

16.II: Nun, Katalin and Jon Stewart (eds.), *Kierkegaard's Literary Figures and Motifs*, Tome II, *Gulliver to Zerlina*, Farnham and Burlington: Ashgate 2015 (*Kierkegaard Research: Sources, Reception and Resources*, vol. 16).

(Frederico Pedreira, "Gulliver: Kierkegaard's Reading of Swift and *Gulliver's Travels*," pp. 1–11; Leonardo F. Lisi, "Hamlet: The Impossibility of Tragedy/The Tragedy of Impossibility," pp. 13–38; Robert B. Puchniak, "Holger the Dane: Kierkegaard's Mention of One Heroic Legend," pp. 39–42; Julie K.

Allen, "Jeppe of the Hill: The Hedonistic Christian," pp. 43–8; Elisabete M. de Sousa, "Niels Klim: Project Makers in a World Upside Down," pp. 49–55; Nicholas John Chambers, "King Lear: Silence and the Leafage of Language," pp. 57–64; Matthew Brake, "Loki. Romanticism, and Kierkegaard's Critique of the Aesthetic," pp. 65–73; Fernando Manuel Ferreira da Silva, "Lucinde: "To Live Poetically Is to Live Infinitely," or Kierkegaard's Concept of Irony as Portrayed in His Analysis of Friedrich Schlegel's Work," pp. 75–83; Malgorzata Grzegorzewska, "Lady Macbeth: The Viscera of Conscience," pp. 85–94; Antonella Fimiani, "Margarete: The Feminine Face of Faust," pp. 95–109; F. Nassim Bravo Jordan, "The Master-Thief: A One-Man Army against the Established Order," pp. 111–20; Will Williams, "Mephistopheles: Demonic Seducer, Musician, Philosopher, and Humorist," pp. 121–31; Anne Louise Nielsen, "Minerva: Kierkegaard's Use of a Greek Motif," pp. 133–7; Anders Rendtorff Klitgaard, "Münchhausen: Charlatan or Sublime Artist," pp. 139–54; Laura Liva, "Nemesis: From the Ancient Goddess to a Modern Concept," pp. 155–62; Sean Anthony Turchin, "Nero: Insatiable Sensualist," pp. 163–7; Karen Hiles and Marcia Morgan, "Papageno: An Aesthetic Awakening of the Ethics of Desire," pp. 169–79; Gabriel Guedes Rossatti, "Per Degn: Towards Kierkegaard's Genealogy of the Morals of the Servitors of the State Church," pp. 181–6; Markus Pohlmeyer, "Prometheus: Thief, Creator, and Icon of Pain," pp. 187–98; Nataliya Vorobyova Jørgensen, "Richard III: The Prototype of the Demonic," pp. 199–213; Telmo Rodrigues, "Robert le Diable: A Modern Tragic Figure," pp. 215–21; David D. Possen, "Typhon: The Monster in Kierkegaard's Mirror," pp. 223–33; Joseph Ballan, "The Wandering Jew: Kierkegaard and the Figuration of Death in Life," pp. 235–47; Ana Pinto Leite, "Xerxes: Kierkegaard's King of Jest," pp. 249–56; Sara Ellen Eckerson, "Zerlina: A Study on How to Overcome Anxiety," pp. 257–67.)

17: Nun, Katalin and Jon Stewart (eds.), *Kierkegaard's Pseudonyms*, Farnham and Burlington: Ashgate 2015 (*Kierkegaard Research: Sources, Reception and Resources*, vol. 17).

(Ryan Kemp, "'A,' the Aesthete: Aestheticism and the Limits of Philosophy," pp. 1–25; Joseph Westfall, "A, B, and A. F.....: Kierkegaard's Use of Anonyms," pp. 27–38; Jakub Marek, "Anti-Climacus: Kierkegaard's 'Servant of the Word,'" pp. 39–50; Gabriel Guedes Rossatti, "Constantin Constantius: The Activity of a Travelling Esthetician and How He Still Happened to Pay for the Dinner," pp. 51–66; Wojciech Kaftański and Gabriel Guedes Rossatti, "Frater Taciturnus: The Two Lives of the Silent Brother," pp. 67–88; Paul Martens, "H.H.: A Guerrilla Writer After Theologians...and More," pp. 89–96; Elisabete M. de Sousa, "Hilarius Bookbinder: The Realm of Truth and the World of Books," pp. 97–105; Joseph Westfall, "Inter et Inter: Between Actress and Critic," pp. 107–15; Lee C. Barrett, "Johannes Climacus: Humorist, Dialectician, and Gadfly," pp. 117–42; Ryan Kemp, "Johannes de silentio: Religious Poet or Faithless Aesthete?," pp. 143–58; Nathaniel Kramer, "Johannes the Seducer: The Aesthete *par Excellence* or on the Way to Ethics?," pp. 159–76; Patricia C. Dip, "Judge William: The Limits of the Ethical," pp. 177–92; Nassim Bravo Jordán, "Nicolaus Notabene: Kierkegaard's Satirical

Mask," pp. 193–204; Matthew Brake, "One Still Living: Life-View, Nihilism, and Religious Experience," pp. 205–14; Thomas J. Millay, "Petrus Minor: A Lowly and Insignificant Ministering Critic," pp. 215–21; Mariana Alessandri, "Quidam: Earnest for Ten Minutes a Week," pp. 223–42; Joaquim Hernandez-Dispaux, "Victor Eremita: A Diplomatic yet Abstruse Editor," pp. 243–57; Lee C. Barrett, "Vigilius Haufniensis: Psychological Sleuth, Anxious Author, and Inadvertent Evangelist," pp. 259–80; Mariana Alessandri, "William Afham: The Line by Which an Ape May Become an Apostle," pp. 281–301; Jochen Schmidt, "Young Man: Voice of Naïveté," pp. 303–10.)

18.I: Stewart, Jon (ed.), *Kierkegaard Secondary Literature*, Tome I: *Catalan, Chinese, Czech, Danish and Dutch*, Farnham and Burlington: Ashgate 2016 (*Kierkegaard Research: Sources, Reception and Resources*, vol. 18).

(Dolors Perarnau Vidal, "Estelrich i Artigues, Joan, *Entre la vida i els llibres*, pp. 3–6; Dolors Perarnau Vidal, "Sáez Tajafuerce, Begonya, (ed.), *Enrahonar. Quaderns de filosofia*, no. 29, 1998, pp. 7–10; Qi Wang, "Xin Ru,《看哪，克尔凯郭尔这个人》[Collected Papers on Kierkegaard]," pp. 13–16; Zizhen Liu, "Qi Wang,《走向绝望的深渊─克尔凯郭尔的美学生活境界》[Unto the Abyss of Despair: A Study of Kierkegaard's Aesthetic Sphere of Existence]," pp. 17–19; Chingshun J. Sheu, "Qi Wang,《生命与信仰──克尔凯郭尔假名写作时期基督教哲学思想研究》[Life and Belief: A Study of Christian Philosophy in Kierkegaard's Pseudonymous Writings], pp. 21–3; Qi Wang, "Shaojun Weng,《人的存在─"存在主义之父"克尔凯戈尔述评》[Existence of the Individual: Kierkegaard as "Forefather of Existentialism"]," pp. 25–8; Qi Wang, "Dachun Yang,《沉沦与拯救─克尔凯戈尔精神哲学研究》[Perdition and Salvation: A Study of Kierkegaard's Philosophy of Spirit], pp. 29–32; Kateřina Marková, "Václav Fiala, *Příkaz a skutek. Dialog o Kierkegaardovi* [Command and Deed: A Dialogue on Kierkegaard], pp. 35–8; Søren Bruun, "Benny Alex, *Søren Kierkegaard. Et autentisk Liv: Kierkegaards lange og trange vej mod åndelig afklaring*," pp. 41–3; Anne Louise Nielsen, "Lars Erslev Andersen, *Hinsides ironi. Fire essays om Søren Kierkegaard*," pp. 45–8; Mads Sohl Jessen, "Jacob Bøggild, *Ironiens tænker—tænkningens ironi: Kierkegaard læst retorisk*," pp. 49–53; Gabriel Guedes Rossatti, "Jørgen Bukdahl, *Søren Kierkegaard og den menige mand*," pp. 55–8; Jon Stewart, "Niels Jørgen Cappelørn, Joakim Garff and Johnny Kondrup, *Skriftbilleder. Søren Kierkegaards journaler, notesbøger, hæfter, ark, lapper og strimler*," pp. 59–63; Jon Stewart, "Henning Fenger, *Kierkegaard-Myter og Kierkegaard-Kilder. 9 kildekritiske studier i de kierkegaardske papirer, breve og aktstykker*," pp. 65–70; Andres Roberto Albertsen, "Eduard Geismar, *Søren Kierkegaard. Hans Livsudvikling og Forfattervirksomhed*, vols. 1–2," pp. 71–9; Anne Louise Nielsen, "Arne Grøn, *Begrebet Angst hos Søren Kierkegaard*," pp. 81–5; Anne Louise Nielsen, "Arne Grøn, *Subjektivitet og negativitet. Kierkegaard*," pp. 87–91; Wenche Marit Quist, "Jørgen Husted, *Wilhelms brev—Det etiske ifølge Kierkegaard*," pp. 93–6; Anne Louise Nielsen, "Anders Kingo, *Analogiens teologi. En dogmatisk studie over dialektikken i Søren Kierkegaards opbyggelige og pseudonyme forfatterskab*," pp. 97–101; Jon Stewart, "Carl Henrik Koch, *En flue på Hegels udødelige næse eller Om Adolph Peter Adler og om Søren Kierkegaards forhold til ham*,"

pp. 103–7; Jon Stewart, "Sejer Kühle, *Søren Kierkegaards Barndom og ungdom*," pp. 109–12; Bjørn Rabjerg, "K.E. Løgstrup, *Opgør med Kierkegaard*," pp. 113–18; Jon Stewart, "Gregor Malantschuk, *Dialektik og Eksistens hos Søren Kierkegaard*," pp. 119–24; Rasmus Rosenberg Larsen, "Gregor Malantschuk, *Frihed og eksistens. Studier i Søren Kierkegaards tænkning*," pp. 125–9; Jon Stewart, "Svend Aage Nielsen, *Kierkegaard og Regensen. Kierkegaards forhold til F.C. Petersen, Poul Martin Møller, D.G. Monrad, Magnus Eiriksson, Carl Ploug, P.L. Møller, Hans Brøchner og J.C. Hostrup*," pp. 131–5; Nathaniel Kramer, "Kresten Nordentoft, *Kierkegaards psykologi*," pp. 137–41; Rasmus Rosenberg Larsen, "Kresten Nordentoft, *"Hvad siger Brand-Majoren?" Kierkegaards opgør med sin samtid*," pp. 143–7; Gabriel Guedes Rossatti, "Peter P. Rohde, *Et geni i en Købstad. Et essay om Søren Kierkegaard*," pp. 149–52; Christopher B. Barnett, "Heinrich Roos, *Søren Kierkegaard og Katolicismen*," pp. 153–6; Jon Stewart, "Paul V. Rubow, *Kierkegaard og hans Samtidige*," pp. 157–60; Christian Fink Tolstrup, "Johannes Sløk, *Kierkegaard—humanismens tænker*," pp. 161–5; Gabriel Guedes Rossatti, "Johannes Sløk, *Da Kierkegaard tav. Fra forfatterskab til kirkestorm*," pp. 167–71; Rasmus Rosenberg Larsen, "Johannes Sløk, *Kierkegaards univers. En ny guide til geniet*," pp. 173–7; Thomas Eske Rasmussen, "Peter Thielst, *Livet forstås baglæns, men må leves forlæns. Historien om Søren Kierkegaard*," pp. 179–83; Jon Stewart, "Niels Thulstrup, *Kierkegaards forhold til Hegel og til den spekulative idealisme indtil 1846*," pp. 185–9; Christian Fink Tolstrup, "Bjarne Troelsen, *Manden på Flydebroen. En fortælling om Søren Kierkegaard og det moderne menneskes tilblivelse*," pp. 191–5; Wolter Hartog, "Bernard Delfgaauw, *Kierkegaard. Waarheid en menselijkheid?*" pp. 199–202; Paul Cruysberghs, "Udo Doedens, *In het teken van tegenspraak. Steekhoudende gedachten van Søren Kierkegaard*," pp. 203–5; Wolter Hartog, "Taeke Dokter, *De structuur van Kierkegaard's oeuvre*," pp. 207–11; Paul Cruysberghs, "Louis Dupré, *Kierkegaards theologie of dialektiek van het christen-worden*," pp. 213–16; Wolter Hartog, "Johan Fetter, *Inleiding tot het denken van Kierkegaard*," pp. 217–18; Desiree Berendsen; "Frits Florin, *Geloven als noodweer. Het begrip "het religieuze" bij S. Kierkegaard*," pp. 219–22; Paul Cruysberghs, "Etienne Laurentius Gertrudis Egbertus Kuypers, *Spelen met beelden; een theoretisch kritische studie over de zin of onzin van een christelijk-religieus-georiënteerde-pedagogie(k) onder auspiciën van S.A. Kierkegaard*," pp. 223–6; Johan Taels, "Cyril Lansink, *Vrijheid en ironie. Kierkegaards ethiek van de zelfwording*," pp. 227–30; Paul Cruysberghs, "Victor Leemans, *Søren Kierkegaard*," pp. 231–3; Wolter Hartog, "Willem Leendertz, *Sören Kierkegaard*," pp. 235–9; Pieter Vos, "Wim Scholtens, *Alle gekheid op een stokje. Kierkegaard als psycholoog*," pp. 241–4; Paul Cruysberghs, "Johan Taels, *Søren Kierkegaard als filosoof. De weg terug naar het subject*," pp. 245–8; Wolter Hartog, "August van Dijk, *Perspectieven bij Kierkegaard*," pp. 249–52; Wolter Hartog, "Hans van Munster, *De filosofische gedachten van de jonge Kierkegaard, 1831–1841*," pp. 253–7; Wolter Hartog, "Hans van Munster, *Søren Aabye Kierkegaard*," pp. 259–60; Wolter Hartog, "Maarten van Rhijn, *Søren Kierkegaard. Een indruk van zijn leven en denken*," pp. 261–2; Pieter Vos, "Karl Verstrynge, *De hysterie van de geest. Melancholie en zwaarmoedigheid in het*

pseudonieme œuvre van Kierkegaard," pp. 263–7; Paul Cruysberghs, "Peter Vogelsang, *Oprecht veinzen. Over Kierkegaards "Over het begrip ironie, vooral met betrekking tot Socrates" (1841),*" pp. 269–71; Johan Taels, "Pieter Vos, *De troost van het ogenblik: Kierkegaard over God en het lijden,*" pp. 273–6.)

18.II: Stewart, Jon (ed.), *Kierkegaard Secondary Literature*, Tome II: *English, A-K*, Farnham and Burlington: Ashgate 2016 (*Kierkegaard Research: Sources, Reception and Resources*, vol. 18).

(Daniel M. Dion, "Edgar Leonard Allen, *Kierkegaard: His Life and Thought,*" pp. 1–4; Matthew Brake, "Albert Anderson, *Kierkegaard: A Brief Overview of the Life and Writings of Søren Kierkegaard, 1813–1855,*" pp. 5–7; Robert Wyllie, "Alison Assiter, *Kierkegaard, Metaphysics and Political Theory: Unfinished Selves,*" pp. 9–12; Thomas J. Millay, "Stephen Backhouse, *Kierkegaard's Critique of Christian Nationalism,*" pp. 13–16; Daniel M. Dion, "John A. Bain, *Sören Kierkegaard: His Life and Religious Teaching,*" pp. 17–20; Jacob Given, "Christopher Barnett, *Kierkegaard, Pietism and Holiness,*" pp. 21–3; Jacob Given, "Christopher Barnett, *From Despair to Faith: The Spirituality of Søren Kierkegaard,*" pp. 25–7; Jennifer Potter, "Lee C. Barrett, *Kierkegaard,*" pp. 29–32; Helene Russell, "Lee C. Barrett, *Eros and Self-Emptying: The Intersections of Augustine and Kierkegaard,*" pp. 33–6; Geoff Dargan, "Gregory R. Beabout, *Freedom and Its Misuses: Kierkegaard on Anxiety and Despair,*" pp. 37–42; Michael Strawser, "Pat Bigelow, *Kierkegaard and the Problem of Writing,*" pp. 43–7; Andrew M. Kirk, "Harold Bloom (ed.), *Søren Kierkegaard,*" pp. 49–52; Matthew Brake, "John D. Caputo, *How to Read Kierkegaard,*" pp. 53–6; Claudine Davidshofer, "Clare Carlisle, *Kierkegaard's Philosophy of Becoming: Movements and Positions,*" pp. 57–61; Robert Puchniak, "Clare Carlisle, *Kierkegaard: A Guide for the Perplexed,*" pp. 63–7; Michael Misiewicz, "Clare Carlisle, *Kierkegaard's 'Fear and Trembling': A Reader's Guide,*" pp. 69–72; Nathaniel Kramer, "J. Preston Cole, *The Problematic Self in Kierkegaard and Freud,*" pp. 73–7; Christopher B. Barnett, "James D. Collins, *The Mind of Kierkegaard,*" pp. 79–82; Lee C. Barrett, "Arnold B. Come, *Kierkegaard as Humanist: Discovering Myself,*" pp. 83–6; Lee C. Barrett, "Arnold B. Come, *Kierkegaard as Theologian: Recovering My Self,*" pp. 87–90; Gudmundur Bjorn Thorbjornsson, "George Connell, *To Be One Thing: Personal Unity in Kierkegaard's Thought,*" pp. 91–5; J. Michael Tilley, "George B. Connell and C. Stephen Evans (eds.), *Foundations of Kierkegaard's Vision of Community: Kierkegaard on Religion, Ethics and Politics,*" pp. 97–101; Thomas J. Millay, "Charles L. Creegan, *Wittgenstein and Kierkegaard: Religion, Individuality, and Philosophical Method,*" pp. 103–7; Christian Kettering, "Stephen Crites, *In the Twilight of Christendom: Hegel vs. Kierkegaard on Faith and History,*" pp. 109–13; Daniel M. Dion, "Thomas Henry Croxall, *Kierkegaard Studies, with Special Reference to (a) the Bible (b) Our Own Age,*" pp. 115–18; Erik M. Hanson, "Benjamin Daise, *Kierkegaard's Socratic Art,*" pp. 119–23; Walter Wietzke, "John Davenport and Anthony Rudd (eds.), *Kierkegaard after MacIntyre: Essays of Freedom, Narrative, and Virtue,*" pp. 125–9; Deidre Nicole Green, "Bradley R. Dewey, *The New Obedience: Kierkegaard on Imitating Christ,*" pp. 131–5; Leo Stan, "Mark Dooley, *The Politics of Exodus: Kierkegaard's*

Ethics of Responsibility," pp. 137–43; Matthew Brake, "Elmer H. Duncan, *Sören Kierkegaard*," pp. 145–8; Andrew M. Kirk, "Stephen N. Dunning, *Kierkegaard's Dialectic of Inwardness: A Structural Analysis of the Theory of Stages*," pp. 149–52; Curtis L. Thompson, "Louis Dupré, *Kierkegaard as Theologian: The Dialectic of Christian Existence*," pp. 153–7; Matthew Brake, "Vernard Eller, *Kierkegaard and Radical Discipleship: A New Perspective*," pp. 159–62; Dean Wm. Lauer, "John Elrod, *Being and Existence in Kierkegaard's Pseudonymous Works*," pp. 163–7; Robert Wyllie, "John Elrod, *Kierkegaard and Christendom*," pp. 169–73; Kyle Roberts, "Steven M. Emmanuel, *Kierkegaard and the Concept of Revelation*," pp. 175–9; Michael D. Stark, "C. Stephen Evans, *Kierkegaard's "Fragments" and "Postscripts": The Religious Philosophy of Johannes Climacus*," pp. 181–4; Adam Buben, "C. Stephen Evans, *Passionate Reason: Making Sense of Kierkegaard's "Philosophical Fragments,"* pp. 185–9; J.D. Mininger, "Peter Fenves, *"Chatter": Language and History in Kierkegaard*," pp. 191–5; Joseph Ballan, "Harvie Ferguson, *Melancholy and the Critique of Modernity: Søren Kierkegaard's Religious Psychology*," pp. 197–201; Lee C. Barrett, "M. Jamie Ferreira, *Transforming Vision: Imagination and Will in Kierkegaardian Faith*," pp. 203–6; Carl S. Hughes, "M. Jamie Ferreira, *Love's Grateful Striving: A Commentary on Kierkegaard's "Works of Love,"* pp. 207–11; Gene Fendt, "Mary E. Finn, *Writing the Incommensurable: Kierkegaard, Rossetti, and Hopkins*," pp. 213–16; Daniel M. Dion, "Francis W. Fulford, *Sören Aabye Kierkegaard: A Study*," pp. 217–20; Roberto Sirvent, "Rick Anthony Furtak, *Wisdom in Love: Kierkegaard and the Quest for Emotional Integrity*," pp. 221–4; Matthew Brake, "Patrick Gardiner, *Kierkegaard*," pp. 225–7; Jennifer Veninga, "David J. Gouwens, *Kierkegaard's Dialectic of the Imagination*," pp. 229–33; Lee C. Barrett, "David J. Gouwens, *Kierkegaard as Religious Thinker*," pp. 235–8; Roe Fremstedal, "Ronald M. Green, *Kierkegaard and Kant: The Hidden Debt*," pp. 239–44; Carl S. Hughes, "Ronald Grimsley, *Kierkegaard and French Literature: Eight Comparative Studies*," pp. 245–7; Matthew Brake, "Ronald Grimsley, *Kierkegaard: A Biographical Introduction*," pp. 249–52; Rafael García Pavón, "Luis Guerrero Martínez, *The Ages of Life: Childhood, Youth and Adulthood*," pp. 253–6; Jesus Luzardo, "Anoop Gupta, *Kierkegaard's Romantic Legacy: Two Theories of the Self*," pp. 257–61; Christina M. Danko, "Amy Laura Hall, *Kierkegaard and the Treachery of Love*," pp. 263–6; Jesus Luzardo, "Kenneth Hamilton, *The Promise of Kierkegaard*," pp. 267–71; Thomas J. Millay, "Alastair Hannay, *Kierkegaard*," pp. 273–7; Erik M. Hanson, "Alastair Hannay, *Kierkegaard: A Biography*," pp. 279–82; Thomas J. Millay, "Alastair Hannay, *Kierkegaard and Philosophy: Selected Essays*," pp. 283–6; Erik M. Hanson, "Alastair Hannay and Gordon Marino (eds.), *The Cambridge Companion to Kierkegaard*," pp. 287–91; Luke Johnson, "Edward Harris, *Man's Ontological Predicament: A Detailed Analysis of Sören Kierkegaard's Concept of Sin with Special Reference to "The Concept of Dread,"* pp. 293–6; Joseph Westfall, "M. Holmes Hartshorne, *Kierkegaard, Godly Deceiver: The Nature and Meaning of His Pseudonymous Writings*," pp. 297–300; Curtis L. Thompson, "Hector Hawton, *The Feast of Unreason*," pp. 301–5; Robert B. Puchniak, "Paul L. Holmer, *The Grammar of Faith*," pp. 307–10; Matthew Brake,

"Jacob Howland, *Kierkegaard and Socrates: A Study in Philosophy and Faith*," pp. 311–14; Joseph Westfall, "Elsebet Jegstrup (ed.), *The New Kierkegaard*," pp. 315–19; Matthew Brake, "Howard A. Johnson and Niels Thulstrup (eds.), *A Kierkegaard Critique*," pp. 321–4; Matthew Brake, "Ralph H. Johnson, *The Concept of Existence in the "Concluding Unscientific Postscript,"* pp. 325–8; Leo Stan, "David J. Kangas, *Kierkegaard's Instant: On Beginnings*," pp. 329–34; Carson Webb, "Abrahim H. Khan, *"Salighed" as Happiness? Kierkegaard on the Concept Salighed*," pp. 335–9; Devon C. Wootten, "Bruce H. Kirmmse, *Kierkegaard in Golden Age Denmark*," pp. 341–4; Thomas J. Millay, "Janne Kylliäinen, *Living Poetically in the Modern Age: The Situational Aspects of Kierkegaard's Thought*, pp. 345–9.)

18.III: Stewart, Jon (ed.), *Kierkegaard Secondary Literature*, Tome III: *English, L-Z*, London and New York: Routledge 2016 (*Kierkegaard Research: Sources, Reception and Resources*, vol. 18).

(Curtis L. Thompson, "David R. Law, *Kierkegaard as Negative Theologian*," pp. 1–4; Matthew Brake, "Lewis A. Lawson (ed.), *Kierkegaard's Presence in Contemporary American Life: Essays from Various Disciplines*," pp. 5–8; Thomas J. Millay, "Céline Léon and Sylvia Walsh (eds.), *Feminist Interpretations of Søren Kierkegaard*," pp. 9–13; Jamie Turnbull, "John Lippitt, *Humour and Irony in Kierkegaard's Thought*," pp. 15–20; Paul Martens, "John Lippitt, *Routledge Philosophy Guidebook to Kierkegaard and 'Fear and Trembling,'*" pp. 21–4; Jon Stewart, "John Lippitt and George Pattison (eds.), *The Oxford Handbook of Kierkegaard*," pp. 25–9; María J. Binetti, "Laura Llevadot, *Kierkegaard through Derrida: Toward a Postmetaphysical Ethics*," pp. 31–5; Thomas Gilbert, "Walter Lowrie, *Kierkegaard*," pp. 37–40; Thomas Miles, "Louis Mackey, *Kierkegaard: A Kind of Poet*," pp. 41–5; Joseph Westfall, "Louis Mackey, *Points of View: Readings of Kierkegaard*," pp. 47–51; Christian Kettering, "Habib C. Malik, *Receiving Søren Kierkegaard: The Early Impact and Transmission of His Thought*," pp. 53–6; Timothy C. Hall, "Ronald J. Manheimer, *Kierkegaard as Educator*," pp. 57–60; Annemarie van Stec, "Gordon D. Marino, *Kierkegaard in the Present Age*," pp. 61–4; David Coe, "Harold Victor Martin, *Kierkegaard: The Melancholy Dane*," pp. 65–7; Andrew M. Kirk, "Roy Martinez, *Kierkegaard and the Art of Irony*," pp. 69–72; Marcia Morgan, "Martin J. Matuštík and Merold Westphal (eds.), *Kierkegaard in Post/Modernity*," pp. 73–6; Marcia Morgan, "Vincent A. McCarthy, *The Phenomenology of Moods in Kierkegaard*," pp. 77–80; Matthew Brake, "David E. Mercer, *Kierkegaard's Living Room: The Relation between Faith and History in "Philosophical Fragments,"* pp. 81–4; Roberto Sirvent, "Thomas P. Miles, *Kierkegaard and Nietzsche on the Best Way of Life: A New Method of Ethics*," pp. 85–9; Geoff Dargan, "Edward F. Mooney, *Knights of Faith and Resignation: Reading Kierkegaard's "Fear and Trembling,"* pp. 91–6; Tamar Aylat-Yaguri, "Edward F. Mooney, *Selves in Discord and Resolve: Kierkegaard's Moral-Religious Psychology, from "Either/ Or" to "Sickness unto Death,"* pp. 97–100; Tamar Aylat-Yaguri, "Edward F. Mooney, *On Søren Kierkegaard: Dialogue, Polemics, Lost Intimacy, and Time*," pp. 100–4; Narve Strand, "Stephen Mulhall, *Inheritance and Originality: Wittgenstein, Heidegger, Kierkegaard*," pp. 105–10; Andrew M. Kirk, "Harry

A. Nielsen, *Where The Passion Is: A Reading of Kierkegaard's "Philosophical Fragments,"* pp. 111–14; Jon Stewart, "Katalin Nun, *Women of the Danish Golden Age: Literature, Theater and the Emancipation of Women*," pp. 115–18; Michael Strawser, "George Pattison, *Kierkegaard: The Aesthetic and the Religious: From the Magic Theatre to the Crucifixion of the Image*," pp. 119–23; Daniel Arruda Nascimento, "George Pattison, *Kierkegaard, Religion and the Nineteenth-Century Crisis of Culture*," pp. 125–9; David D. Possen, "George Pattison, *Kierkegaard's Upbuilding Discourses: Philosophy, Literature, and Theology*," pp. 131–4; Narve Strand, "George Pattison and Steven Shakespeare (eds.), *Kierkegaard: The Self in Society*," pp. 135–9; Thomas J. Millay, "Simon D. Podmore, *Kierkegaard and the Self before God: Anatomy of the Abyss*," pp. 141–4; Michael D. Stark, "Louis P. Pojman, *The Logic of Subjectivity: Kierkegaard's Philosophy of Religion*," pp. 145–9; Lee C. Barrett, "Timothy Houston Polk, *The Biblical Kierkegaard: Reading by the Rule of Faith*," pp. 151–4; Carl S. Hughes, "Roger Poole, *Kierkegaard: The Indirect Communication*," pp. 155–8; Andrew Torrance, "Hugh Pyper, *The Joy of Kierkegaard: Essays on Kierkegaard as a Biblical Reader*," pp. 159–63; Andrew Torrance, "Murray Rae, *Kierkegaard's Vision of the Incarnation: By Faith Transformed*," pp. 165–9; Luke Tarassenko, "Joel D.S. Rasmussen, *Between Irony and Witness: Kierkegaard's Poetics of Faith, Hope and Love*," pp. 171–5; Jon Stewart, "Gregory L. Reece, *Irony and Religious Belief*," pp. 177–80; Robert M. Riordan, "Robert C. Roberts, *Faith, Reason and History: Rethinking Kierkegaard's "Philosophical Fragments,"*" pp. 181–5; Jamie Turnbull, "Anthony Rudd, *Kierkegaard and the Limits of the Ethical*," pp. 187–92; Leo Stan, "Bartholomew Ryan, *Kierkegaard's Indirect Politics: Interludes with Lukács, Schmitt, Benjamin, and Adorno*," pp. 193–8; Gene Fendt, "Anne T. Salvatore, *Greene and Kierkegaard: The Discourse of Belief*," pp. 199–203; Annemarie van Stee, "Genia Schönbaumsfeld, *A Confusion of the Spheres: Kierkegaard and Wittgenstein on Philosophy and Religion*," pp. 205–9; Kyle Roberts, "Steven Shakespeare, *Kierkegaard, Language and the Reality of God*," pp. 211–14; Devon C. Wootten, "K. Brian Soderquist, *The Isolated Self: Truth and Untruth in Søren Kierkegaard's "On the Concept of Irony,"*" pp. 215–18; Marcia Morgan, "Leo Stan, *Either Nothingness or Love: On Alterity in Søren Kierkegaard's Writings*," pp. 219–23; Paul Martens, "Jon Stewart, *Kierkegaard's Relations to Hegel Reconsidered*," pp. 225–30; K. Brian Soderquist, "Jon Stewart, *The Cultural Crisis of the Danish Golden Age: Heiberg, Martensen and Kierkegaard*," pp. 231–4; Devon C. Wootten, "Jon Stewart (ed.), *Kierkegaard und His Contemporaries: The Culture of Golden Age Denmark*," pp. 235–8; Jesus Luzardo, "Michael Strawser, *Both/And: Reading Kierkegaard from Irony to Edification*," pp. 239–43; Thomas Gilbert, "David F. Swenson, *Something About Kierkegaard*," pp. 245–8; Curtis L. Thompson, "Mark C. Taylor, *Kierkegaard's Pseudonymous Authorship: A Study of Time and the Self*," pp. 249–52; Jon Stewart, "Mark C. Taylor, *Journeys to Selfhood: Hegel and Kierkegaard*," pp. 253–7; Luke Johnson, "John Heywood Thomas, *Subjectivity and Paradox: A Study of Kierkegaard*," pp. 259–62; Jon Stewart, "Curtis L. Thompson, *Following the Cultured Public's Chosen One: Why Martensen Mattered to Kierkegaard*," pp. 263–6; Aaron Edwards,

"Josiah Thompson, *Kierkegaard*," pp. 267–71; Aaron Edwards, "Peter Vardy, *Kierkegaard*," pp. 273–7; John Louis Haglund, "Jeremy D.B. Walker, *To Will One Thing: Reflections on Kierkegaard's 'Purity of Heart,'*" pp. 279–82; Curtis L. Thompson, "Jeremy D.B. Walker, *The Descent into God*," pp. 283–6; Leo Stan, "Sylvia Walsh, *Living Poetically: Kierkegaard's Existential Aesthetics*," pp. 287–92; Geoff Dargan, "Sylvia Walsh, *Living Christianly: Kierkegaard's Dialectic of Christian Existence*," pp. 293–7; Thomas J. Millay, "Julia Watkin, *Kierkegaard*," pp. 299–302; Dean Wm. Lauer, "Julia Watkin, *Historical Dictionary of Kierkegaard's Philosophy*," pp. 303–5; Thomas J. Millay, "Michael Weston, *Kierkegaard and Modern Continental Philosophy: An Introduction*," pp. 307–11; Margherita Tonon, "Merold Westphal, *Kierkegaard's Critique of Reason and Society*," pp. 313–17; Tony Kim, "Merold Westphal, *Becoming a Self: A Reading of Kierkegaard's "Concluding Unscientific Postscript*," pp. 319–23.)

18.IV: Stewart, Jon (ed.), *Kierkegaard Secondary Literature*, Tome IV: *Finnish, French, Galician and German*, London and New York: Routledge 2016 (*Kierkegaard Research: Sources, Reception and Resources*, vol. 18).

(Olli Mäkinen, "Torsti Lehtinen, *Søren Kierkegaard, intohimon, ahdistuksen ja huumorin filosofi* [Søren Kierkegaard, a Philosopher of Passion, Anxiety and Humor]," pp. 3–6; Olli Mäkinen, "Kalle Sandelin (Sorainen), *Søren Kierkegaardin persoonallisuusaatteen kehittyminen Tanskan filosofisten virtausten yhteydessä viime vuosisadan alkupuolella* [The Development of Søren Kierkegaard's Idea of Personality in Connection with the Danish Philosophical Currents of the Early Nineteenth Century]," pp. 7–10; Olli-Pekka Vainio, "Helge Ukkola, *Eksistoiva ihminen. Ihmisen ongelma Søren Kierkegaardin ajattelussa* [Existing Man: The Problem of Man as Presented in Søren Kierkegaard's Thought]," pp. 11–14; Olli-Pekka Vainio, "Helge Ukkola, *Lähimmäisenrakkaus Søren Kierkegaardin ajattelussa* [The Love of the Neighbor in the Thought of Søren Kierkegaard]," pp. 15–18; Mélissa Fox-Muraton, "Rodolphe Adam, *Lacan et Kierkegaard*," pp. 21–6; Joaquim Hernandez-Dispaux, "André Bellesort, *Le crépuscule d'Elseneur*," pp. 27–30; Frédéric Dubois, "Gerta Berberich, *La notion métaphysique de la personne chez Kant et Kierkegaard*," pp. 31–4; Mélissa Fox-Muraton, "Rachel Bespaloff, *Cheminements et Carrefours. Julien Green, André Malraux, Gabriel Marcel, Kierkegaard, Chestov devant Nietzsche*," pp. 35–40; Margherita Tonon, "Patrice Bollon, (ed.), *Søren Kierkegaard—Philosophe et dandy*, special issue of *Le Magazine Littéraire*," pp. 41–4; Kjell Bleys, "Philippe Chevallier, *Être soi: Actualité de Søren Kierkegaard*," pp. 45–9; Margherita Tonon, "André Clair, *Pseudonymie et paradoxe. La pensée dialectique de Kierkegaard*," pp. 51–3; Mélissa Fox-Muraton, "André Clair, *Kierkegaard. Existence et éthique*," pp. 55–9; Noreen Khawaja, "Jacques Colette, *Kierkegaard, chrétien incognito. La Neutralité armée*," pp. 61–4; Joaquim Hernandez-Dispaux, "Jacques Colette, *Histoire et absolu. Essai sur Kierkegaard*," pp. 65–8; Margherita Tonon, "Jacques Colette, *Kierkegaard et la non-philosophie*," pp. 69–72; Fleur Van Bocxlaer, "Michel Cornu, *Kierkegaard et la communication de l'existence*," pp. 73–7; Mélissa Fox-Muraton, "Vincent Delecroix, *Singulière philosophie. Essai sur Kierkegaard*," pp. 79–83; Joaquim Hernandez-Dispaux, "Victor Deleuran, *Esquisse d'une étude sur Soeren Kierkegaard*," pp. 85–8;

Claudine Davidshofer, "Alain Douchevsky, *Médiation et singularité: Au seuil d'une ontologie avec Pascal et Kierkegaard*," pp. 89–93; Joaquim Hernandez-Dispaux, "Juliette Favez-Boutonier, *L'angoisse. Contribution à la psychologie et la métaphysique de l'angoisse*," pp. 95–8; Mélissa Fox-Muraton, "Benjamin Fondane, *La conscience malheureuse*," pp. 99–104; Mélissa Fox-Muraton, "Benjamin Fondane, *Rencontres avec Léon Chestov*," pp. 105–9; Claudine Davidshofer, "Darío González, *Essai sur l'ontologie kierkegaardienne. Idéalité et determination*," pp. 111–15; Frédéric Dubois, "Françoise Heinrich, *Kierkegaard: le devenir chrétien*," pp. 117–20; Joaquim Hernandez-Dispaux, "Régis Jolivet, *Introduction à Kierkegaard*," pp. 121–4; Joaquim Hernandez- Dispaux, "Régis Jolivet, *Les doctrines existentialistes de Kierkegaard à J. P. Sartre*," pp. 125–9; Mélissa Fox-Muraton, "*Kierkegaard*, special issue of *Kairos*," pp. 131–136; Mélissa Fox-Muraton, "*Kierkegaard vivant. Colloque organisé par l'Unesco à Paris du 21 au 23 avril 1964*," pp. 137–41; Mélissa Fox-Muraton, "Aude-Marie Lhote, *La notion de pardon chez Kierkegaard ou Kierkegaard lecteur de l'Épître aux Romains*," pp. 143–9; Vasco Baptista Marques, "Jean-François Marquet, *Miroirs de l'identité. La littérature hantée par la philosophie*," pp. 151–4; Joseph Ballan, "Emmanuel Mounier, *Introduction aux existentialismes*," pp. 155–8; Susanne Rimstad, "Hélène Politis, *Kierkegaard*," pp. 159–61; Fleur Van Bocxlaer, "Hélène Politis, *Le vocabulaire de Kierkegaard*," pp. 163–7; Mélissa Fox-Muraton, "Hélène Politis, *Kierkegaard en France au XXe siècle: Archéologie d'une réception*," pp. 169–73; Nicolae Irina, "Hélène Politis, *Le concept de philosophie constamment rapporté à Kierkegaard*," pp. 175–9; Mélissa Fox-Muraton, "Henri-Bernard Vergote, *Sens et répétition: Essai sur l'ironie kierkegaardienne*, vols. 1–2," pp. 181–5; Anna Fioravanti and Carlos Raúl Cordero, "Nelly Viallaneix, *Kierkegaard. L'unique devant Dieu*," pp. 187–91; Dolors Perarnau Vidal, "Oscar Parcero Oubiña, *Søren Kierkegaard*," pp.195–8; Esther Oluffa Pedersen, "Hjördis Becker-Lindenthal, *Die Wiederholung der Philosophie. Kierkegaards Kulturkritik und ihre Folgen*," pp. 201–5; Heiko Schulz, "Tilman Beyrich, *Ist Glauben wiederholbar? Derrida liest Kierkegaard*," pp. 207–12; Ulrich Lincoln, "Hermann Deuser, *Sören Kierkegaard. Die paradoxe Dialektik des politischen Christen. Voraussetzungen bei Hegel. Die Reden von 1847/48 im Verhältnis von Politik und Ästhetik*," pp. 213–17; Ulrich Lincoln, "Hermann Deuser, *Dialektische Theologie. Studien zu Adornos Metaphysik und zum Spätwerk Kierkegaards*," pp. 219–23; David Coe, "Hermann Diem, *Die Existenzdialektik von Sören Kierkegaard*," pp. 225–8; Magnus C. Nagel, "Helmut Fahrenbach, *Kierkegaards existenzdialektische Ethik*," pp. 229–33; Ulrich Lincoln, "Gerd-Günther Grau, *Die Selbstauflösung des christlichen Glaubens. Eine religionsphilosophische Studie über Kierkegaard*," pp. 235–9; Magnus C. Nagel, "Wilfried Greve, *Kierkegaards maieutische Ethik. Von "Entweder/Oder II" zu den "Stadien*," pp. 241–6; Henning Nörenberg, "Jochem Henningfeld and Jon Stewart (eds.), *Kierkegaard und Schelling. Freiheit, Angst und Wirklichkeit*," pp. 247–52; Klaus Viertbauer, "Jann Holl, *Kierkegaards Konzeption des Selbst. Eine Untersuchung über die Voraussetzungen und Formen seines Denkens*," pp. 253–6; Hjördis Becker-Lindenthal, "Madeleine Kim, *Der Einzelne und das Allgemeine. Zur Selbstverwirklichung des Menschen*

bei S. Kierkegaard," pp. 257–61; Ulrich Lincoln, "Klaus-Michael Kodalle, *Die Eroberung des Nutzlosen. Kritik des Wunschdenkens und die Zweckrationalität im Anschluß an Kierkegaard*," pp. 263–7; Bjørn Rabjerg, "Knud Ejler Lögstrup, *Kierkegaards und Heideggers Existenzanalyse und ihr Verhältnis zur Verkündigung*," pp. 269–73; Gerhard Thonhauser, "Olaf P. Monrad, *Sören Kierkegaard. Sein Leben und seine Werke*," pp. 275–8; Gerhard Thonhauser, "Gerhard Niedermeyer, *Sören Kierkegaard und die Romantik*," pp. 279–83; Ulrich Lincoln, "Smail Rapic, *Ethische Selbstverständigung. Kierkegaards Auseinandersetzung mit der Ethik Kants und der Rechtsphilosophie Hegels*," pp. 285–9; Gerhard Thonhauser, "Walter Ruttenbeck, *Sören Kierkegaard. Der christliche Denker und sein Werk*," pp. 291–5; Wolter Hartog, "Klaas Schilder, *Zur Begriffsgeschichte des 'Paradoxon'. Mit besonderer Berücksichtigung Calvins und des nach-kierkegaardschen 'Paradoxon,'*" pp. 297–301; Harald Steffes, "Henning Schröer, *Die Denkform der Paradoxalität als theologisches Problem. Eine Untersuchung zu Kierkegaard und der neueren Theologie als Beitrag zur theologischen Logik*," pp. 303–7; Henning Nörenberg, "Heiko Schulz, *Eschatologische Identität. Eine Untersuchung über das Verhältnis von Vorsehung, Schicksal und Zufall bei Sören Kierkegaard*," pp. 309–15; Hjördis Becker-Lindenthal, "Johannes Sløk, *Die Anthropologie Kierkegaards*," pp. 317–20; Thomas Posch, "Michael Theunissen and Wilfried Greve (eds.), *Materialien zur Philosophie S. Kierkegaards*," pp. 321–6; Gerhard Thonhauser, "Helmuth Vetter, *Stadien der Existenz. Eine Untersuchung zum Existenzbegriff Sören Kierkegaards*," pp. 327–31.)

18.V: Stewart, Jon (ed.), *Kierkegaard Secondary Literature*, Tome V: *Greek, Hebrew, Hungarian, Italian, Japanese, Norwegian, and Polish*, London and New York: Routledge 2016 (*Kierkegaard Research: Sources, Reception and Resources*, vol. 18).

(Georgios Patios, "Δημήτρης Κ. Φαρμάκης, [Dimitris K. Farmakis], *Ὕπαρξη καὶ ἀπελπισία στὴ φιλοσοφία τοῦ S. Kierkegaard* [Existence and Despair in S. Kierkegaard's Philosophy]," pp. 3–6; Vasiliki Tsakiri, "Μιχάλης Κ. Μακράκης, [Michalis K. Makrakis], *Ἐμμένεια καὶ ὑπέρβαση στὴ φιλοσοφία τοῦ Kierkegaard* [Immanence and Transcendence in Kierkegaard's Philosophy]," pp. 7–11; Vasiliki Tsakiri, "Νίκος Ἀγγ. Νησιώτης, [Nikos Agg. Nissiotis], *Ὑπαρξισμός καὶ χριστιανικὴ πίστις ἡ ὑπαρκτικὴ σκέψις ἐν τῇ φιλοσοφίᾳ καὶ ἡ χριστιανικὴ πίστις ὡς τὸ ἀναπόφευκτον καὶ βασικὸν πρόβλημα αὐτῆς κατὰ τὸν Soren Kierkegaard καὶ τοὺς συγχρόνους ὑπαρξιστὰς φιλοσόφους Karl Jaspers, Martin Heidegger καὶ Jean-Paul Sartre* [Existentialism and Christian Faith, or The Existential Thought in Philosophy and Christian Faith as the Inevitable and Basic Problem for Thought according to Søren Kierkegaard and the Modern Existential Philosophers Karl Jaspers, Martin Heidegger and Jean-Paul Sartre)]," pp. 13–17; Jacob Golomb, Tamar Aylat-Yaguri, דיאלוג אנושי עם המוחלט: הסולם של קירקגור לפסגת הקיום הרוחני ירושלים: הוצאת ספרים ע"ש י"ל מאגנס, האוניברסיטה העברית [Human Dialogue with the Absolute: Kierkegaard's Ladder to the Climax of Spiritual Existence] pp. 21–3; Zoltán Gyenge, "Judit Bartha, *A szerző árnyképe. Romantikus költőmítosz Kierkegaard és E. T. A. Hoffmann alkotásesztétikájában* [The Shadow of the Author: The Romantic Myth of the Poet in the Creation Aesthetics of Kierkegaard

and E.T.A. Hoffmann]," pp. 27–31; András Nagy, "Béla Brandenstein, *Kierkegaard. Tanulmány* [Kierkegaard: A Study]," pp. 33–7; Zoltán Gyenge, "István Czakó, *Hit és egzisztencia. Tanulmány Søren Kierkegaard hitfelfogásáról* [Faith and Existence: A Study of Søren Kierkegaard's Conception of Faith]," pp. 39–43; Anita Soós, "István Dévény, *Sören Kierkegaard,*" pp. 45–9; István Czakó, "Zoltán Gyenge, *Kierkegaard élete és filozófiája* [Kierkegaard's Life and Philosophy]," pp. 51–6; István Czakó, "Zoltán Gyenge, *Kierkegaard és a német idealizmus* [Kierkegaard and German Idealism]," pp. 57–61; Sarolta Püsök, "Sándor Koncz, *Kierkegaard és a világháború utáni teológia* [Kierkegaard and Post-War Theology]," pp. 63–7; Anita Soós, "András Nagy, *Az árnyjátékos. Sören Kierkegaard irodalomtörténet, eszmetörténet és hatástörténet metszéspontjain* [The Shadowplayer: Søren Kierkegaard at the Crossroads of Literary History, History of Ideas and Reception History]," pp. 69–73; Judit Bartha, "András Nagy (ed.), *Kierkegaard Budapesten. A Kierkegaard-hét előadásai 1992. december 1–4* [Kierkegaard in Budapest: Proceedings of the Kierkegaard Week, December 1–4, 1992]," pp. 75–9; András Nagy, "Sarolta Püsök, *Søren Kierkegaard teológiájának súlypontjai* [The Focal Points of Kierkegaard's Theology]," pp. 81–5; Judit Bartha, "Anita Soós, *."Ha egy arcot sokáig és figyelmesen szemlélünk. . ."* ["If We Watch a Face Long and Carefully Enough. . ."]," pp. 87–91; András Nagy, "Lajos Zsigmond Szeberényi, *Kierkegaard élete és munkái* [Kierkegaard's Life and Works]," pp. 93–7; Sarolta Püsök, "László Széles, *Kierkegaard gondolkozásának alapvonalai* [The Basic Lines of Kierkegaard's Thought]," pp. 99–102; Sarolta Püsök, "Sándor Tavaszi, *Kierkegaard személyisége és gondolkodása* [Kierkegaard's Personality and Thought]," pp. 103–6; Laura Liva, "Isabella Adinolfi Bettiolo, *Poeta o testimone? Il problema della comunicazione del cristianesimo in Søren Aabye Kierkegaard* [Poet or Witness? The Problem of the Communication of Christianity in Søren Aabye Kierkegaard]," pp. 109–13; Ingrid Basso, "Remo Cantoni, *La coscienza inquieta. Søren Kierkegaard* [The Restless Consciousness: Søren Kierkegaard]," pp. 115–18; Alessio Santoro, "Simonella Davini, *Il circolo del salto. Kierkegaard e la ripetizione* [The Circle of the Leap: Kierkegaard and Repetition]," pp. 119–22; Laura Liva, "Simonella Davini, *Arte e critica nell'estetica di Kierkegaard* [Art and Criticism in Kierkegaard's Aesthetics]," pp. 123–6; Cristian Benavides, "Cornelio Fabro, *Tra Kierkegaard e Marx. Per una definizione dell'esistenza* [Between Kierkegaard and Marx: Towards a Definition of Existence]," pp. 127–31; Alessandra Granito, "Roberto Garaventa, *Angoscia e peccato in Søren Kierkegaard* [Anxiety and Sin in Søren Kierkegaard]," pp. 133–6; Laura Liva, "Anna Giannatiempo Quinzio, *L'estetico in Kierkegaard* [Aesthetics in Kierkegaard]," pp. 137–41; Alessandra Granito, "Massimo Iiritano, *Disperazione e fede in Søren Kierkegaard. Una "lotta di confine"* [Despair and Faith in Søren Kierkegaard: A Border Struggle]," pp. 143–6; Alessio Santoro, "Alessandro Klein, *Antirazionalismo di Kierkegaard* [Kierkegaard's Anti-Rationalism]," pp. 147–50; Simonella Davini, "Giuseppe Modica, *Fede libertà peccato. Figure ed esiti della "prova" in Kierkegaard* [Faith, Freedom, Sin: Figures and Outcomes of the "Trial" in Kierkegaard]," pp. 151–4; Silvia Vignati, "Giuseppe Modica, *Una verità per me. Itinerari kierkegaardiani* [A Truth for Me:

Kierkegaardian Itineraries]," pp. 155–9; Laura Liva, "Enzo Paci, *Relazioni e significati. II. Kierkegaard e Thomas Mann* [Relations and Meanings, vol. 2, Kierkegaard and Thomas Mann]," pp. 161–5; Silvia Vignati, "Luigi Pareyson, *L'etica di Kierkegaard nella prima fase del suo pensiero* [Kierkegaard's Ethics in the First Phase of His Thought]," pp. 167–72; Silvia Vignati, "Luigi Pareyson, *L'etica di Kierkegaard nella "Postilla"* [Kierkegaard's Ethics in the *Postscript*]" pp. 173–7; Alessandra Granito, "Giorgio Penzo, *Kierkegaard. La verità eterna che nasce nel tempo* [Kierkegaard: The Eternal Truth which is Born in Temporality]," pp. 179–81; Silvia Vignati, "Ettore Rocca, *Tra estetica e teologia. Studi kierkegaardiani* [Between Aesthetics and Theology: Kierkegaardian Studies]," pp. 183–188; Silvia Vignati, "Ettore Rocca, *Kierkegaard*," pp. 189–95; Keisuke Yoshida, "Hiroshi Fujino, キルケゴール―美と倫理のはざまに立つ哲学 [Kierkegaard: The Philosophy of Standing in between the Aesthetic and the Ethical]," pp. 199–203; Yusuke Suzuki, "Jun Hashimoto, キェルケゴールにおける「苦悩」の世界 ["Suffering" in the Life and Authorship of Søren Kierkegaard]," pp. 205–7; Tomomichi Baba, "Shosyu Kawakami, ドイツにおけるキルケゴール思想の受容―20 世紀初頭の批判哲学と実存哲学 [The Reception of Kierkegaard's Thought in Germany: Critical Philosophy and Existential Philosophy in the Early Twentieth Century]," pp. 209–13; Michio Ogino, "Hidehito Otani, キルケゴール青年時代の研究、正続 [A Study of Kierkegaard's Youth]," pp. 215–19; Michio Ogino, "Hidehito Otani, キルケゴール著作活動の研究　前篇―青年時代を中心に行われた文学研究の実態 [A Study of Kierkegaard's Authorship, Part 1: The Realities of Young Kierkegaard's Own Studies of Literature]," pp. 221–4; Michio Ogino, "Hidehito Otani, キルケゴール著作活動の研究　後編―全著作構造の解明 [A Study of Kierkegaard's Authorship, Part 2: Investigation into the Structure of the Entirety of his Works]," pp. 225–8; Keisuke Yoshida, "Takaya Suto, キルケゴールと「キリスト教界」 [Kierkegaard and "Christendom"]," pp. 229–33; Hans Herlof Grelland, "Trond Berg Eriksen, *Søren Kierkegaard. Den fromme spotteren* [Søren Kierkegaard: The Pious Mocker]," pp. 237–41; Morten Dahlback, "Harald Beyer, *Søren Kierkegaard og Norge* [Søren Kierkegaard and Norway]," pp. 243–6; Morten Dahlback, "Harald Beyer, *Søren Kierkegaard*," pp. 247–9; Nathaniel Kramer, "Hans Herlof Grelland, *Tausheten og øyeblikket. Kierkegaard, Ibsen, Munch* [Silence and the Moment: Kierkegaard, Ibsen, Munch]," pp. 251–5; Morten Dahlback, "Karstein Hopland, *Virkelighet og bevissthet. En studie i Søren Kierkegaards antropologi* [Actuality and Consciousness: A Study of Søren Kierkegaard's Anthropology]," pp. 257–60; Morten Dahlback, "Kjell Eyvind Johansen, *Begrebet Gjentagelse hos Søren Kierkegaard* [The Concept of Repetition in Søren Kierkegaard]," pp. 261–5; Katalin Nun, "Finn Jor, *Kjærlighetens gjerninger. En roman om Søren og Regine* [Works of Love: A Novel about Søren and Regine]," pp. 267–70; Narve Strand, "Finn Jor (ed.), *Filosofi & samfunn: Søren Kierkegaard* [Philosophy and Society: Søren Kierkegaard]," pp. 271–6; Morten Dahlback, "Per Lønning, *Samtidighedens situation. En studie i Søren Kierkegaards Kristendomsforståelse* [The Situation of Contemporaneity: A Study in Søren Kierkegaard's Understanding of Christianity]," pp. 277–80; Wojciech Kaftański, "Edward Kasperski, *Kierkegaard.*

Antropologia i dyskurs o człowieku [Kierkegaard. Anthropology and Discourse on Man]," pp. 283–7; Andrzej Słowikowski, "Stefania Lubańska, *Pascal i Kierkegaard-filozofowie rozpaczy i wiary* [Pascal and Kierkegaard: The Philosophers of Despair and Faith]," pp. 289–94; Katarzyna Krawerenda-Wajda, "Hubert Mikołajczyk, *Kierkegaard, Kant a antropologia filozoficzna* [Kierkegaard, Kant and Philosophical Anthropology]," pp. 295–9; Katarzyna Krawerenda-Wajda, "Hubert Mikołajczyk, *Antropologia Kierkegaarda w świetle Kantowskiej filozofii praktycznej* [Kierkegaard's Anthropology in the Perspective of Kantian Practical Philosophy]," pp. 301–5; Andrzej Słowikowski, "Jacek Aleksander Prokopski, *Søren Kierkegaard: dialektyka paradoksu wiary* [Søren Kierkegaard's Dialectics of the Paradox of Faith]," pp. 307–12; Wojciech Kaftański, "Antoni Szwed, *Między wolnością a prawdą egzystencji: studium myśli S. Kierkegaarda* [Between Freedom and the Truth of Existence: A Study of S. Kierkegaard's Thought]," pp. 313–17; Wojciech Kaftański, "Karol Toeplitz, *Kierkegaard*," pp. 319–24.)

18.VI: Stewart, Jon (ed.), *Kierkegaard Secondary Literature*, Tome VI: *Portuguese, Romanian, Russian, Slovak, Spanish, and Swedish*, London and New York: Routledge 2016 (*Kierkegaard Research: Sources, Reception and Resources*, vol. 18).

(Joana Cordovil Cardoso, "Agustina Bessa-Luís, *Estádios Eróticos Imediatos de Sören Kierkegaard* [Søren Kierkegaard's Immediate Erotic Stages]," pp. 3–8; Marcio Gimenes de Paula, "Ricardo Quadros Gouvêa, *Paixão pelo paradoxo: Uma introdução a Kierkegaard* [Passion for Paradox: An Introduction to Kierkegaard]," pp. 9–13; Arthur Bartholo Gomes, "Ricardo Quadros Gouvêa, *A Palavra e o Silêncio: Kierkegaard e a relação dialética entre a razão e a fé em Temor e Tremor* [The Word and the Silence: Kierkegaard and the Dialectical Relation between Reason and Faith in *Fear and Trembling*]," pp. 15–20; Arthur Bartholo Gomes, "Guiomar de Grammont, *Don Juan, Fausto e o Judeu Errante em Kierkegaard* [Don Juan, Faust and the Wandering Jew in Kierkegaard]," pp. 21–5; Humberto Araujo Quaglio de Souza, "Alceu Amoroso Lima, *O Existencialismo e Outros Mitos do Nosso Tempo* [Existentialism and Other Myths of Our Time]," pp. 27–31; Vasco de Jesus, "Márcio Gimenes de Paula, *Socratismo e cristianismo em Kierkegaard: o escândalo e a loucura* [Socratism and Christianity in Kierkegaard: Offense and Foolishness]," pp. 33–7; Rodrigo Carqueja de Menezes and Thiago Costa Faria, "Marcio Gimenes de Paula, *Subjetividade e objetividade em Kierkegaard* [Subjectivity and Objectivity in Kierkegaard]," pp. 39–42; Rodrigo Carqueja de Menezes and Thiago Costa Faria, "Miguel Reale (ed.), *Søren Kierkegaard*, special issue of *Revista Brasileira de Filosofia*," pp. 43–7; Sara Ellen Eckerson, "Elisabete Sousa, *Formas de Arte: A prática crítica de Berlioz, Kierkegaard, Liszt e Schumann* [Forms of Art: The Practical Criticism of Berlioz, Kierkegaard, Liszt and Schumann]," pp. 49–53; Rodrigo Carqueja de Menezes and Thiago Costa Faria, "Alvaro Luiz Montenegro Valls, *Entre Sócrates e Cristo: ensaios sobre a ironia e o amor em Kierkegaard* [Between Socrates and Christ: Essays on Irony and Love in Kierkegaard]," pp. 55–9; Marcio Gimenes de Paula, "Alvaro Valls, *Kierkegaard cá entre nós* [Kierkegaard, Just Between Us]," pp. 61–5; Marcio Gimenes de Paula, "Alvaro

Valls, *O crucificado encontra Dionísio: ensaios sobre Kierkegaard e Nietzsche* [The Crucified Meets Dionysus: Studies on Kierkegaard and Nietzsche]," pp. 67–71; Leo Stan, "Mădălina Diaconu, *Pe marginea abisului. Søren Kierkegaard și nihilismul secolului al XIX-lea* [On the Edge of the Abyss: Søren Kierkegaard and Nineteenth-Century Nihilism], pp. 75–80; Leo Stan, "Grigore Popa, *Existență și adevăr la Sören Kierkegaard* [Existence and Truth in Søren Kierkegaard's Thought], pp. 81–6; Irina Kruchinina, "Piama Pavlovna Gaidenko, *Трагедия эстетизма. О миросозерцании Серена Киркегора* [The Tragedy of Aestheticism: On the World-View of Søren Kierkegaard]," pp. 89–92; Darya Loungina, "Sergey Alexandrovich Isaev, *Философско-эстетическое учение С. Кьеркегора (критический анализ)* [The Philosophico-Aesthetic Teaching of S. Kierkegaard (A Critical Analysis)]," pp. 93–8; Darya Loungina, "Valery Podoroga, *Метафизика ландшафта. Коммуникативные стратегии в философской культуре XIX – XX вв* [Metaphysics of the Landscape: Communicative Strategies in the Philosophical Culture of the Nineteenth and Twentieth Centuries]," pp. 99–104; Zuzana Blažeková, "Andrej Démuth (ed.), *Postskriptum ku Kierkegaardovi* [A Postscript to Kierkegaard]," pp. 107–10; Peter Šajda, "Milan Petkanič, *Filozofia vášne Sørena Kierkegaarda* [Søren Kierkegaard's Philosophy of Passion]," pp. 111–16; Milan Petkanič, "Peter Šajda, *Buberov spor s Kierkegaardom. O vzťahu náboženstva k etike a politike* [Buber's Polemic with Kierkegaard: On the Relation of Religion to Ethics and Politics]," pp. 117–22; Zuzana Blažeková, "František Sirovič, *Søren A. Kierkegaard: Filozoficko-kritická analýza diela* [Søren A. Kierkegaard: A Philosophical-Critical Analysis of his Authorship]," pp. 123–6; María J. Binetti, "Cèlia Amorós, *Søren Kierkegaard o la subjetividad del caballero. Un estudio a la luz de las paradojas del patriarcado* [Søren Kierkegaard or the Subjectivity of the Knight: A Study in the Light of the Paradoxes of Patriarchy]," pp. 129–33; Juan Evaristo Valls Boix, "María José Binetti, *El itinerario hacia la libertad. Un estudio basado en el Diario de Søren Kierkegaard según la interpretación de Cornelio Fabro* [The Itinerary of Freedom: A Study Based on the Diary of Søren Kierkegaard According to Cornelio Fabro's Interpretation]," pp. 135–9; Alejandro González Contreras, "María José Binetti, *El Poder de la Libertad. Una introducción a Kierkegaard* [The Power of Freedom: An Introduction to Kierkegaard]," pp. 141–4; Rafael García Pavón, José Luis Cañas Fernández, *Søren Kierkegaard. Entre la inmediatez y la relación* [Søren Kierkegaard: Between Immediacy and Relation]," pp. 145–8; Fernanda Rojas, "Catalina Elena Dobre, *La experiencia del silencio* [The Experience of Silence]," pp. 149–52; Rafael García Pavón, "Catalina Elena Dobre, *La repetición en Kierkegaard. O cómo recuperar lo imposible* [Repetition in Søren A. Kierkegaard: Or How to Recover the Impossible]," pp. 153–6; Manfred Svensson, "Luis Farré, *Unamuno, William James y Kierkegaard y otros ensayos* [Unamuno, William James and Kierkegaard and Other Essays]," pp. 157–60; Rafael García Pavón, "María García Amilburu (ed.), *El concepto de la angustia: 150 años después* [The Concept of Anxiety: 150 Years Later], special issue of *Thémata, Revista de Filosofía*," pp. 161–4; Juan Evaristo Valls Boix, "Rafael García Pavón, *El problema de la comunicación en Søren A. Kierkegaard. El debate con Hegel en El concepto de la angustia* [The Problem of Communication in Søren A. Kierkegaard:

The Debate with Hegel in The Concept of Anxiety]," pp. 165–9; Azucena Palavicini Sánchez, "Rafael García Pavón and Catalina Elena Dobre, *Søren Kierkegaard y los ámbitos de la existencia* [Søren Kierkegaard and the Areas of Existence]," pp. 171–5; Juan Evaristo Valls Boix, "Rafael García Pavón, Catalina Elena Dobre, Luis Guerrero Martínez, and Leticia Valadez (eds.), *Conversaciones sobre Kierkegaard* [Conversations about Kierkegaard]," pp. 177–80; Juan Evaristo Valls Boix, "Carlos Goñi, *El filósofo impertinente. Kierkegaard contra el orden establecido* [The Impertinent Philosopher: Kierkegaard against the Established Order]," pp. 181–5; Fernanda Rojas, "Luis Guerrero Martínez, *Kierkegaard. Los límites de la razón en la existencia humana* [Kierkegaard: The Limits of Reason in Human Existence]," pp. 187–90; Azucena Palavicini Sánchez, "Luis Guerrero Martínez, *La verdad subjetiva. Søren Kierkegaard como escritor* [The Subjective Truth: Søren Kierkegaard as Writer]," pp. 191–5; Juan Evaristo Valls Boix, "Luis Guerrero Martínez (ed.), *Kierkegaard. Individualidad versus globalización* [Kierkegaard: Individuality versus Globalization], special issue of *El garabato*," pp. 197–200; Guadalupe Pardi, "Luis Guerrero Martínez (ed.), *Søren Kierkegaard. Una reflexión sobre la existencia humana* [Søren Kierkegaard: A Reflection on Human Existence]," pp. 201–4; Juan Evaristo Valls Boix, "Asunción Herrera Guevara, *La historia perdida de Kierkegaard y Adorno. Cómo leer a Kierkegaard y Adorno* [The Lost History of Kierkegaard and Adorno: How to Read Kierkegaard and Adorno]," pp. 205–9; Manfred Svensson, "Claudio Gutiérrez Marín, *Dios ha hablado. El pensamiento dialéctico de Kierkegaard, Brunner y Barth* [God has Spoken: The Dialectical Thought of Kierkegaard, Brunner and Barth]," pp. 211–13; Patricia Dip, "Rafael Larrañeta Olleta, *La interioridad apasionada. Verdad y amor en S. Kierkegaard* [Passionate Inwardness: Love and Truth in S. Kierkegaard]," pp. 215–19; Oscar Parcero Oubiña, "Rafael Larrañeta Olleta, *La lupa de Kierkegaard* [Kierkegaard's Magnifying Glass]," pp. 221–4; Juan Evaristo Valls Boix, "Fernando Pérez-Borbujo (ed.), *Ironía y destino. La filosofía secreta de Kierkegaard* [Irony and Destiny: The Secret Philosophy of Søren Kierkegaard]," pp. 225–9; Azucena Palavicini Sánchez, "Francesc Torralba, *Kierkegaard en el laberinto de las mascaras* [Kierkegaard in the Labyrinth of Masks]," pp. 231–5; Juan Evaristo Valls Boix, "Leticia Valadez (ed.), *Las publicaciones de Søren Kierkegaard de 1843* [Søren Kierkegaard's Publications from 1843], special issue of *Tópicos. Revista de Filosofía*," pp. 237–40; Matthew T. Nowachek, "John Björkhem, *Sören Kierkegaard i psykologisk belysning* [Søren Kierkegaard Seen from a Psychological Perspective]," pp. 243–7; Anders Kraal, "Torsten Bohlin, *Sören Kierkegaard. Drag ur hans levnad och personlighetsutveckling* [Søren Kierkegaard: His Life and Personality Development]," pp. 249–52; Anders Kraal, "Torsten Bohlin, *Sören Kierkegaards etiska åskådning med särskild hänsyn till begreppet "den enskilde"* [Søren Kierkegaard's Ethical View with Special Reference to the Concept of the Single Individual]," pp. 253–6; Anders Kraal, "Torsten Bohlin, *Sören Kierkegaard och nutida religiöst tänkande* [Kierkegaard and Contemporary Religious Thought]," pp. 257–60; Matthew T. Nowachek, "Torsten Bohlin, *Kierkegaards dogmatiska åskådning i dess historiska sammanhang* [Kierkegaard's Dogmatic View in its Historical Context],"

pp. 261–5; Anders Kraal, "Torsten Bohlin, *Sören Kierkegaard. Mannen och verket* [Sören Kierkegaard: The Man and His Work]," pp. 267–270; Matthew T. Nowachek, "Torsten Bohlin, *Kierkegaards tro och andra Kierkegaardstudier* [Kierkegaard's Faith and Other Kierkegaard Studies]," pp. 271–275; Matthew T. Nowachek, "Allan Green, *Kierkegaard bland samtida. Personhistoriska skisser* [Kierkegaard among His Contemporaries: Outlines of Personal Histories]," pp. 277–81; Matthew T. Nowachek, "Edward A. Harris, *Gör ditt val. En introduktion till Kierkegaards subjektivitetsteori* [Make Your Choice: An Introduction to Kierkegaard's Theory of Subjectivity]," pp. 283–7; Matthew T. Nowachek, "Ted Harris and Ann Lagerström, *Konsten att leva innerligt. Existentialism för den moderna människan* [The Art of Living Inwardly: Existentialism for the Modern Human Being]," pp. 289–93; Matthew T. Nowachek, "Jonna Hjertström Lappalainen, *Den enskilde. En studie av trons profana möjlighet i Sören Kierkegaards tidiga författarskap* [The Single Individual: A Study of Faith's Profane Possibility in Søren Kierkegaard's Early Authorship]," pp. 295–9; Matthew T. Nowachek, "Lennart Koskinen, *Tid och evighet hos Sören Kierkegaard. En studie i Kierkegaards livsåskådning* [Time and Eternity in Søren Kierkegaard: A Study in Kierkegaard's Philosophy of Life]," pp. 301–5; Matthew T. Nowachek, "Lis Lind, *Søren Kierkegaard själv. Psykoanalytiska läsningar* [Søren Kierkegaard Himself: Psychoanalytic Readings]," pp. 307–11; Matthew T. Nowachek, "Arnold Ljungdal, *Problemet Kierkegaard* [The Problem Kierkegaard]," pp. 313–17; Anders Kraal, "Waldemar Rudin, *Sören Kierkegaards person och författarskap. Ett försök* [Søren Kierkegaard's Personality and Writings: An Essay]," pp. 319–22; Matthew T. Nowachek, "Ingmar Simonsson, *Kierkegaard i vår tid* [Kierkegaard in Our Time]," pp. 323–7.)

19.I: Šajda, Peter and Jon Stewart (eds.), *Kierkegaard Bibliography*, Tome I, *Albanian to Dutch*, London and New York: Routledge 2016 (*Kierkegaard Research: Sources, Reception and Resources*, vol. 19).

(Paul Cruysberghs and Karel Th. Eisses, "Afrikaans," p. 1; Gjergji Pendavinji, "Albanian," pp. 3–4; Faezeh Moieni, "Arabic," pp. 5–8; Dolors Perarnau Vidal and Óscar Parcero Oubiña, "Basque," p. 9; Peter Šajda and Jon Stewart, "Bulgarian," pp. 11–15; Dolors Perarnau Vidal, "Catalan," pp. 17–21; Qi Wang and Chingshun J. Shen, "Chinese," pp. 23–37; Hrvoje Barić, "Croatian, Serbian, and Serbo-Croatian," pp. 39–43; Kateřina Marková, "Czech," pp. 45–53; Esben Lindemann, Emma Sørgaard and Jon Stewart, "Danish," pp. 55–154; Karel Th. Eisses, "Dutch," pp. 155–215.)

19.II: Šajda, Peter and Jon Stewart (eds.), *Kierkegaard Bibliography*, Tome II, *English*, London and New York: Routledge 2016 (*Kierkegaard Research: Sources, Reception and Resources*, vol. 19).

(Luke Johnson, Katalin Nun, Jamie Turnbull, and Jon Stewart, "English," pp. 1–255.)

19.III: Šajda, Peter and Jon Stewart (eds.), *Kierkegaard Bibliography*, Tome III, *Estonian to Hebrew*, London and New York: Routledge 2016 (*Kierkegaard Research: Sources, Reception and Resources*, vol. 19).

(Mikael Munk Lyshede, "Estonian," p. 1; Janne Kylliäinen, "Finnish," pp. 3–6; Leo Stan, "French," pp. 7–55; Óscar Parcero Oubiña, "Galician,"

pp. 57–8; Eva Kaminski, Gerhard Schreiber, and Heiko Schulz, "German," pp. 59–212; Daphne Giofkou, "Greek," pp. 213–28; Tamar Aylat-Yaguri and Roi Benbassat, "Hebrew," pp. 229–35.)

19.IV: Šajda, Peter and Jon Stewart (eds.), *Kierkegaard Bibliography*, Tome IV, *Hungarian to Korean*, London and New York: Routledge 2016 (*Kierkegaard Research: Sources, Reception and Resources*, vol. 19).

(Judit Bartha and István Czakó, "Hungarian," pp. 1–22; Kristian Guttesen, "Icelandic," pp. 23–5; Laura Liva, "Italian," pp. 27–95; Yusuke Suzuki, "Japanese," pp. 97–178; Jae-myeong Pyo and Min-Ho Lee, "Korean," pp. 179–204.)

19.V: Šajda, Peter and Jon Stewart (eds.), *Kierkegaard Bibliography*, Tome V, *Latvian to Ukrainian*, London and New York: Routledge 2016 (*Kierkegaard Research: Sources, Reception and Resources*, vol. 19).

(Viestarts Vidins, "Latvian," pp. 1–3; Jolita Adomeniene Pons, "Lithuanian," pp. 5–7; Trajce Stojanov, "Macedonian," pp. 9–10; Siv Frøydis Berg and Øivind Berg, "Norwegian," pp. 11–29; Hussein Ismailzadeh, "Persian," pp. 31–3; Wojciech Kaftański, Jacek Aleksander Prokopski, Antoni Szwed, and Karol Toeplitz, "Polish," pp. 35–69; Marcio Gimenes de Paula and Elisabete M. de Sousa, "Portuguese," pp. 71–105; Nicolae Irina, "Romanian," pp. 107–10; Darya Loungina, "Russian," pp. 111–27; Zuzana Blazeková and Peter Šajda, "Slovak," pp. 129–42; Primož Repar, "Slovenian," pp. 143–50; Nassim Bravo, Dolors Perarnau Vidal, Oscar Parcero, "Spanish," pp. 151–95; Joseph Ballan, "Swedish," pp. 197–233; Turker Armaner, "Turkish," pp. 235–7; Serhii Shevchenko, "Ukranian," pp. 239–48.)

19.VI: Šajda, Peter and Jon Stewart (eds.), *Kierkegaard Bibliography*, Tome VI, *Figures*, London and New York: Routledge 2016 (*Kierkegaard Research: Sources, Reception and Resources*, vol. 19).

19.VII: Šajda, Peter and Jon Stewart (eds.), *Kierkegaard Bibliography*, Tome VII, *Figures*, London and New York: Routledge 2016 (*Kierkegaard Research: Sources, Reception and Resources*, vol. 19).

20: Nun, Katalin, Gerhard Schreiber, and Jon Stewart (eds.), *The Auction Catalogue of Kierkegaard's Library*, Farnham and Burlington: Ashgate 2015 (*Kierkegaard Research: Sources, Reception and Resources*, vol. 20).

21.I: Stewart, Katalin Nun, *Cumulative Index to Kierkegaard Research: Sources, Reception and Resources*, Tome I, *Index of Names, A–K*, London and New York: Routledge 2018.

21.II: Stewart, Katalin Nun, *Cumulative Index to Kierkegaard Research: Sources, Reception and Resources*, Tome II, *Index of Names, L–Z*, London and New York: Routledge 2018.

21.III: Stewart, Katalin Nun, *Cumulative Index to Kierkegaard Research: Sources, Reception and Resources*, Tome III, *Index of Subjects. Overview of the Articles in the Series*, London and New York: Routledge 2018.